REQUIRED READING

Required Reading

THE LIFE OF EVERYDAY TEXTS
IN THE BRITISH EMPIRE

PRIYASHA MUKHOPADHYAY

PRINCETON UNIVERSITY PRESS
PRINCETON & OXFORD

Copyright © 2024 by Princeton University Press

Princeton University Press is committed to the protection of copyright and the intellectual property our authors entrust to us. Copyright promotes the progress and integrity of knowledge. Thank you for supporting free speech and the global exchange of ideas by purchasing an authorized edition of this book. If you wish to reproduce or distribute any part of it in any form, please obtain permission.

Requests for permission to reproduce material from this work should be sent to permissions@press.princeton.edu

Published by Princeton University Press
41 William Street, Princeton, New Jersey 08540
99 Banbury Road, Oxford OX2 6JX

press.princeton.edu

All Rights Reserved

ISBN 978-0-691-25769-3
ISBN (pbk.) 978-0-691-25770-9
ISBN (e-book) 978-0-691-26154-6

British Library Cataloging-in-Publication Data is available

Editorial: Anne Savarese and James Collier
Production Editorial: Jill Harris
Cover Design: Haley Chung
Production: Lauren Reese
Publicity: William Pagdatoon
Copyeditor: Leah Caldwell
Cover image © Dayanita Singh

This book has been composed in Arno

10 9 8 7 6 5 4 3 2 1

CONTENTS

Acknowledgments vii
A Note on Names xi

Introduction. Reading for History, circa 1857   1

1   Reading for Survival   26

2   Reading for the Record   56

3   Reading for Time   90

4   Reading for Company   128

Epilogue   168

Notes 173
Selected Bibliography 201
Index 205

ACKNOWLEDGMENTS

THIS BOOK BEGAN AS a vague idea when I was a DPhil student at the University of Oxford. Elleke Boehmer, my adviser, provided the guidance and support to turn it into a project with legs. Many years on, I remain grateful for her unflinching enthusiasm, her meticulous readings of multiple drafts of every chapter of this book, and most of all, for her time.

Elsewhere in Oxford, I found intellectual homes that made my experience of graduate school anything but lonely. At Ertegun House, Bryan Ward-Perkins was a model of generosity and good humor. He also continues to hold the distinction of being one of the few people who read this manuscript voluntarily. For stimulating conversation and all-round good company, I thank Annina Loets, Jacob Meister, Thomas Newbold, Kelsey Rubin-Detlev, Sam Shearn, and Tobias Tan. At the Postcolonial Theory and Writing Seminar, Elleke Boehmer and Ankhi Mukherjee ran a tight ship, creating the conditions for vibrant discussions and fast friendships, as I'm sure Erica Lombard, Eleni Philippou, and Alex Bubb would agree. For his support and encouragement, I thank Faisal Devji. Lipika Kamra and Aashique Iqbal made Oxford home.

I began rethinking my vague idea for a book as a Junior Fellow at the Society of Fellows, Harvard University. Conversations with Simion Filip, William Todd, Peter McMurray, Amartya Sen, and Moira Weigel kept Monday evenings lively. I cannot imagine my time in Cambridge without my "scientist" friends, Xin Jin and Vedika Khemani.

It was at Yale that I finally began rewriting my vague idea into a book manuscript. I'd like to thank the chairs of the Department of English, Langdon Hammer, Jessica Brantley, and Marc Robinson, for helping me navigate the bureaucratic and paperwork worlds of the university, immigration, and beyond. I'm lucky to work alongside brilliant and wonderful colleagues like Ardis Butterfield, Jill Campbell, Joe Cleary, Marcel Elias, Greg Ellermann, Marta Figlerowicz, Ben Glaser, Catherine Nicholson, Joe North, John Durham Peters, Emily Thornbury, Katie Trumpener, Juno Richards, and Sunny Xiang. I'm grateful for

Stephanie Newell's guidance, incisive feedback on many drafts, and unbridled enthusiasm for cake. I'd like to think that Naomi Levine, Tasha Eccles, and I would be friends even if we weren't colleagues. Beyond Linsly-Chittenden Hall, I have incurred other debts on campus. I owe much to Ayesha Ramachandran, whose encouragement and support was integral to finishing this project. Over on Hillhouse Avenue at the South Asia Council, I've been glad to find friends like Sarah Khan and Naveena Naqvi. No question was too silly for me to ask Rohit De, and for him to answer. A Zoom writing group with Adeem Suhail kept me sane in 2020.

Countless interlocutors—many of them unknown to me—read drafts-in-progress and listened to the conference talks that went into the making of this manuscript. Their feedback made it a better book. Among those whom I can name, I thank: Sukanya Banerjee, Tasha Eccles, Jacqueline Goldsby, Isabel Hofmeyr, Priya Joshi, Cajetan Iheka, David Kastan, Peter McDonald, Aakriti Mandhwani, and Michael Warner. Leah Price's *How to Do Things with Books* was published my first year of graduate school and immediately converted me to book history.

At Princeton University Press, I thank Anne Savarese for her support of and belief in the project, and James Collier for his careful editorial assistance. Jill Harris oversaw the book's transformation from immaterial text to material object; Leah Caldwell copyedited the manuscript scrupulously.

A great deal of the research for this book was made possible because of the efforts of librarians and archivists, in particular those at the Bodleian Library, Oxford; the British Library, London; the National Library, Kolkata; the Beinecke Rare Book and Manuscript Library, Yale University; and the Sri Lanka National Archives, Colombo. I'd like to make special mention of Arijit Roy Chowdhury, the director of the Gupta Press, who has let me try and make sense of his extraordinary collections of books every year since 2014.

The many years of research that went into this book were generously funded by grants from the University of Oxford, including the Vice Chancellor's Fund and the Grimstone Foundation, as well as numerous travel grants and bursaries from the Department of English and Wolfson College. An Ahmet and Mica Ertegun Graduate Scholarship in the Humanities made a DPhil at Oxford an actual possibility. A Morse Junior Faculty Fellowship at Yale gave me the time and space to reimagine the book, and A. Whitney Griswold and South Asia Faculty Research awards allowed me to conduct additional archival research. The publication of this book, especially the inclusion of its many images, was made possible through a Frederick Hilles Publication Award, also from Yale University.

Chapter 1 is derived in part from my article "On Not Reading *The Soldier's Pocket-book for Field Service*," published in *Journal of Victorian Culture* 22.1 (2017): 40–56, © Leeds Trinity University. An earlier version of chapter 2 was published as "Of Greasy Notebooks and Dirty Newspapers: Reading the Illegible in *The Village in the Jungle*," *Journal of Commonwealth Literature* 50.1 (2015): 59–73, © Priyasha Mukhopadhyay. I thank Leeds Trinity University and Sage Publishing for their permission to reuse this material in the book.

Writing this book was easier because of Apoorva Bhandari, Susan Christi, Naina Dayal, Morgan Day Frank, Aruni Kashyap, Aakriti Mandhwani, Stuti Mehta, and Abhimanyu Tewari. With sincere gratitude, I thank the numerous aunts, uncles, and family friends who indulgently sent me books from across the world whenever I wanted them as an undergraduate student in Delhi. My parents, Paromita and Monojit, have given me a lifetime of support and encouragement, even as trips back to India became filled with endless visits to the archive. In the last twenty years I have lived on three continents, but their house in Cal will always be my home. My brother Mayukh's good humor has never failed to cheer me up. My grandfather, Prodyot Kumar Talukdar, filled my childhood with poetry, music, art, and ice cream. Finally, I'm happy to report that Zack Barnett-Howell survived the writing of this book. He has read it more times than anyone, and it has benefited from his exacting editorial eye. If he will allow me one last material metaphor, he is the spine that holds this book together. He also made the map and graphs you will see in chapter 3.

A NOTE ON NAMES

THE NAMES OF SEVERAL South Asian cities and countries I refer to have changed since the historical period on which this book focuses.

- I use Calcutta to refer to the city before 2001, and Kolkata to refer to the city after this date.
- I use Bombay to refer to the city before 1995, and Mumbai to refer to the city after this date.
- I use Madras to refer to the city before 1996, and Chennai to refer to the city after this date.
- I use Ceylon to refer to the country before 1972, and Sri Lanka to refer to the country after this date.

REQUIRED READING

Introduction

READING FOR HISTORY, CIRCA 1857

RUDYARD KIPLING'S *Departmental Ditties and Other Verses* (1886) was an instant hit.¹ Kipling, just shy of twenty-one, had already spent close to four years in India, writing for *The Civil and Military Gazette*, a newspaper with offices in Lahore and Shimla, and a forum for some of his first poems and stories.² A slim volume of twenty-six poems, the collection brought together some of Kipling's earliest observations about the social life of the British in the colonial outposts of South Asia, a subject that he would continue to document and satirize mercilessly throughout his literary career. The primary target of his acerbic tongue in *Departmental Ditties* was the institution of the government office—the hub of Britain's administration abroad—and the civil servants who handled its daily business. The government office was ostensibly crucial to the retention of empire, but Kipling's series of comical sketches recasts it as a staging ground for scandal, nepotism, and indolence. Its world is stacked with pompous pretenders with inflated egos, lazy bureaucrats idling away their time with piles of unimportant papers, and unfaithful wives plotting and scheming behind their husbands' backs. This portrait of Anglo-Indian life, in short, is characterized less by colonial might than by dissatisfying marriages, dullness of mind, boredom of routine, and the claustrophobic heat of the Indian subcontinent. The collection helped claim a colonial readership, and ultimately a metropolitan one, for the young writer. It was published in a print run of no more than five hundred copies. Kipling sent out order forms to readers, tracing familiar routes of imperial trade: from Aden to Singapore, from Quetta to Colombo. Within a few weeks, every copy was sold.³

In the fall of 2019, I called up a copy from the first run of *Departmental Ditties* to the reading room of the Beinecke Rare Book & Manuscript Library at

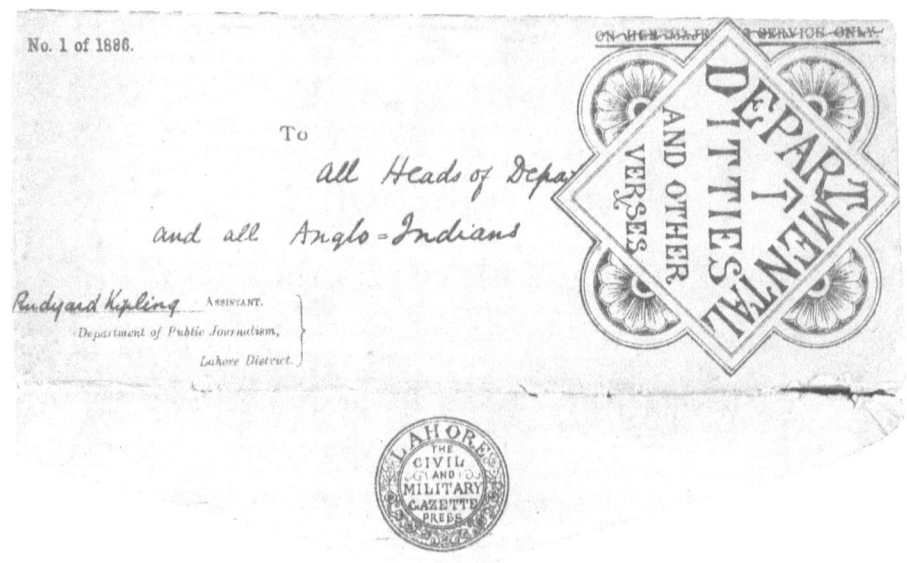

FIGURE I.1. Rudyard Kipling, *Departmental Ditties and Other Verses* (Lahore: The Civil and Military Gazette Press, 1886), David Alan Richards Collection of Rudyard Kipling, Beinecke Rare Book & Manuscript Library, Yale University. Limited First Edition.
The red tape to which Kipling alludes is missing.

Yale University. I laughed when I saw it, not just because the poems were funny, but because the object in front of me was exactly the kind of joke a book historian would appreciate. Writing about the production of the book, Kipling chuckled that the narrow quarto volume was meant "to imitate a D[istrict]. O[ffice]. Government envelope," its light brown wrappers bound together by iconic red tape.[4] A perfect coalescing of form and content, the similarities to an envelope on "official" business continue. The dedication—"To All the Heads of Depar[tments] and all Anglo-Indians"—declares an addressee (or a reading public). The ornate presentation of the book's title transforms what would have otherwise been an ordinary envelope into one holding a governmental missive. Kipling's name, signifying his authorial claim to the collection, doubles up as a return address, muddying the boundaries between poet and clerk. The mock stamp of The Civil and Military Gazette Press, a nod to the fact that the book was printed in the workshop of his employer, replaces a customary government seal on the flap of the envelope. As anyone who has worked with bureaucratic archives will spot, the publication date of 1886 merges with the official document number, No. 1, reminding us that this is just the first of many letters that the office will send as the year progresses, just as it is the first of many works to come from Kipling over the course of his career. Opening the envelope reveals a pamphlet with writing printed on only one side of each page, as per official prescription. We're invited to read the poems as individual sheaves. Tied together in Kipling's docket, they make up a bureaucratic collection. Kipling proudly declared that the imitation was so convincing that "among a pile of papers," it would have "deceived a clerk of twenty years' service."[5]

The poems in *Departmental Ditties* knitted together references to survey maps and charts, official reports and letters, directories, and books of Euclidean geometry. What better to hold a literary rendition of these documents, all part of the professional life of being a servant of empire, than a bureaucratic envelope? I suggest that Kipling's *Departmental Ditties* performs what we might call a material poetics of empire. This is a poetics that not only speaks to the inseparability of the book-as-object and the book-as-text, but also takes seriously the relationship between the literary text and its mundane counterparts, embedding both in colonial networks of production and circulation. The imperial conditions that made literary production possible—Kipling's included—were bolstered by a foundation of thick stacks of everyday books and documents: bureaucratic files and forms, statistical accounts, survey reports, ethnographic compendia, military manuals, and almanacs. Such forms of writing served crucial, functional purposes in the daily life of the colonizers and the colonized. They were also ubiquitous, circulating in unprecedented numbers that dwarfed literary print runs. Kipling's *Departmental Ditties*, a literary portrait of empire bound in a bureaucratic spine, is a material acknowledgment of the mundane textual infrastructure of the colonial world. The imbrication of poem and bureaucratic document can be described in bibliographical terms: the faux envelope is the paratext of *Departmental Ditties*. Attesting to Kipling's familiarity with the colonial institution of the office, the cover of the volume sparks a moment of recognition between the author and reader. Without the framing context of the envelope, the poems and their satire on bureaucratic routine fall flat.

The design of *Departmental Ditties* also tells us something about Kipling's imagined readers, an anglophone public scattered across Britain's empire. Kipling knew that nothing quite commanded attention like an envelope bearing government insignia. Such an envelope inevitably contained something that *had to be read*: a request, a summons, an official notice. Repositories of actionable information, such envelopes demanded that recipients open them immediately. Imagine a copy of the book in the hands of a nineteenth-century reader. Our hypothetical reader would have first been worried, then confused, and then amused as the prank was revealed. This progression certainly explains the readers' complaints that poured in about the difficulties the configuration of the book posed. Reports that the "wire binding cut the pages, and the red tape tore the covers" conjure up an image of a panicked reader hastily tearing open the envelope, only to be relieved to find nothing more than a set of poems.[6] *Departmental Ditties* cleverly borrows the urgency of a communication from the government and lends it to a work of literature, intended for leisure and enjoyment. Kipling's gimmick, in short, framed his debut collection of poetry as *required reading*.

Required Reading recovers the story of how everyday forms of writing, from the bureaucratic report to the almanac, came to dominate the cultural imagination of the British empire in South Asia in the late nineteenth and early twentieth centuries. It tracks the journeys of boisterous soldiers posted on treacherous frontiers, bored colonial administrators languishing in colonial outposts, peasants confused by the regulations governing licenses and permits, office clerks racing to catch public transport to work, and lonely women eager to excel in their social and literary circles. For each of these publics, daily life in colonial South Asia was inextricable from a tangled stream of print and manuscript, ranging from instruction manuals to railway timetables, petitions to magazines. Generated both by and in response to colonial institutions such as the army, the bureaucratic office, and the Indian railways, these everyday forms of writing formed a material "contact zone," an uneven playing ground on which both British agents and South Asian subjects grappled with the enormity of empire, acknowledged the challenges it presented, and formulated strategies of self-preservation.[7]

Starting in the mid-nineteenth century, the coupling of the modern state with the widespread availability of cheap printing technologies meant that everyday forms of writing in English, Bengali, Urdu, and other South Asian languages circulated in enormous numbers across colony and metropole to create what I term the *functional archive*. An interface between the British empire and its inhabitants, it was a crucial conduit through which historical readers came to understand imperial relationships as they were made and unmade in colonial

South Asia. Linking acts of reading to actions in the world, the constituents of the functional archive, ranging from licenses to handbooks, acquired the status of *required reading*. They were essential practical guides to navigating an imperial landscape. Across their differing goals and audiences, these texts provided blueprints for an imperial life, working through prescription and proscription to shape the range of actions possible under the aegis of the British empire.

Required Reading is a history of reading under *duress*. I use *duress* to lay bare the visible and invisible pressures of the colonial state that coerced readers into textual relationships that weren't always of their own making. Duress is a constant presence from which there is little respite. It operates in the realm of the everyday, eroding people's sense of self and well-being.[8] The bureaucratization of village life, for example, meant that local inhabitants needed to apply for licenses and permits to engage in age-old agricultural practices. Sometimes outrightly forced, at other times strongly suggested, to read under duress was to acknowledge the environments of power in which texts were produced, circulated, and made compulsory. I uncover the intimate connections that readers formed with texts, connections that manifested as anger, exhaustion, helplessness, expediency, and playfulness. The line from requirement to actual compliance, however, was far from straight. Just because a book or document was mandated didn't mean that people read it. It also didn't mean that these texts were even readable. I chart a history of reading under duress that comes hand in hand with a history of readerly resourcefulness, with readers bending regulations, deliberately flouting requirements, and finding creative ways to compensate for the failures of texts and the limits of their own skills.

Required Reading asks: What happens to our histories of empire and our histories of reading if we route them through ordinary forms of writing? This book makes two arguments. First: it argues that the functional archive offers us new ways to think about people's relationships to empire. For the inhabitants of colonial South Asia, empire wasn't an abstract institution of political authority. Empire had a textual form: the petitions and handbooks they encountered in their daily lives. Mandated by professional needs and necessitated by social ones, how readers responded to timetables or account books provides us with a window into contemporary conversations about the military, bureaucracy, and women's rights. It was through these forms of writing that colonial subjects and colonial agents came to understand themselves as compliant, dissident, or indifferent imperial actors.

Second: this book argues that the itineraries of the functional archive challenge our very conception of what interpretative and noninterpretative acts count as reading. Readers' encounters with an almanac or an account book activated a range of unexpected affective and intellectual responses that borrowed from the feeling and vocabulary ascribed to reading literary texts. Selectively read almanacs and impenetrable account books were springboards for intimate, world-shaping readerly relationships. These relationships deserve attention, not simply to diversify the range of responses we include in a reception history, but rather to acknowledge that these modes of engagement—material, textual, aural, circulatory—had readerly and literary effects.

By foregrounding the functional archive, my aim is not to sideline literary texts or literary methods of reading. I resist the impulse to see the functional archive merely as informational, turning instead to its rich aesthetic life in the colonial world. Late nineteenth- and early twentieth-century colonial literature, written in English and South Asian vernacular languages, responded to the historical surfeit of paper by folding references to petitions and handbooks into their plots. Even beyond their literary representations, the material and textual forms of the functional archive had literary resonances, carefully deploying metaphors, tropes, and material format to achieve their desired ends. *Required Reading* is committed to reproducing the commingling of the functional archive and its more conventionally literary counterparts that we find in the world of colonial South Asia.

Unreadable Empire

In 1852, John Stuart Mill was asked about the reasons for the phenomenal success of the East India Company. His answer—unequivocal in its emphasis—was that India was governed by writing:

> All the orders given, and all the acts of the executive officers, are reported in writing, and the whole of the original correspondence is sent to the Home Government; so that there is no single act done in India, the whole of the reasons for which are not placed on record. This appears to me a greater security for good government than exists in almost any other government in the world, because no other probably has a system of recordation so complete.[9]

Mill's self-congratulatory opinion highlights an administrative problem at the heart of the British empire: the distance between the colony and the metropole. Any empire, as Thomas Richards argues, is a "nation in overreach," struggling to control seized territory spread across the world.[10] One solution to this problem was the bureaucratic universalism that Mill echoes: that every single action should have its very own paper trail. Laying bare the inextricable connection between the written word and imperial rule, Mill's response points to an empire of accountability that depended on the mobility of letters, reports, memos, minutes, contracts, and multiple copies of each, across local and international networks of offices and institutions.[11] Office manuals and codes of instruction outlined how and when to draft, copy, attest, and destroy documents. If there was a birth, death, or marriage in a village in South Asia, the local office would have to keep a record of it. Extensive correspondences grew out of the work of setting up reading rooms and libraries for soldiers. J. Emerson Tennent, the colonial secretary of Ceylon between 1845 and 1850, complained about the levels of scrutiny and documentation that even the most trivial tasks required. Official written permission was required for "two skeins of thread to sew [together] the records of a district court" and a single measuring ruler for an assistant agent. The need for one pewter inkstand in a police station generated thirteen dispatches.[12]

When the East India Company transferred its holdings in South Asia to the British Crown in 1858, it also transferred its penchant for paperwork and anxieties about imperial rule. The historian Ranajit Guha traces these proclivities in the writings of the military officer Francis Yeats-Brown. In Yeats-Brown's accounts, South Asia emerges as a claustrophobic presence, a force that is at once inchoate and real. Yeats-Brown "shivered at the millions and immensities and secrecies of India." Its "magical plains" stretching to the Himalayas were both awe-inspiring and wholly indecipherable. Unlike the Anglo-Indian gentlemen's club—"a world whose limits were known"—empire appeared unbounded and unmanageable.[13] Yeats-Brown's sense of alienation was not unique; echoes of it can be found across the writings of colonial administrators of the period. One historical origin for this feeling, what Guha calls being "not at home in empire," is the Revolt of 1857, an unsuccessful military rebellion against the British that was nevertheless significant in precipitating the dissolution of the East India Company. As the newly formed British Raj reflected on the events of 1857, concerns about imperial control escalated to a feverish pitch. Despite a British victory against the rebels, the revolt left the British with a lurking feeling of unease. Stemming from a premise of insurmountable difference between the colonizer and the colonized, the Revolt of 1857 reminded the British that despite their efforts, South Asia remained an unreadable empire. In the eyes of its colonial rulers, its vistas bore marks of the terrifying sublime, its religious practices were wholly inscrutable, its languages were too numerous to count, much less learn. South Asia, the jewel in the British crown, seemed more like a set of traps, waiting to ensnare the unsuspecting colonizer.

South Asia might have been ultimately unreadable, but that did little to stymie British attempts. The feeling of being not at home in empire came hand in hand with the creation of a surveillance state, built on decades of data collection projects. Intertwined with the birth of modern disciplines like anthropology, archaeology, and geography, these epistemic projects were aimed at collecting, categorizing, and codifying all aspects of South Asia's territorial and cultural histories. Raw, unprocessed data from multiple years of collecting efforts were neatly transformed into different textual forms: official reports, ethnographic taxonomies, directories, geographic compendia, encyclopedias, maps, and dictionaries. As the work of scholars like Bernard Cohn has shown us, these projects didn't necessarily lead to more efficient modes of imperial rule. Rather, the act of building an archive of information allowed the British to entertain fantasies of control that didn't always comport with reality.[14]

The textual projects of control and surveillance, attempting to make the colonies readable, varied in scale and emphasis. There were ones like George Grierson's ambitious *Linguistic Survey of India* (1903–1928), a systematic sampling of over 723 South Asian languages and dialects, which took over thirty years to complete and yielded over eight thousand pages of prose organized in eleven volumes.[15] Similarly, William Wilson Hunter's historical compendium, *The Imperial Gazetteer of India,* started off in nine volumes in 1881 and morphed into twenty-six by 1909.[16] Majestic in both their scope and material appearance, these authoritative imperial tomes were the definition of a "book": printed and hardbound, and meant to last. In short, these colonial tomes were seen as synonymous with the unflinching backbone of British rule.[17] High profile as they were, such printed projects were elite productions. For the most part, they sat undisturbed on bookshelves, read sparingly and almost exclusively by government officials and scholars.

In this book, I turn instead to the scrappier textual forms spurred on by the informational turn in the colonial imagination. The uncharismatic minutiae of colonial life, these official and unofficial kinds of writing included but weren't limited to permits and licenses, instructional texts and household manuals, and self-help volumes for audiences as varied as soldiers and equestrian breeders.[18] Unlike the impressive *Imperial Gazetteer*, these texts took on a variety of material forms: single sheets of paper, files, pocket-sized paperback books, and serialized publications. Some, like military handbooks published in London and bureaucratic documents produced on the ground, were linked to local institutions of governance, garnering both British and South Asian readerships.

There were also texts produced by South Asians that catered to predominantly South Asian readerships. If the British collected information to discipline an unreadable empire, that same empire, transformed and reconfigured via foreign intervention, seemed alien and formidable to their colonial subjects. As printing technologies became cheaper and more widely available, colonial subjects turned to knowledge production and data collection endeavors of their own, with local print shops in cities and towns across the colony churning out hastily sewn-together almanacs and directories, periodicals, and anthologies. Rather than merely being statistics listed in the pages of governmental reports, South Asians began to create their own textual tools to navigate a world shaped by colonial modernity. The functional archive of this book was as much a construction of South Asian subjects as it was their colonial overlords.

Defining the Functional Archive

The concept of the *functional archive* underpins this book. Beyond merely providing the raw material for my research, it offers a framework through which to understand the relationship between texts and their circulation in the world. In one sense, the functional archive is a material manifestation of ideology, accreting and diffusing into the cultural milieu and popular imagination.[19]

Here are four concepts that can help us unpack the functional archive:

Network

Much like empire itself, the functional archive was a textual construct, a series of files and folders held together by precarious relationships of reading. More than just a loose agglomeration, it formed a material infrastructure of texts that crisscrossed and networked throughout the space of empire. Texts in the functional archive never worked in isolation; they overlapped and mutually reinforced each other. Obtaining a gun license in Ceylon in 1909, for example, would have required the orchestration of a range of everyday forms of writing: multiple, attested copies of the application form, a copy of the Gun License Ordinance of

1908 (published in the *Ceylon Government Gazette*), the license itself with a counterfoil copy, and the official register in which the details of the license would be recorded. None of these documents could have stood alone; none of them could have performed their roles without the others. These supportive linkages also point to the generative nature of the archive, with written objects mushrooming and multiplying, mandating the creation of more and more texts. My archival research for this book has continuously impressed upon me that even simple bureaucratic infractions—like not having a valid license—could spawn pages and pages of petitions, letters, reports, and investigations. That these texts always worked in concert with each other meant that the functional archive was always an archive-in-process, expanding and buckling—but never collapsing—under the weight of added texts.

Transaction

The purpose of the functional archive was to broker transactions made necessary by the institutional structures of the colonial state. I use the word *transaction* because it captures the dynamic nature of these interactions, the push and pull, the give and take.[20] After all, what makes a transaction a transaction is that all parties involved aim to get *something*, whether material or ideological, out of the exchange. Each node in the functional archive was the result of multiple interconnected transactions between subjects, agents, and intermediaries across the spectrum of colonial society. In this way, the functional archive's textual network overlaid a social one, reflecting the conflicts and contracts that made up colonial South Asia.

Most of the transactions I narrate in this book were not among equals. They were negotiated along very steep power gradients, determined by an individual's racial and occupational proximity to the colonial state. For disenfranchised colonial subjects, to participate in a transaction was to participate in a system that was slated against them and to their disadvantage. More often than not, they found themselves in transactions not of their choosing, just one of the many consequences of living in a violent empire. The costs of engagement were unequally distributed and were often magnitudes higher for parties not acting on behalf of the state. This isn't, of course, to suggest that the disenfranchised party in a transaction had no levers to pull. Some of the most meaningful moments in my research for this book were discovering how people triumphed despite the odds being against them, finding loopholes and fixes by which to tilt situations in their favor.

Dispersion

Studying the functional archive poses a unique challenge. How do we reconstruct its networks and connections, its linkages and iterations? One of the singular features of the functional archive was that it defied the logics of site. It wasn't designed to be a single physical repository, to be housed in a university library or a government institution. As a networked formation, its scattered nature enabled its primary role: to connect different institutions and individuals. To an extent, this dispersion was built into the mechanics of colonial offices, which tracked correspondence through "despatch diaries," creating a record of all official letters sent, tagged by date and branch.[21]

But the generative nature and staggered growth of the functional archive means that its scope is undefined. It would take a real feat of the imagination to truly conjure up the functional archive—nodes, branches, and all—in its entirety. As researchers, we encounter its parts scattered across the world, filling up cupboards and shelves in storage facilities. Transnational, multi-sited archival research is necessary, but not sufficient, to trace the functional archive's ever-expanding networks. Each chapter of this book provides a snapshot of a small part of the functional archive, stitched together from collections in South Asia (Kolkata, Colombo), the United Kingdom (London, Brighton, and Oxford), the United States (New Haven), and numerous digital repositories. In the process, I have learned to think of archival research not in terms of narratives, but in terms of constellations, following the discontinuous growth of parts of the functional archive in its historical moment and beyond.

Ephemerality

The historical incarnation of the functional archive was characterized by paper excess and information overflow. Yet the functional archive that I see, as a scholar in the twenty-first century, is chronically fragmented. Historians have always had to work around the problems posed by incomplete archives. In the postcolonial world, this challenge presents itself in an extreme form. As Ulrike Stark has pointed out, historians of the book in South Asia are faced with the lack of reliable empirical evidence about every stage of a book's lifecycle.[22] Paucity is a result of material degradation, the result of natural processes and human neglect. White ants, silverfish, and humid weather have systematically contributed to the rapid disintegration of physical evidence, often misstored in damp, overcrowded rooms. Facing storage crises, bureaucrats have ordered files deemed unimportant be burned to make room for others. Sometimes, with insidious intent, they also have burned important files to hide crimes. One way or the other, the texts of the functional archive were likely to vanish into the proverbial and literal dustbins of history. While the historical value of the functional archive was predicated on its ability to help readers do things, the conditions of its physical storage have jeopardized that very purpose for its unintended audience of scholarly readers in the present.

But even in its time, most of the functional archive wasn't built to last. Its constituent texts tended toward the cheaply produced: printed on poor quality paper, hastily bound together in files and folders, or clumsily sewn together between paper covers. These were mobile, traveling texts, shunted between bureaucratic offices and railway station platforms. Linked to the repeated performance of daily activities, these material objects bore the brunt of frequent use in the form of torn pages, frayed edges, and ripped covers. Even when copies escaped wear and tear, there was little reason for a reader to preserve them. These texts expired and became outdated; they needed to be revised and reissued regularly. For this reason, most had a short shelf life. Almanacs were useful for a single calendar year, newspapers for a single day. Replaced by new and improved editions, they met a destructive fate: up in flames as tinder or turned into wastepaper.[23] One of the paradoxes of the history of the book is that the examples of everyday writing that *do* survive were probably those that were least consulted.[24]

A progression from plethora to paucity characterizes the functional archive over time. Lamentations for the loss of materials and gaps in the historical record are appropriate. After all, what we have access to today is minuscule when compared to historical circulation. Digitization, too, doesn't promise unregulated access to what does remain. Laurel Brake notes that a decade of digitizing efforts has opened up access to less than 1 percent of surviving nineteenth-century newspapers.[25] Nevertheless, my research for this book has been made possible by acts of preservation that render the functional archive's ephemerality moot. It has relied on official archives, public institutions, and digital repositories, but it has just as often been enriched by the efforts of individuals to preserve the functional archive's ephemeral components. Victorian readers, like Garnet Wolseley in chapter 1, pushed back against the ephemerality of print objects, ranging from newspapers to greeting cards, by creating archives of their own, cut and pasted into scrapbooks. Similarly, chapter 3's discussion of almanacs was made possible by the collecting efforts of one contemporary almanac publisher in Kolkata.

Empire's Histories of Reading

Histories of reading, whether in empire or beyond, have tended to be histories of reading literary texts.[26] Since Thomas Macaulay infamously declared that the value of a "single shelf of a good European library" far outweighed the "whole native literature of India and Arabia," postcolonial scholars have suggested that the ideological underpinnings of literary texts were the connective tissue holding the British empire together.[27] Following Macaulay's blueprint, colonial rulers conceived of reading works of English literature as an act of imperial interpellation, creating a class of indispensable native informants, "Indian in blood and colour, but English in tastes, in opinions, in morals, and in intellect."[28] As we know from Gauri Viswanathan's *Masks of Conquest* (1989), these historical forces led to the institutionalization of English literature as a discipline: first in South Asia, then in the metropole.[29] Through the 1990s, postcolonial scholarship, most notably, Edward Said's *Culture and Imperialism* (1993), has explored how the historical condition of empire was inextricable from the rise of the novel, even as the form worked to make this interdependency invisible.[30] Though from opposing sides of the political spectrum, Macaulay and Said build their arguments on a shared assumption. English literature—its valuation, its weightiness—was both an instrument and measure of colonial power relations. The literary text, in short, is framed as an apparition of colonial desires and cultural capital.

Over the last two decades, a pioneering body of revisionist scholarship on the history of reading in South Asia has emerged. These works center the figure of the colonial reader and transform literary taste into an expression of readerly agency. For example, Priya Joshi's *In Another Country* (2002) draws on extensive library circulation figures from nineteenth-century South Asia to show that the English novel of "serious standards" had a less successful career abroad than arrogant administrators would have us believe. Canonical nineteenth-century novels faced stiff competition from sentimental novels by the likes of Marie Corelli, F. Marion Crawford, and G.W.M. Reynolds.[31] While such writers were relegated to insignificance in Britain, as Stephanie Newell shows, they were also popular in West Africa.[32] This revisionism about what was being read, however, doesn't shift the overall literary bent of these histories of reading. Reframed instead as a debate between the highbrow and the lowbrow in which the lowbrow wins, the literary text remains the primary object under scrutiny.

This also holds true for scholarship on print cultures in South Asian languages. Anindita Ghosh's *Power in Print* (2006) undoes the image of nineteenth-century Calcutta as a city occupied exclusively by the Bengali *bhadralok* (literally "genteel folk"). Underneath its surface teemed subversive pockets that churned out *Battala* books, ephemeral genres of literature named after the part of the city where they were produced and sold. These included sentimental novels, books of black magic, satirical farces, detective stories, and pornographic writings. Challenging "respectable" literary tastes with colloquial language and tackling subjects considered obscene, such texts catered to the emergent middle and lower classes, functionally literate in the vernaculars, overworked and in need of entertainment. On the sly, elite readers read them, too.[33] Francesca Orsini's *Print and Pleasure* (2009) sketches a similar landscape for Hindi and Urdu publications in North India. In her account, pulpy genres such as the detective novel and romance were the common reader's daily go-to books, not canonical literary masterpieces.[34]

I share with this body of scholarship an investment in archival recovery, a commitment to foregrounding readerly agency, and a strong belief in the power of material and textual history to uncover the many fractures under the surface of the colonial world. I turn this commitment to the functional archive. Incorporating these forms of writing into our histories of reading allows us, I argue, to think of textual relationships more expansively. The people who read detective stories and sentimental fiction *also* read almanacs and instructional manuals. Literary readers were embedded in and influenced by the messy, entangled print world that this book uncovers. The relationships that those readers forged with everyday forms of writing elicited contradictory feelings of anxiety, compliance, resistance, and wish fulfillment. Magazines were described as friends; account books denigrated as enemies. Even the absence of a traditional literary text—whether a novel or a volume of erotic poetry—didn't stop readers from forming intimate relationships with their everyday reading material.

Not Really Reading

All histories of reading rely on the responses of readers. Most scholars rely on textual evidence: detailed marginalia in a novel signal deep engagement; a letter sent to a friend recommending a book (or suggesting that it's a waste of time) answers questions about a reader's taste. We take *Things Fall Apart* as confirmation that Chinua Achebe read Conrad and Yeats, just as *Midnight's Children* tells us that Salman Rushdie read García Márquez and Grass. Textual evidence is paired with material details. Food stains on a page indicate multitasking;

torn pages represent the frequency and carelessness with which readers approached a book. Taken together, these textual and material clues are the smoking guns of book historical research. Because they exist, we know that someone performed an act of reading.[35] Many of the readers I study left these kinds of crumbs for me to find: dated notes in the margins of bureaucratic files, additions and corrections to their almanacs, short stories complaining about handbooks, and book reviews lauding literary texts. For the most part, these precious forms of evidence were created by elite and, it goes without saying, literate readers. Individuals of this sort dominate histories of reading, as if the only people who had thoughts or feelings about a text were the people who were capable of—and willing—to read it.

I collect responses to the functional archive from individuals ranging across the literacy spectrum. A key thread through the book is illiteracy, most prominently discussed in chapter 2. Scholars have always grappled with the ineluctable gaps illiterate subjects leave in the historical record. In his account of the experiences of Indian soldiers in World War I, Santanu Das laments the lack of extensive literary works from the soldiers themselves, overwhelmingly due to their lack of literacy skills.[36] Elizabeth McHenry's hunt for black readers presents the stumbling block of Anna Murray Douglass, Frederick Douglass's wife, who never learned how to read or write. "Without the ability to write letters or otherwise create a lasting record of her experience," McHenry notes, it's difficult to understand what her experience as an illiterate member of a literary club, the East Baltimore Mental Improvement Society, might have been like.[37]

One way in which historians of colonial South Asia have included the region's unlettered population in their accounts is by exploring practices of reading aloud. A familiar scene is a literate person, book in hand, surrounded by a mass of illiterate people hanging on their every word.[38] In this scenario, an illiterate person's only access to the content of a text is by listening to it, read out in the voice of another. In these relationships, texts are disembodied objects reconfigured as aurality.[39] But this approach doesn't encompass the full range of ways in which illiterate subjects came to interact with forms of writing.[40] While the aural experiences of illiterate subjects are an important part of the puzzle, they're not the only part. Despite their lack of reading abilities, illiterate people in colonial South Asia came into frequent and direct contact with many kinds of written and printed materials, demanding that we develop a more nuanced vocabulary with which to describe their textual interactions. One avenue is to explore moments in which the book-as-object presses in on the book-as-text. While for the illiterate, a text's content could only be mediated through the voice of others, the rest of the text—its appearance, its size and weight, the feel of its paper, the arrangement of writing—was up for grabs. After all, not being able to read doesn't preclude tactile, material relationships with books and documents, whether as fetish objects or dead weight.

For historians of the colonial and postcolonial book, an emphasis on the material life of writing is a much-needed course correction for a literary field saturated in discourse analysis.[41] My inquiry extends recent scholarship that takes seriously the meanings that books make as objects, even in opposition to those they make as texts. Representative of this body of work is Leah Price's *How to Do Things with Books in Victorian Britain* (2012), which urges us to turn our attention to the ways in which books were repurposed as physical things: screens and shields, grease paper, and interior decoration.[42] In a similar vein, the medievalist Mark Amsler argues for what he calls affective literacy, an economy of reading driven by somatic and emotional responses to texts that could subvert lettered, literate ones.[43] In *Dockside Reading* (2022), Isabel Hofmeyr shows us how customs officials in Southern African ports treated imported books as "a form of miniature cargo," one item among a consignment of many.[44] For these bureaucratic readers, books were "cargo to be moved, objects to be classified and taxed, and items to be checked for potential danger, whether ideological or epidemiological."[45] Across these three works of scholarship, reading the content emerges as just one way—and not necessarily the predominant way—of engaging with a text. In the course of my own research, this point has been driven home by the marks of illiterate subjects that I see creeping into books and documents. Petitions, written by official scribes, are "signed" by the thumbprints of their illiterate petitioners. Bureaucratic reports describe how, during the Deccan Riots of 1875, the anger of farmers found a material target: the account books of their moneylenders, which they burned to erase any trace of their debts.

Illiterate readers present a limit case. They challenge our understanding of how people can form relationships with written material even when they can't literally access the content for themselves. Methodologically, illiteracy serves as a starting point for thinking about moments in the archive in which the ability to read doesn't neatly map onto understanding. It sits alongside other barriers to reading: the refusal to exercise one's literacy (discussed in chapter 1), the realization that literacy isn't a guarantee of understanding (chapter 2) or social acceptance (chapter 4), and the inability to read, stymied by the inhospitable material trappings of a text (chapter 3). Collectively, the readers in my book make us pause to ask: What counts as a response to a text? Holding it? Owning but never opening it? Never reading the whole, but only bits and pieces, extracts, and summaries? Listening to someone else talk about it? These questions push me to take into consideration the full range of responses that readers, irrespective of their literacy skills, generated to make sense of the forms of writing they encountered every day. By exploring the varied ways in which people from across the literacy spectrum dealt with books and documents, my aim is to expand the kinds of evidence we use to construct histories of reception. Rather than confining ourselves to lettered communities who leave traces of their intellectual work in the margins of pages, in diaries, and in literary works, I demonstrate how even readers who teeter on the brink of illiteracy had meaningful, world-shaping encounters with texts. Readers, not-readers, book handlers, selective readers, and sometimes-readers all come together to populate my history of reading for colonial South Asia.

You may have noticed that I use the term "illiterate reader." I am fully aware of the implications of this oxymoronic construction, and I want to embrace them in the spirit of expanding our disciplinary categories. To this end, my book is a small stab at a big question: What, exactly, is reading? My aim is not to provide a counterdefinition, but to claim the label of "reading" for the range of affective and intellectual responses that people had to the functional archive: an acknowledgment of what I see as the porousness of reading, its ability to encompass an array of different practices, values, and effects. In this light, I claim practices of half-reading, not reading, and handling, not simply as reading adjacent, but as integral to how we understand our interpretative methods of meaning-making.

Reading, as Leah Price writes, is an "activity that's too close for critical distance, and perhaps for comfort."[46] Our own proximity to the functional archive makes this statement even more true. While ordinary forms of writing, from petitions to handbills, lurk in the margins of scholarly works, they aren't seen to require histories of reading of their own. Lisa Gitelman, for example, puts the job-printed bureaucratic form center stage in the history of printing and reproduction, but separates these material developments from developments in reading by arguing that the writing on such forms becomes "naturalized" through the tasks we use them to perform.[47] Put differently, we know what these documents say without having to read the fine print. In these accounts, novels acquire readers; documents acquire users.[48] Extending this vocabulary of pragmatism, it could be said that we don't really read bureaucratic documents or refer to instruction manuals, and that we only superficially consult almanacs.

Where the functional archive does make an appearance, it's to lay the ground for future literary relationships.[49] In Richard Altick's landmark study, *The English Common Reader* (1957), for example, nineteenth-century English children could only become "regular readers" when they moved past mundane acts of literacy, such as "deciphering handbills and legends in shop windows."[50] This tendency is indicative of, to borrow Daniel Henkin's words, "the disproportionate weight" given to the novel as the "paradigmatic object of literate consumption."[51] As a result, what historical readers—or even contemporary ones—do with the constituents of the functional archive appears as a foil to acts of "really reading."

The overdetermination of the novel form has also led to a narrower understanding of the many different kinds of reading practices a text can elicit. I share Peter Stallybrass's frustrations: "The novel has only been a brilliantly perverse interlude in the long history of discontinuous reading."[52] The novel is synonymous with continuous reading; thrilling stories and detective fictions are driven by the linear consumption of a plot and, by extension, the linear navigation of a book. Yet, as Stallybrass notes, the technology of the codex—the material format of most novels—was developed precisely to encourage modes of *discontinuous* reading. Unlike a scroll, which needed to be rolled out to be read, the codex form allowed readers to move randomly across a text, skipping and skimming as they so chose.[53]

If scholars agree that there is no singular normative reading experience, the dominant portrait of the reader is still a portrait of a reader lost in a book.[54] Literature, especially the form of the novel, drowns out the world around us; the more we read, the less we notice it.[55] To read a novel is to enter another consciousness, to "read as though we were someone else."[56] These ideas draw on a phenomenological approach to reading, exemplified by the work of Georges Poulet. In his "Phenomenology of Reading" (1969), Poulet describes reading as a concatenation of the twin processes of identification and transformation:

> Reading, then, is the act in which the subjective principle which I call *I*, is modified in such a way that I no longer have the right, strictly speaking, to consider it as my *I*. I am on loan to another, and this other thinks, feels, suffers, and acts within me.[57]

In Poulet's account, we step into the mind of another—the book, the author—to identify with the fictional characters about whom we read and, in turn, reflect on ourselves.[58] This is what is at the heart of reading: its capacity to enthrall us, its ability to change us, its potential for community both within and outside of the covers of the book.

My intention isn't to contest Poulet's description of reading, but instead to extend his characterization of reading to the functional archive. The relationships that readers formed with the functional archive were intimate and transformative, rendering distinctions between reading and use irrelevant.[59] Circulating as affectively charged objects, the functional archive and its offshoots generated responses in readers that hewed closely to those generated by their more recognizably literary counterparts. While the readers of the functional archive may not have used the word "literary" to describe the forms of writing with which they interacted, they experienced their entanglements with the archive as an intimate literary phenomenon. Collectively, the chapters of this book show that what we might call the literary *effects* of reading can crop up even in response to the most mundane of texts, with no aspirations or pretensions to the literary. Put boldly, *Required Reading* is a literary history of reading that is anchored in the functional archive.

Literature and the Uses of History

I take seriously Ben Kafka's assessment that many scholars have "discovered all sorts of interesting and important things looking *through* paperwork, but seldom paused to look *at* it."[60] That is, old-school historical research mined paperwork for content—the raw materials required to write other histories—without necessarily thinking about the histories of paperwork themselves.[61] Over the past decade, historians and anthropologists have become increasingly self-reflexive about their sources, turning them into objects of scholarly inquiry, too.[62] Consider a petition about a land dispute between two groups in early-twentieth-century Ceylon. Looking *through* this document, we could glean evidence for a study of agricultural practices or notions of private property. Looking *at* it, the petition becomes a catalyst for thinking about the readers and texts entangled in the bureaucratic process of petitioning, the details of its content aside. As Ann Stoler argues in *Along the Archival Grain* (2009), a study of colonial documents from nineteenth-century Indonesia under Dutch rule, we should take archival forms "less as stories for a colonial history than as active, generative substances with histories, as documents with itineraries of their own."[63]

Taking inspiration from Kafka (a media historian) and Stoler (an anthropologist), what do these challenges look like for me (a book historian and a literary critic)? They lead me to a series of interconnected questions: How can we look at the functional archive, not simply through the eyes of scholars, but through the eyes of historical readers? What does this tell us about the reading practices they cultivated? How might my own disciplinary practices be deployed as tools of reconstruction and recovery? For me, these questions are methodological. As a scholar trained in literary studies, I am in the habit of performing close readings, paying attention to the linguistic structure and detail of a text. As a historian of the book, I think beyond a text's content, turning instead to how the material shape and form of a book or document might impact how it was read (or not). Stemming from the acknowledgment that every form of writing has generic conventions that generate aesthetic effects in the hands of readers, *Required Reading* is the result of my two disciplinary homes, mobilizing the productive overlaps between their different models of close attention, and considering what these can reveal about how a text generates social and cultural effects in the world.

The history of the functional archive is closely imbricated with questions of its materiality. After all, texts don't exist outside of their physical forms, which actively shape readers' responses. Kipling's *Departmental Ditties* might have made a much smaller splash if it first appeared as a standard print volume instead of a novelty envelope. But even more fundamental things like the size of a bound book or the presence of an authorized signature on a government document are meaningful signifiers of how a text was expected to circulate in the world. To this end, I use bibliographical tools to identify the physical features of the functional archive and to understand how these features structured the interactions readers had with it. I think of the constituent texts of the functional archive as evolving technologies, their material characteristics adapting in response to evolutionary pressure. Many of the material developments recorded in this book were the result of historical shifts. The widespread availability of cheap printing technologies, for example, propelled almanacs from handwritten scrolls to mass printed volumes. Audience feedback from sales figures and reviews drove changes to size and layout. Sometimes readers made corrections and additions to texts themselves, in an effort to make their reading material more accessible.

Alongside my close readings of the functional archive as an object, I present close readings of the functional archive as a textual construct, grafting the literary critic's methodological toolkit of close reading onto this unlikely recipient. I read for metaphors, tropes, and descriptions, all of which feature across a range of even the most ordinary forms of writing. In this light, a petition complaining about the confiscation of a farmer's buffalo herd in early-twentieth-century Ceylon is less a document about animal husbandry than it is a complex drama, replete with characters, plot, and dramatic tension.[64] Often, rhetorical flourishes were established parts of a specific genre. Petitions filed in colonial South Asia, for example, began and ended with florid, self-abasing addresses and pleas from petitioners. The presence of these patterned beginnings and endings across the official archive transforms them into part of the bureaucratic infrastructure of the petition. They were practical devices mobilized as part of the affective apparatus of the genre, a conventional way through which the petitioner sought to generate sympathy and pity in the person reading their appeals. That these elements were carefully crafted and repeatedly deployed reminds us that the aesthetic tropes and effects of the functional archive were crucial, rather than incidental, to its role.

Recall that the bulk of the functional archive is composed of informational texts: how-to manuals, reports, almanacs. In the hands of its scholarly readers, its status as information has obviated the need to explore its aesthetic value. Bluntly, the functional archive has been framed as all surface, no depth. It has no hidden secrets to plumb; it wears its intentions on its sleeve. Its iconic incarnation, the bureaucratic form, relies on blanks, a universal technology of limiting expression.[65] (Chapter 2's discussion of the bureaucratic document might leave you with second thoughts about this.) At best, the functional archive is considered "historical." At worst, it's considered "nonliterary." But whether the functional archive says what it means or means what it says, I show that it has undeniable aesthetic effects that are worthy of literary attention and that help us understand how these objects worked in the world.

If I am intentional in matching one discipline's methods to another discipline's objects, my approach is necessitated by the historical context of late nineteenth- and early twentieth-century South Asia. Policing the boundaries of the literary is antithetical to the spirit of the colonial archive, where bureaucratic forms, novels, and instructional manuals comingle, bleeding into each other in surprising and powerful ways, as the example of Kipling's *Departmental Ditties* shows us. Similarly, policing the boundaries of our methods would, too, be antithetical to the spirit of the objects I encounter. It is my hope that this book will provide some impetus and inspiration for others to turn to their functional archives and think about their methods of reading.

A Reader's Guide

To uncover how the functional archive circulates in the hands of its readers in colonial South Asia, I have organized *Required Reading* into four chapters. Each shows the reach of the functional archive in a different domain of colonial life under the British empire: the military, the bureaucratic, the temporal, and the literary. Each focuses on a different bibliographical object: a military handbook, a sheaf of bureaucratic documents, a cupboard of almanacs, and the print run of a magazine. I position these objects as nodes in the functional archive, starting points from which to track the relationships they form with other texts and the networks in which they participate.

Required Reading probes the relationship between the functional archive and its more conventional literary counterparts. In some chapters, I place the functional archive in conversation with how it is depicted in literary texts. This allows me to show how literary representations can drive historical reception (chapter 1) or to remark on the artificial separation of the functional and literary archives of the late nineteenth and early twentieth centuries (chapter 2). At other moments, the functional archive eschews its informational role to take on literary qualities (chapters 2 and 3). Occasionally, the functional archive performs the role of the literary text better than the text itself (chapter 4). The aim of these pairings is to insist on the literary value of the functional archive, which resonates in its form, content, and reception.

The functional archive's organic quality—its persistent ability to bring together a multitude of different texts from unlikely places—has determined this book's geographical focus. Simply, I have followed the functional archive's paper trail wherever it has taken me. While all four chapters are grounded in the British empire's territorial holdings in South Asia, they also roam widely across it, from the barracks of the North-West Frontier Provinces and Burma, and jungles and back offices of district magistrates in Ceylon and Orissa, to the households of the aspirational middle-classes in Calcutta, and the drawing rooms of newly literate, elite women in Madras. Occasionally, they also roam beyond South Asia, taking us to nineteenth-century Boston, London, or China.

This book cannot serve as a comprehensive history of reading for South Asia; the region's linguistic and cultural disjointedness would make that a fool's errand. At the broadest scale, my focus on the British empire means that I cannot take into account the role that South Asia's other European empires— the Portuguese, the Danish, the Dutch, and the French—played historically in the dissemination of print technologies and books. Conversely, by not focusing on the ramifications of reading in one particular part of South Asia, my research doesn't fit area studies models either.[66] I have been inspired by the careful and ambitious work such studies contain, even as I ultimately depart from the regional foci that have shaped their arguments about print. Rather, by offering a series of comparative snapshots, I aim to register what is similar across all of my examples: the entanglement of self and book within the institutional frameworks of the British empire.

Scholarly monographs, too, are part of our functional archive, and I understand that readers will come to this book for different reasons and with different interests. To help you quickly find what you are looking for, here is a short breakdown of the stakes of each chapter. If you would like to learn more about British soldiers posted in colonial South Asia, Rudyard Kipling, and vicious book reviews, turn to chapter 1. If you'd like to know about the long history of bureaucratic frustrations, illiteracy, and some stolen buffalo, start with chapter 2. Chapter 3 is for enthusiasts of the Indian Railways, schedules, and doodling. Chapter 4 is for the most literary-minded reader, with an investment in the histories of gender, loneliness, and the English canon. If you are bored, there are puzzles to solve.

Chapter 1, "Reading for Survival," is about the refusal to read. It tracks the reception history of Garnet Wolseley's military handbook, *The Soldier's Pocket-book for Field Service* (1869), to unpack the relationship between reading, education, and print in the making of the British army at the end of the nineteenth century. Despite its widespread circulation and ostensible success, the *Pocket-book* had a controversial life. It was a book much talked about but little read. Rejected by professional readers and zealously discussed by lay ones, the handbook was accused of being incorrect, ineffectual, immoral, as well as long and boring. By tracking how the *Pocket-book* became entangled in relationships of refusal, denial, and misappropriation, I argue that moments of not reading determined the purposes to which readers put a technical manual. In turn, this challenged the moral and military imperatives of empire. The chapter uncovers the responses of historical and fictional readers to Wolseley's manual, reconstructed from letters, antiwar pamphlets, newspaper articles, scrapbooks, and short stories by Rudyard Kipling.

Chapter 2, "Reading for the Record," is about not being able to read. I turn to a range of bureaucratic documents—account books, licenses, and petitions—to explore the relationship between reading, bureaucracy, and local authorities. Set in late nineteenth- and early twentieth-century Ceylon (present-day Sri Lanka), "Reading for the Record" focuses on the nonelite, barely literate section of the Sinhalese population, for whom daily life was inseparable from written documents that they couldn't read. I show how in moments when content eluded them, these readers fell to alternative practices of meaning-making—ranging from the tactile, material feeling of paper to outsourcing their reading and writing to professionals—to yield interpretive outcomes. I juxtapose these responses with those of highly trained, professional readers, such as colonial officers and scribes. Even for elite readers, bureaucratic writing presented difficulties of volume, clarity, and falsification. Taken collectively, I argue that elite and nonelite readers' responses challenge the distinction between the literate and the illiterate. I show how readers nevertheless harnessed the impenetrability of the bureaucratic form to their own profits and ends, learning to work the system by manipulating practices of reading and duplication. The chapter's material and literary analysis draws from archival research in the Sri Lanka National Archives, anchoring them in readings of Leonard Woolf's *The Village in the Jungle* (1913) and H. E. Beal's *Indian Ink* (1954), which formally and thematically engage with the unreadability of colonial bureaucracy.

Chapters 1 and 2 explore the relationship between the functional archive and colonial institutions, focusing on readerly engagements with texts produced by the colonial state as part of its daily official business. Chapters 3 and 4 take us into the world of commercially produced forms of print published for and by South Asians, aimed at guiding them through a landscape modified by colonial rule.

Chapter 3, "Reading for Time," is about trying and sometimes failing to read. It takes as its focus the form of the *panjika*, a Bengali Hindu almanac, among the best-selling books of the late nineteenth century. These volumes contained astrological guidelines, directory-style bureaucratic information, and advertisements. I argue that we should read panjikas, which were guides to organizing time efficiently and auspiciously, as life-writing manuals that helped readers align their traditional routines with the temporal transformations of capitalist modernity. Drawing on close examinations of Bengali-language panjikas, I explore how even as these volumes encouraged selective, repetitive reading, they thwarted readers with the poor quality of their print, ungenerously spaced layouts, and cramped tables of information. I study marginalia as crucial evidence of readerly attempts to navigate the unreadability of these essential texts and, more broadly, the unreadability of empire. I suggest that while the panjika was a genre almost exclusively associated with women, its printed nineteenth-century form opened it up to an English-educated Bengali male readership navigating between astrological time and the fast-paced demands of the imperial bureaucracy. My readings draw primarily on the archives of the offices of the Gupta Press, a Kolkata-based publishing house, but I have also examined almanacs in the National Library of India, the Bodleian Library, and the offices of P. M. Bagchi, another publisher of the genre.

Chapter 4, "Reading for Company," examines the functional archive of English literature in colonial South Asia through an exploration of practices of reading together. Consequent to Thomas Macaulay's 1835 "Minute on Indian Education," English literature's role as an instrument of colonialism was inextricable from debates about education in South Asia. The chapter explores how *The Indian Ladies' Magazine*, Kamala Satthianadhan's Madras-based, English-language monthly (est. 1901), placed English literature at the heart of questions about gender reform, education, and nationalism. Even for elite, English-literate women readers, English literature felt like a daunting object, stirring up deep feelings of inadequacy and provinciality. By publishing literary puzzles, lists of reading suggestions, and literary essays, the magazine provincialized English literature for South Asians, offering it up in bite-size and manageable pieces. Through these different genres, the magazine offered a helping hand, assisting readers as they made their way through difficult texts or, alternatively, congratulating them on their knowledge. Reducing the English literary canon to a functional form aided in the political project of the magazine by allowing women to construct intellectual and affective relationships with other readers through the shared consumption of its thin printed pages. I end the chapter with a discussion of Rabindranath Tagore's Bengali-language novella, *Nashtanirh* [The Broken Nest] (1901), in which literary magazines become functional props for forging intimate relationships, but ultimately fail miserably.

The epilogue examines a photograph from Dayanita Singh's *File Room* (2013) to show that the functional archive is as much a contemporary presence as it is a historical one. I return to the central questions that animate this book, highlighting how the anxieties that surrounded the history of writing and imperial rule continue to percolate through postcolonial life in South Asia. The history of any text is the history of different readers with widely varying literacy skills seeking different outcomes for different reasons. A re-attunement to the circulatory patterns of the functional archive shows us that our histories of reading do not have to be divided into demographic siloes, but rather can be characterized by an unequal simultaneity. The epilogue ends by claiming a literary methodology for a historical archive. It is my belief that close reading—its capacity to parse metaphor and form—is an indispensable tool to understand the loaded ways in which a text works and fails in the world.

1

Reading for Survival

Slide One

In 2009, a PowerPoint slide that was leaked from a military briefing in Kabul, Afghanistan, caused an international stir (Figure 1.1). The slide contained a visual representation of the United States' military strategy of counterinsurgency in Afghanistan, a doctrine that focuses on defeating insurgent movements by winning the "hearts and minds" of the local population.[1] As the US Army's Field Manual 3-24 on counterinsurgency—or COIN, in its abbreviation—argues, such operations are built on cooperation between the invaders and the invaded. They require soldiers to be "nation builders" as well as "warriors," trained to be "greeted with either a handshake or a hand grenade."[2] The catchword of COIN is restraint. To this end, Field Manual 3-24 is self-reflexively full of contradictory koans: "Sometimes, the More Force Is Used, the Less Effective It Is." "Sometimes Doing Nothing Is the Best Reaction." "Some of the Best Weapons for Counterinsurgents Do Not Shoot."[3] Modern-day counterinsurgency movements and their attempts to gain the loyalty of local informants are inseparable from the history of empire building. In fact, counterinsurgency doctrine as it was practiced by the US Army, first in Vietnam and then in Afghanistan, was modeled on British tactics in Malaya, where the colonial government successfully reconstituted the local police force to squash insurgency efforts by the Malayan Communist Party between 1948 and 1960.[4]

The image of the leaked slide from the Afghanistan briefing looks very little like a systematic exercise in restraint. The slide is part of the functional archive of the American military apparatus, an archive that was generated in response to Afghanistan's unintelligibility to US forces. As Martin Bayly writes in his history of British interventions in the Afghan region in the nineteenth century, "Nothing terrifies empire quite like an unknown space."[5] Just like the British

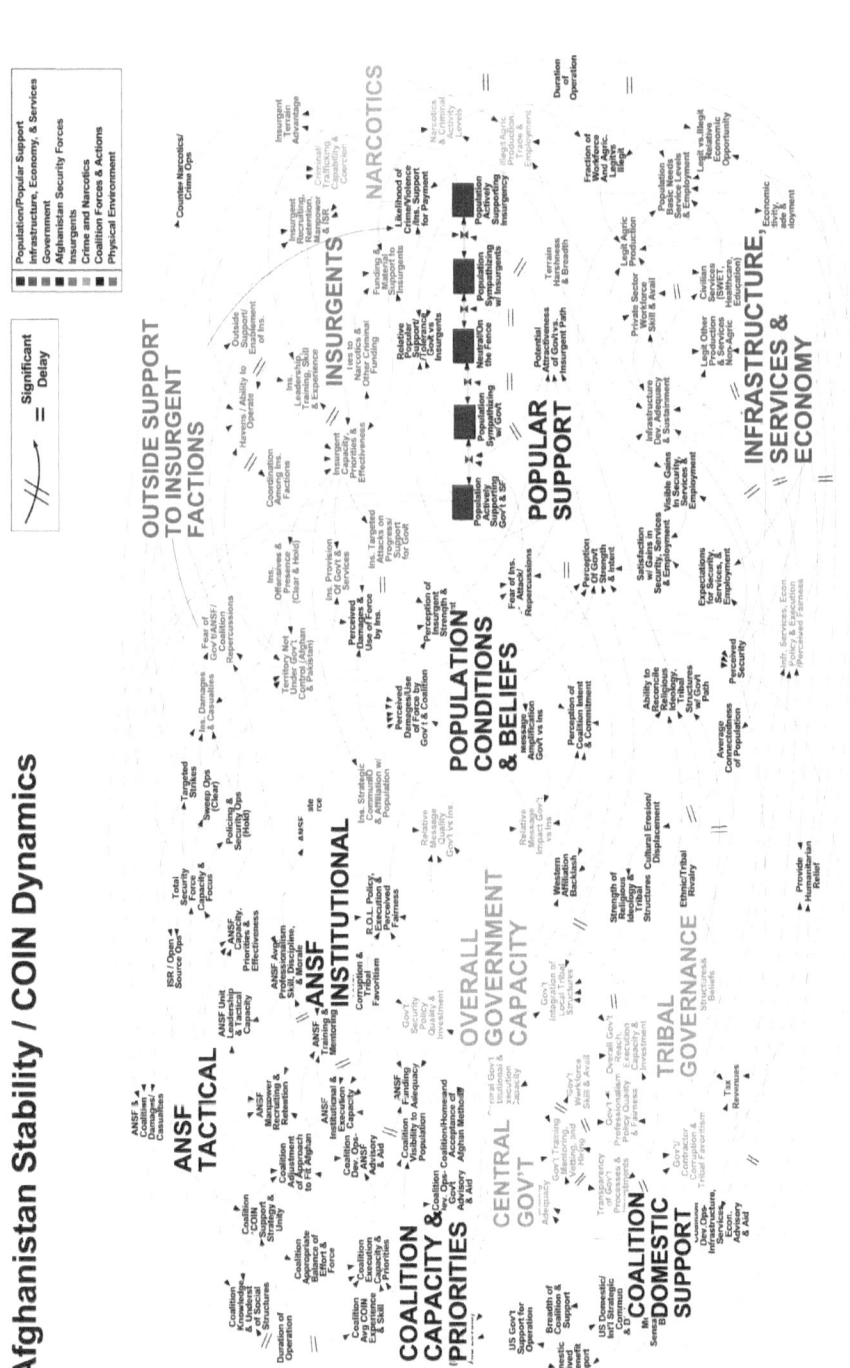

FIGURE 1.1. Slide titled "Afghanistan Stability / COIN Dynamics."

strategically collected knowledge and information to bolster their military operations in Afghanistan through the nineteenth and twentieth centuries, so did their twenty-first-century American counterparts.[6] In the slide, the region's stability appears dependent on a multitude of tangled connections between different groups of people, infrastructures of rule, and economic considerations. The unreadability of Afghanistan—its hostile landscape and its inscrutable population—is mirrored in the chaos of the slide. More than a blueprint for military action, the slide embodies the precarity of empire, held together by tenuous strings. Snap one, snap two, and the whole system could begin to unravel. Indeed, Stanley McChrystal, general and then commander of the US and NATO forces in Afghanistan, apparently chuckled when he saw it: "When we understand that slide, we'll have won the war."[7]

There have been endless forensic examinations by journalists, political scientists, and military strategists of the aftermath of the 2001 invasion of Afghanistan: dissections of McChrystal's hubris, the impossibility of effective counterinsurgency, and the arrogance of American empire. But through the eyes of a book historian, McChrystal's quip reframes the problem of war as a problem of reading. Described by its creators as a "causal loop diagram," the slide nevertheless obscures causality. It's unclear where counterinsurgency starts and where it ends. It's unclear, too, which connections in the diagram are load-bearing and which are superfluous. The slide represents not only the challenge of on-the-ground counterinsurgency tactics, but also the challenge of representing these tactics in lucid, decipherable ways. In McChrystal's book, reading the slide is a precondition to winning. It's also an impossible task.

For some critics, the slide was a failed exercise, unreadable and therefore of no use. For others, its unreadability was a perfect crystallization of the complexities of war. The image of the leaked slide and these issues took on a stormy life of their own. A technical, highly specialized object meant for the expert eyes of a military audience, the slide nevertheless became something of a cultural touchstone. Newspaper commentators smirked at the military's attempts to make war legible. "We have met the Enemy and he is PowerPoint," screamed a *New York Times* headline.[8] In others, it stirred up feelings of concern about the direction the war was heading. "I think I may have felt better about the build-up in Afghanistan before I saw this DOD-commissioned chart that explains it," remarked another commentator.[9] *The New Yorker* turned the slide into an object of literary criticism, marveling at its aesthetic qualities and comparing it to a map of the world.[10] In *War Machine* (2017), a film about the invasion of Afghanistan in which Brad Pitt plays a thinly fictionalized version of McChrystal, the slide hangs in the background of briefings and press conferences, a specter of the general's impending failure.[11]

The leaked slide exists in a cloud of different readings by its intended and unintended audience of generals, journalists, and scholars. Its controversial reception reminds us that war itself is a matter of reading. The success or failure of any military encounter, irrespective of its time and place, is intimately entangled with acts of reading terrain, people, and situations. For the same reason, military institutions have always responded to the unpredictability of war by generating printed texts and written documents, ranging from manuals and strategy maps to, in the twenty-first century, PowerPoint slides. Propelling this textual production is the hope that these objects will help soldiers make sense of otherwise nonsensical situations. Put another way, they're props against anxieties of unreadability. Things were no different in the nineteenth century, when Garnet Wolseley decided to write his pioneering *The Soldier's Pocket-book for Field Service* (1869), a military manual directed at soldiers posted in the colonial outposts of the British empire. As we will see, the uproar that came to define Wolseley's *Pocket-book* anticipated the dramatic reception of the leaked US military slide.

Not Reading for Survival

The Soldier's Pocket-book for Field Service, published by Macmillan in 1869, was a comprehensive military handbook written to assist the British army in times of war overseas.[12] Its author, Garnet Wolseley, was a larger-than-life military phenomenon. His name was inseparable from colonial might; the phrase "All Sir Garnet" was synonymous with efficiency and order. Beginning his career in 1852 as an ensign in the Second Anglo-Burmese War, Wolseley went on to participate in just about every major British colonial war in the second half of the nineteenth century. When he retired as the commander in chief of the British Armed Forces in 1900, he was a household name as the public face of many British military campaigns, the author of a considerable number of journalistic and historical works, and a celebrity endorser of brands of tobacco and tea.[13]

The Pocket-book was an experimental text that greatly exceeded the brief of a dry run-of-the-mill military manual. It was, first, a guide to strategic armed military operations. With each new edition, Wolseley included more and more technical information: how to destroy (and repair) railroads and bridges, how to transport arms, how to perform quick-and-dirty calculations to survey

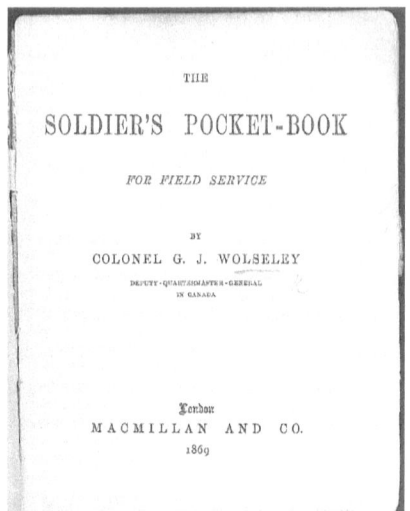

FIGURE 1.2. The first edition of *The Soldier's Pocket-book for Field Service* (London: Macmillan, 1869), © British Library Board, 8825.aa.33. Note that the pencil loop is damaged.

territory. It was also an encyclopedia filled with "minute details on everything connected with the wild life one has to lead in the field, when cut adrift, perhaps, entirely from civilization, but, at any rate, from cooks, clubs, tailors, and bootmakers."[14] It included pep talks to motivate disillusioned officers (and in turn, inspire their men), listed recipes (for beef and mutton pudding), suggested that the army bake bread in three-pound loaves, and reminded soldiers not to strap more than 250 pounds of supplies onto a mule's back.[15] For British soldiers removed from their homes and shuttled to South Asia, the rugged Afghan landscape of the North-West Frontier Provinces or the monsoonal jungles of Burma proved terrifying and unknowable.[16] The *Pocket-book* made that terrain, foreign and hostile as it was, manageable. The expanse of the colony could be controlled and surmounted if soldiers followed the book's instructions carefully. Its eclectic supply of information, both military and quotidian, gleaned from field experience, distinguished the *Pocket-book* from its predecessors, *The Queen's Regulations* and *The Field Exercise Book*.[17] Wolseley's handbook wasn't meant to languish on a shelf, opened only occasionally for reference. It was meant to be the soldier's go-to handbook: carried on their person, thumbed-through and marked-up.

The *Pocket-book* quickly rose to the status of required reading in British colonial military circles. Indeed, many of the suggestions proffered in the first edition were made into regulations formally adopted by the British army.[18] Among these was the recommendation of a small field kit that included a copy of the *Pocket-book*.[19] Through this mandate, the *Pocket-book* gained global circulation, reaching all corners of the British empire in the bags and pockets of its soldiers. By 1874, Wolseley claimed that the book had gained the status of a "regular textbook" and was being "bought by every officer now" and "used in all military schools."[20]

In this chapter, I chart a reception history of the *Pocket-book*. This endeavor quickly devolves into what Leah Price has called a "rejection history."[21] For while many soldiers owned a copy of the *Pocket-book*, very few of them felt inclined to read it. At some level, this is unsurprising. The fate of most manuals, ranging from recipe collections to etiquette guides, is to go unread, gathering dust on a shelf or in a cupboard and vanishing into oblivion.[22] The *Pocket-book*, too, was very much dead weight, lying unopened in the bags of soldiers. Legend has it that, sent to inspect the kits of a regiment, Wolseley asked a private, "If you had to lighten your knapsack, what is the first thing you would throw away?" The answer was, "The *Pocket Book* [sic], Sir."[23]

But what distinguishes the *Pocket-book* from other examples of unread manuals was the public outcry it caused. This was puzzling and perhaps disproportionate to a technical manual intended for circulation in the military. Instead, like a sensational novel or an infamous news article, the book instigated lively discussions of its merits in mainstream Victorian newspapers, religious pamphlets, literary fiction, and satirical magazines. These conversations remained energetic throughout the print life of the book's five editions.[24] Written for soldiers, its public of readers nevertheless ranged well beyond the military.[25] The explorer Henry Morton Stanley read it (with "disgust") aboard the *Benin* on his way to the Gold Coast.[26] Rudyard Kipling lampooned the manual mercilessly as a book that no sensible soldier would deign to open. The *Pocket-book* was accused of being riddled with errors, ineffectual preparation for the horrors of a hostile colonial environment, and of encouraging immoral behavior. It was also considered too long and incredibly boring.

If ordinary forms of writing provide an index for imperial relationships, the *Pocket-book* and the eccentric routes of circulation it took bore the weight of anxieties about nineteenth-century empire, moral character, and class. The text's readers—soldiers, religious leaders, writers, artists, and journalists—collectively undermined its status as required reading by reconfiguring its relationship with survival. While military brass thought the book was lifesaving, pacifists and Christians argued it would destroy soldiers' souls. In the space of the military classroom, reading the *Pocket-book* meant soldiers would die of boredom. Soldiers stationed on the colonial frontier felt that the manual's guidance was best left at home, though making fun of it generated some good laughs, at least. Framed as a universal object of derision, the deliberate neglect of the *Pocket-book* wasn't a neutral decision. It was a principled one. If Wolseley hoped that reading his handbook would mold resourceful individuals capable of independent thought, *refusing* to read it paradoxically provided readers with the tools to undermine its lessons and, in the process, reframe the moral and military imperatives of empire. As it fell into the hands of angry, ungenerous, and mocking readers, the case of the *Pocket-book* turned a popular maxim upside down. In the eyes of its detractors, you were what you refused to read.

The purpose of Wolseley's *Pocket-book* was to educate soldiers; it claimed no distinctions "on the score of literary merit."[27] Yet, I contend, the *Pocket-book* did create something of a literary figure in its pages: the figure of the ideal soldier. While a far cry from the romanticized image of the soldier that circulated in children's adventure stories and travel narratives of the time, Wolseley's imagined soldier was meant to create relationships of identification with its readers. Like a character in a novel, officers were meant to see themselves in him; privates and noncommissioned soldiers were meant to aspire to be like him. Instead, soldiers formed ambivalent relationships with the *Pocket-book*, angrily distancing themselves from the figure of the general's ideal soldier, even as they still found themselves trapped in the orbit of the text.

As I've argued in the introduction, histories of reading the functional archive require us to take seriously histories of not reading. In what follows, I show that under the surface of the *Pocket-book* teemed an entire host of meaning-making practices that weren't always connected to the desire to engage with the text. Caustic reviewers, begging their audiences to throw away their copies of the book, had to subject the volume to close readings of their own to justify their claims of its insidiousness. Even as they were adamant in their refusal to read it, soldiers found themselves surrounded by a cloud of the *Pocket-book*'s content, refracted and circulated beyond the bounds of the text. They came across extracts and reprints, quotations of quotations, snippets overheard secondhand and thirdhand floating in training camps and military mess halls. These textual encounters allowed them to feign knowledge of the book, if needed. Put bluntly, even as soldiers refused to read the *Pocket-book*, there was no escaping it. It was a constant material and physical presence in their lives. The *Pocket-book*'s reception history, then, is an acute reminder that books may well have vibrant intellectual lives, even in moments when they aren't read.

This chapter uncovers the responses of historical and fictional readers to Wolseley's handbook, reconstructed from nineteenth-century literary and archival materials: publishers' correspondence, bureaucratic reports, letters, autobiographies, religious pamphlets, satirical drawings, and short stories. I connect a network of readers located in South Asia and its neighboring regions—Himachal Pradesh, the North-West Frontier Provinces, and Burma—to others reading in various parts of Britain and the United States. I deliberately include the imagined readers of the *Pocket-book* alongside its historical ones. Here, my intention isn't to sidestep or undermine the experience of actual readers. Rather, as will become clear as the chapter unfolds, much of the reputation of the *Pocket-book* as an unreadable text was instigated by the circulation of popular accounts that made such claims (fictional or otherwise). How the nineteenth-century British soldier was imagined and portrayed as reading (or not) had as much bearing on the place of the *Pocket-book* in late nineteenth-century colonial culture as how it was actually read.[28]

Helping Soldiers Help Themselves

The *Pocket-book* entered military discourse at a crucial historical juncture, both reflecting and participating in the transformative changes the British army underwent in the years around its publication. The first such intervention was a targeted investment in the education of soldiers. J. H. Lefroy, the author of an 1859 report on reading practices among British soldiers, remarked on the limited literacy and vocabulary of British soldiers, specifically the vast "number of words there are in common use of whose meaning they have no idea or a false one."[29] Subsequently, as a result of Forster's Education Act of 1870, legislation that made primary education compulsory and freely available in Britain, national literacy rates increased from 63.3 percent in 1841 to a phenomenal 92.2 percent by 1900.[30] The army also instated complementary educational requirements. By 1861, soldiers required an army certificate of education of at least the third (and lowest) level for a promotion to corporal. By 1889, 85.4 percent of Britain's soldiers could read and write.[31]

An increasingly literate army was central to the Cardwell Reforms (1868–74). Initiated the year before the *Pocket-book* was published, this series of legislative measures was primarily responsible for abolishing the practice of purchasing commissions. In doing so, it responded to growing voices of dissent in the ranks of military reformers who maintained that the army needed to be reorganized as a professional entity. The Council on Military Education's 1860 report argued that

> [t]he character of military or professional education is totally distinct from that of general education; and therefore, whilst the latter may be best confided to the public schools or other instructional agencies of the country, the former can only be effectually carried on under the superintendence of officers who have specially devoted their attention to the subject, and have added to acquired knowledge practical experience, or, in other words, at a military college . . . [Military education] must be special in character, totally inapplicable to any other profession, and as necessary to an officer of the army as the drill and instruction of a recruit are to the private soldier.[32]

As W. J. Reader points out, the qualities an officer was traditionally expected to possess intrinsically were those of a country gentleman: courage, loyalty, and physical strength. Instead, the Cardwell Reforms, echoing the report above, radically suggested that one could, even had to, be educated into military practice through specialized training.[33] They prioritized technical knowledge over birth and wealth and, in doing so, opened high-ranking positions in the army to anyone who could prove to hold the requisite qualifications.

Wolseley was a passionate supporter of reform and meritocracy in the army, and the *Pocket-book* was very much a book written for the Cardwell era. It circulated within an army that, like the imperial government it served, was increasingly reliant on collecting information and turning it into written genres.[34] It wasn't intended to be simply a vehicle to disseminate military regulations. It was meant to be an informal guide to the process of voluntary reeducation for the soldier. The British soldier, Wolseley wrote in its opening pages, was not "a machine, incapable of noble impulses," but instead, a person whose unique talents and dispositions could compensate for the shortcomings of his cohort, creating a stronger, unified regiment.[35] The more soldiers were reminded of the roles they had to play in the smooth functioning of their units, the more likely they were to perform to their highest abilities. Importantly, while the *Pocket-book* was ostensibly addressed to army officers, Wolseley's vision for it extended through the army to its lowest levels, the rank-and-file divisions. On the very first page, Wolseley made a grand antihierarchical gesture: "Let us sink as far as possible the respective titles of officers, sergeants and privates, merging them into the one great professional cognomen of soldier, causing all ranks to feel that it is a noble title of which the general as well as the private may well be proud."[36] Urging them to believe that hierarchy was but a "ladder, the rungs of which all can equally aspire to mount," Wolseley hoped to entice soldiers of all classes, not just officers, to read his book, on the assumption that it would facilitate their upwardly mobile journeys.[37]

A close reading of the lessons of the *Pocket-book*, coupled with some good common sense in the field, could serve as an appropriate substitute for the training that others may have received through an elite education. With rising literacy levels and the abolition of purchasing commissions, a military vocation suddenly came within the grasp of the middle classes, as well as those aspiring to that status. In positioning itself as both a technical manual and a text for self-improvement, the *Pocket-book* joined an unlikely genealogy of nineteenth-century self-help guides. Like volumes such as Samuel Smiles's *Self Help* (1859) and even Isabella Beeton's classic *Book of Household Management* (1861), it ascribed to the belief that ambitious individuals could be their own educators, if given the right instructions to follow. It taught its readers that, like being middle class, being a good soldier was dependent on the cultivation of character and resourcefulness, qualities that could very much be learned.[38]

For the Victorians, you were what you read. Soldiers were no exception.[39] As Sharon Murphy's work on the establishment of libraries for soldiers of the East India Company has shown us, even before the publication of the *Pocket-book*, the connection between one's occupation and one's reading habits created considerable debate at the time. Writing about imperial soldiers, Maria Edgeworth, for example, suggested in 1812 that

> a species of reading, which may be disapproved of for other pupils, should be recommended to the young soldier. His imagination should be exalted by the adventurous and the marvellous. Stories of giants, and genii, and knights and tournaments, and "pictured tales of vast heroic deeds," should feed his fancy. He should read accounts of ship-wrecks and hairbreadth scapes, voyages and travels, histories of adventures, beginning with Robinson Crusoe, the most interesting of all stories, and one which has sent many a youth to sea.[40]

For Edgeworth, while it's not a form of professional or technical reading, being captivated by literature marks the first step of military recruitment: the desire to be a soldier in a foreign land. She draws a straight line from fantastical adventure tales and imperial romances—intended to cultivate a restlessness for travel and exotic encounters—to the creation of effective colonial soldiers. By inviting young men to insert themselves into a highly orientalized fantasy of danger and pleasure in the East, Edgeworth suggests that the hunt for adventure, wealth, and novelty is one of the primary motivating forces behind imperial conquest. Her prescribed syllabus for aspiring soldiers is not just a canny recruitment tool, promising soldiers the entirety of the colonial world; it molds them into the kinds of colonial agents who were most effective at defending empire.

The transformative potentials of reading and the uses to which they could be put in empire continued to be cited through the nineteenth century. Vociferous advocates for reading rooms and libraries attached to units and regiments argued for their role in curbing profligacy and immoral behavior. An 1870 report from the Council of Military Education draws on the statements of an officer posted at Fort St. George in the Madras Presidency of British India: "The more I see of soldiers the more convinced I am that they require some strong counter-attraction to keep them from dens of vice and infamy; and so far as my experience has gone, nothing approaches so nearly to the purpose as comfortable and attractive reading rooms."[41] By extension, officials were also wary of the harm reading could do, highly suspicious of the frivolity encouraged by "light" literature (such as the works Edgeworth recommends), the soldiers' preferred reading material. If books had a reforming and positive influence and could make men better human beings as well as soldiers, a poor choice of reading material could also, by extension, turn them into rogue—or worse, sloppy—soldiers.

The Soldier's Pocket-book for Field Service was published in the thick of these debates and at a time when the British army was the largest employer in colonial South Asia.[42] Nestled between information about food rations and surveillance strategies, Wolseley propounded in the *Pocket-book* the need for "correct" methods of textual engagement. Take, for example, these lines from the *Pocket-book*:

> Often have I blushed for my profession, when I have seen officers sitting down under some shelter reading a book, whilst their men were working, or rather, I should say supposed to be working; for after a little time, when the men see that their officers do not take an interest in what is going on, they soon follow suit.[43]

In his autobiography, *The Story of a Soldier's Life* (1903), a competing image emerges:

> Of these [soldiers] a small proportion, taking their profession seriously, studied hard at all military sciences, and spent many of those deadly midday hours of the Indian summers in reading *military history* and the *lives of great commanders*. Happy, indeed, is the young officer who so loves his work as to find in such literature a high form of pleasure.[44]

The second image qualifies the first. The exposed and suffering soldier who spends "many of those deadly midday hours of the Indian summers in reading *military history* and the *lives of great commanders*" grasps the true value of reading. Reading, in this account, is work, but when done "correctly" may also be a "high form of pleasure," collapsing the literary and the practical. By contrast, the officer who is an embarrassment to his profession is found evading the sun while reading an unnameable book, experiencing a low form of pleasure that comes at the cost of his duties ("sitting down under some shelter," Wolseley sneers). The image of the leisure reader from the *Pocket-book* further anticipates the chain reaction of actions and responses that characterize the reception of Wolseley's text. If officers do not read correctly, neither do the soldiers under their command. From one incorrect reader follows an army of them.

In describing resourceful soldiers as those who realize the importance of reading, Wolseley reveals himself to be of the same caliber. He boasts in *The Story of a Soldier's Life* that he "could have passed a high competitive examination in all the then commonly known books on light infantry, and its mode of employment in the field as practiced by our army in the Peninsula."[45] The dedicated Wolseley grows up reading Hume's *History of England*, Alison's *History of Europe*, and Napier's *The Peninsular War*.[46] That he is the exception rather than rule is evident. J. H. Lefroy noted in his 1859 report on the regimental and garrison schools of the army that soldiers did not have the time to begin "larger works": "It is curious to observe how entirely thrown away for the most part are such classics as Napier's *History of the Peninsular War*, the Wellington *Despatches*, and others of the solid and standard character."[47] Instead, like the shirking officer Wolseley evokes in the *Pocket-book*, they chose to read "inappropriate" works of fiction and sentimental novels.[48] By contrast, "books of travels, military works (except the historical records of regiments), and works of general literature, with comparatively few exceptions, repose[d] undisturbed on the shelves."[49]

Lefroy's account was not the only one to come to these conclusions. A range of reports on military reading and education published in the years in and around the publication of the *Pocket-book* repeatedly point out how unpopular histories and military technical works were among soldiers with access to a library. H. L. Grove, an army school inspector in the Madras Presidency, for example, criticized the poor arrangement of books in the Battery army library, whose paltry holdings amounted to 312 volumes. With three rows of books to a shelf, the second and third rows were effectively obscured from sight by the first. But he also realized his censure was irrelevant, for very few of the books—historical, biographical, and scientific works and travelogues—were likely to be read.[50] Wolseley's *Pocket-book*, circulating in a world hostile to "useful reading," was destined to fight a losing battle.

Reading Materiel

Wolseley was very much aware of the distractions that existed in the lives of soldiers and of the challenge that lay before him to counter their reluctance to read. Parallel to the *Pocket-book*'s growing reputation as unreadable were Wolseley's continued efforts to make the handbook easy to buy and use. He started with cost, suggesting that Macmillan reduce the volume's price from its initial five shillings to three shillings and sixpence. This, Wolseley argued, would make the book more accessible, allowing it to "find its way with the volunteer ranks . . . for if it was cheap, a very large proportion of the noncommissioned officers, and even of the privates in some corps, would buy it . . . if sold cheap it would be a book that would sell well on all Railway book stalls."[51] The evocation of the railway book stall points to Wolseley's expansive vision of an audience for the *Pocket-book*: not just the higher-ups of the army, but also its noncommissioned officers and its privates. But the manual would also rub shoulders with the other reading material commonly sold at these stalls, including popular novels, travel books, and thrillers. Taking it out of the technical, professional world of the army, Wolseley imagined the *Pocket-book* to be mundane, everyday reading. This was echoed in a recommendation for the book, printed as part of Macmillan's advertisement for it: that "many of its pages [were] replete with interest even to those who [were] not directly connected with the military profession."[52] That said, Wolseley failed to remember the associations that Victorian readers made with the books they read on trains: as transient, disposable distractions from their long and boring journeys.[53]

If the *Pocket-book* was intended to be a useful railway companion, its next priority was to remain true to its name as a pocket-book. Since it was included in a list of essentials items for an officer's kit, portability was key to its success, especially when the list was officially approved by the army.[54] A small rectangular volume with a red cover and a reasonable weight of just under 236 grams, it could easily be slipped into a pocket or bag.[55] Its unobtrusive appearance, however, was quickly seen as a negative by Wolseley. He was intent on giving it a more "official" appearance in subsequent editions. For example, he instructed Macmillan to make the edges of the pages of the third edition red, evidently oblivious to the negative associations of red tape.[56]

Wolseley's book also proved to be a container for all kinds of other texts, notes, and objects. It wasn't simply an aggregation of anecdotal stories of Wolseley's own military experience, but an organized compilation of these along with extracts (either as direct quotations or paraphrased sections) from other military histories and guides (such as *The Queen's Regulations*), mathematical textbooks, and administrative rule books, among other relevant textual sources. *The Soldier's Pocket-book for Field Service*, as Wolseley wrote in the preface to the second edition, was written as a book to "dispense with other books," qualified by a hasty rejoinder, "[other] than this one."[57] As a matter of practicality, it aimed to save the soldier from having to read hundreds of books on military history and tactics. Instead, it provided a means of glancing through neatly arranged material, whether in narrative prose, tables, or, where necessary, diagrams. The task of locating information was made simple by the incorporation of various finding aids such as a systematic table of contents and index, as well as a running header system that indicated the subject to which the information on any given page pertained. The promise of the *Pocket-book* was to offer abbreviated and easily navigable plenitude. Put another way, its readability was derived from its capacity to render other texts unnecessary.

Wolseley's *Pocket-book* styled itself as a dynamic, changing text. It went through five editions in less than twenty years, and Wolseley's letters to Macmillan reveal a steady flow of anxieties about the need to update the information it contained.[58] Constantly evolving, the *Pocket-book* further invited readers to participate in the process of updating their personal copies. To this end, the first edition included thirty-four blank pages at the end, intended for the reader's notes. Further, correspondence about the second edition reveals information about the form of the first. In a letter to Macmillan, Wolseley suggests that the publishers "do away with the pencil" in the next edition, substituting it was a clasp to hold the increasingly bulky volume.[59] (They didn't listen.) Since the library copies of the *Pocket-book* I examined were damaged, I didn't immediately realize that what seemed to be a stray piece of leather dangling from the side of the front cover was, in fact, a loop into which a pencil could have been easily slipped. The literal imperative to "write!" thus came physically manifest with the *Pocket-book*, as an irrevocable part of the lesson of how to read it, as a text and an object.[60] In later years, the fact that Wolseley felt that many of these innovations should be discarded—the pencil loop, the blank pages— indicates his own shifting thinking about how soldiers might use their volumes.[61] The *Pocket-book* was slowly being transformed into the kind of curtailed, static text that its audience accused it of being.

Despite Wolseley's efforts to make the *Pocket-book* accessible to soldiers of all ranks, it was predominantly perceived as a text that was read, even if superficially, only by men in power rather than those who faced the brunt of military action. An article in the *Taunton Courier and Western Advertiser* in 1876 counted the prime minister among the readership of Wolseley's handbook; during times of war, he is reported to have "never [slept], and [to have] devote[d] his few moments of leisure to a hasty perusal of Sir Garnet Wolseley's *Soldier's Pocket Book* [sic]."[62] The *Pocket-book*, read in his official residence rather than on the battlefield, becomes part of the absurd paraphernalia that surrounds war. Connoting hierarchy rather than aspiration, bureaucracy rather than battlefield, in the view of many of its critics, the *Pocket-book* seemed an ineffectual preparation for both life and war. In examining the negative reception of the *Pocket-book*, it becomes increasingly clear that accepting or rejecting Wolseley's handbook was about much more than a soldier's reading choices. It determined his relationship to self, authority, and empire.

The Moral Life of the Soldier

When John J. Wilson entered a secondhand bookstore in Boston, Massachusetts, he was not expecting to leave with a copy of the third edition of *The Soldier's Pocket-book for Field Service* (1874). He documented his chance encounter with Wolseley's manual and his thoughts on it in a short pamphlet, *Construction and Destruction; or The Devilry of War* (1891).[63] On a bookshelf, a casual browser may have confused the two texts. *Construction and Destruction* shared some physical similarities with Wolseley's handbook, to which Wilson subtly draws our attention. The *Pocket-book*, we are reminded, was a small red book (we are given exact dimensions: four inches by five), and it "fit[s][his] pocket."⁶⁴ Similarly, *Construction and Destruction*'s sixteen pages, sewn between red paper covers, could have been rolled easily into a portable paper tube, or made for a large, though lightweight, stack of pamphlets for convenient distribution (and relatively inexpensive too: three shillings and four pence could buy a hundred copies), making it possible for the pamphlet to circulate widely.

But to draw our attention to these physical similarities is only to highlight the difference in the content of the two publications. For Wolseley, his military instruction manual was, as we have seen, meant as a map by which young soldiers could navigate a socially mobile military world. Wilson disagreed. His reaction to the *Pocket-book* was violent; his commentary on it in *Construction and Destruction* vitriolic. In his account, the manual was both the cause and symptom of the human and material wastefulness of war.

It's not difficult to understand why Wilson reacted as he did. While little is known of him, references to George Fox in the pamphlet and the fact that an expanded version was reprinted by the Friends Peace Committee was part of their antiwar publication series in 1914 strongly suggest that he was a Quaker and a pacifist.⁶⁵ But by labeling the *Pocket-book* as an exercise in the "*studious inculcation of deceit,*" Wilson frames his critique as a problem of reading, balking at the imagined vision of a soldier, hunched and poring over the pages of the red manual.⁶⁶ His own intended target audience is the "candid reader," the reader pure and untainted by the manipulations of Wolseley's *Pocket-book*, to whom he will "prove . . . *the unspeakably Satanic nature of war from first to last.*"⁶⁷ Programmatically going through the text's four parts, he summarizes sections that, according to him, go against the ethical system of any Christian and make the army an unfit home for a believer.⁶⁸ These include Wolseley's discussion of the effectiveness of different kinds of guns, and of the destruction of invaded villages (including tearing up the floorboards of houses to provide material to construct temporary bridges).

Wilson wasn't the only one to reprimand the *Pocket-book* for the ethical infractions it encouraged or to attribute the degradation of military morals to reading it. Keir Hardie, a Scottish trade unionist best known for founding the British Labour Party, wasn't too pleased either. In May 1900, he published an article in the *Labour Leader*, a newspaper he edited. The article, "Peculiar Animals and How to Train Them," was a takedown of the *Pocket-book*, four years after its fifth and final edition had been issued. Its title responded sarcastically to Wolseley's provocation in the manual's introduction that the "soldier is a peculiar animal" who could be transformed into, in Hardie's words, a "bloodthirsty man-killing machine."[69] The prevailing "military educational ideal," Hardie writes, is an

> instructive object-lesson in how a man who presumably in private life conforms to the conventional code of honour, which includes truthfulness, honesty, and an appearance of chivalry, can, in obedience to the supposed demands of his profession, reduce himself to the level of the meanest and most contemptible cut-purse that ever infested a community of decent folk.[70]

Hardie reminds us emphatically that, in Wolseley's code, "[b]efore a man can be a model soldier he must learn to forget that he is a human being subject to ethical laws."[71] We see echoes of Wilson's moral rhetoric here, with truthfulness and honesty being replaced by their antitheses, meanness and indecency. But what stands out is the "instructive object-lesson." Hardie presumably intended this phrase to be understood figuratively (as a "striking practical example of a principle or ideal").[72] But as a book historian, I can't resist the opportunity to read it literally, too. The object-lesson of the military ideal is the *Pocket-book*. It is the material thing to which Hardie traces back the transformation of the honest man into the destructive soldier. We become, Hardie suggests, what we read.

Hardie and Wilson exhort their audiences in the imperative: REFUSE to read this book! Take, for instance, the introductory sections of Wilson's pamphlet that narrate his chance discovery of the text. Wilson attempts to frame the *Pocket-book* as forgotten and irrelevant. The shop from which he buys his copy is a "real old book store where the volumes were piled so closely that it was scarcely possible to read their titles;" the shopkeeper, an "old woman, worn and haggard, in perfect keeping with her surroundings" emerges from "an inner recess."[73] The dusty interior of the shop provides the perfect setting for the book that is soon after revealed to be secondhand—given away as unwanted, and hidden between other books to be forgotten—a book clearly not worth anyone's time.

Nevertheless, to Wilson's disappointment, he opens his copy of the *Pocket-book* to find the names of not one, but three, previous owners on its flyleaf.[74] The *Pocket-book* has changed hands three times, participating in a military brotherhood built on the exchange of words of advice, as well as personal items. Further, when he flips through the book, he realizes these soldiers had engaged with Wolseley's handbook, at least in part. Not only are some sections marked in pencil, but the blank concluding pages also reveal a rough note recording a loan from the paymaster.[75] While the *Pocket-book* may not have been every soldier's go-to notebook or reference work, as Wolseley had hoped, the marginalia in the copy Wilson finds reveals at least one instance in which it served its intended role.

Crucially, Wilson's call to boycott the *Pocket-book* draws together different modes of reading and response, but it also reveals the rich inconsistencies inherent in these practices. Viewing the pamphlet through the lens of reading practices introduces a paradox. Against the widely circulating image of the unread *Pocket-book*, Wilson presumes his nightmare to be true: that the *Pocket-book* is being read and its lessons put into practice. (Hopefully this chapter will disabuse my readers of that notion.) But he also subjects the text to his own form of fine-grained antagonistic close reading, complete with elaborate cross references and marginal glossing. His verdict is that the *Pocket-book* is unreadable—not in the sense of being poorly printed, difficult, or boring—but in the sense of being dangerous. It is unfit for human, readerly consumption. To support his opinion, Wilson produces a reading of the *Pocket-book* that digs beneath its veneer of efficiency and practicality to find another uncomfortable set of meanings lurking.

Wilson's opinion of the *Pocket-book* turns Wolseley's text into a book its author would hardly recognize. What the author of the *Pocket-book* labeled expedient and central to the ambitious spirit of the soldier, Wilson reads as a pervasive disregard for human life and possessions, exacerbated by feelings of self-worth and pride. By the time we come to the end of the review, Wilson's act of substitution is complete. He has replaced Wolseley's text in the minds of its audience with his own version of it. To use Pierre Bayard's term, the *Pocket-book* as it appears in Wilson's pamphlet is less the "real" book than it is a "screen": "What we talk about is not the books themselves, but substitute objects we create for the occasion."[76] Reading, even in its most conventional form, already contains elements of nonreading, and, in this particular instance, what Wolseley thought of as a manual for self-help is radically transformed, in Wilson's account, into a guide to self-destruction.[77]

As I've noted, at the heart of Wilson's and Hardie's commentaries is the fundamental assumption that the *Pocket-book*—a specialized, military manual—had the power to influence and transform its readers. This assumption is even more clear when the writers compare it (unfavorably, of course) to another book intended to affect readers and shape their worldviews: the Bible. The *Pocket-book* is notably silent on religion, worship, or even on the desirability of including a Bible in officers' kits.[78] When it does mention the Bible—twice—it is in the context of military intelligence. Wolseley suggests that a copy with a page missing, "a Testament with the 3rd or the 7th leaf torn out," could be used in espionage as a coded message.[79] Similarly, since the possession of a Bible would not be considered suspicious, he argues that its pages could also be used "to write secret correspondence in lemon juice," escaping detection.[80] Wilson rejoins: "One might suggest to the Major-General that it would be expedient to tear out the Sermon on the Mount, or the First Epistle of St John, where love is substituted for revenge," and that "[c]onsidering all the foregoing, it is surprising that *'perjury'* should be *one of the gravest court-martial offences.*"[81] Wilson's comments point out what Wolseley's appropriation of the Bible obscures: that the actions into which it is co-opted, violent and propagating falsehood, are antithetical to the message of the New Testament.

Wilson's comments demonstrate to his readers that Wolseley sees the Bible as a useful object rather than a text. With this instrumental behavior, the *Pocket-book*'s author demonstrates the same expediency with which Victorian readers used books.[82] For the tasks to which the Bible is put, its meaning is irrelevant, even though its symbolic appearance is eminently exploitable. Put in the terms of my own argument, the *Pocket-book* calls for the use of the Bible as a functional, even incidental, text. To identify oneself in times of war by a willfully mutilated Bible is to declare one's identity unequivocally as a soldier first, and a Christian second.

In "Peculiar Animals and How to Train Them," Hardie noticed Wolseley's complex deployment of the Bible in military espionage, too. But while Wolseley may have paid religious matters short shrift, that hadn't stopped him from writing a preface to *Cromwell's Soldier's Bible*, an 1895 reissue of *The Soldier's Pocket Bible* (1643) compiled for distribution among the ranks of the Commonwealth Army.[83] This was the edition, bound in khaki, handed to British soldiers in the Second Anglo-Boer War, the military backdrop to Hardie's article.[84] In his preface to the edition, Wolseley declared:

> The soldier who carries this Bible in his pack possesses what is of far higher value to him than the proverbial marshal's baton, for if he carries its teaching in his head and lets it rule his heart and conduct, he will certainly be happy, and most probably eminently successful.[85]

At first glance, Wolseley seems to be in agreement with his detractors: the Bible is of "far higher value" than the "proverbial marshal's baton" or the

Pocket-book. But what stood out to Hardie was the "most probably" in the final line. For Wolseley, the religious soldier will *certainly* be happy, but his professional success remains more precarious. Like *Construction and Destruction*, Hardie's article does not simply pit the Bible and the *Pocket-book* against each other as representatives of competing life choices. Rather, it all comes down to the choice of which to read, a choice that assumes that the *Pocket-book* and Bible could, potentially, act on a reader with equal, if contradictory, force. "Before a man can allow the teachings of the Scriptures to rule his heart and conduct," Hardie tells us, "he will require to forget and unlearn all that Wolseley has taught him in *The Soldier's Pocket-book*," substituting the book in the soldier's mind with an erased, blank slate.[86] Until then, the Cromwell Bible would remain in the soldier's knapsack, literally present and figuratively empty.

Blank Stares in the Classroom

Wilson and Hardie built a case for the *Pocket-book* as dangerous, poisonous, and corrupting. Their alarm, however, may have been misplaced. The two were working from the premise that the *Pocket-book* was *actually* being read by soldiers susceptible to its rhetoric. But just as many of the handbook's detractors claimed the opposite. In their accounts, the *Pocket-book* was left unread by soldiers, despite official mandates to procure—and presumably read—the text.

Some of the antipathetic representations of the *Pocket-book* were preserved by Wolseley himself. Like many of his fellow Victorians, Wolseley was an avid scrapbooker. As part of the general's project of personal documentation, few items escaped the scissors of Frances, his daughter and partner-in-compilation. The pair collected newspaper articles that referred to him, sycophantic poems written by those hoping to ingratiate themselves to him, reviews of his books, satirical write-ups and cartoons, and general pieces of Victorian ephemera. The scrapbook collection totals thirty-three volumes.[87] Tucked away in Scrapbook 18 is a set of satirical drawings titled "Okehampton-1897."[88] In their process of archiving, Wolseley and Frances excluded the identity of the artist and where the drawings were originally published.[89] As their title suggests, the sketches depict scenes set in Okehampton, which, even today, is a central British military training camp in West Devon. Each sketch offers a depiction of the ludicrously futile "training" of the soldiery for the unpredictability of war. In them, we see inadequately trained soldiers standing awkwardly on poorly made wheeled contraptions to spy on the enemy. We see them shooting at unrealistic targets

FIGURE 1.3. "The Pow-Wow," from "Okehampton-1897," in Scrapbook 18, n.d., Wolseley Special Collections, Brighton & Hove Libraries. Reproduced with kind permission from Brighton & Hove City Council, Library Services.

and scattering in all directions in the face of imaginary hostile fire. Humor is, if nothing else, a useful strategy of deflection and critique.

Writing is everywhere in the scenes of training depicted in the series, from instructional signposts on the training field to blackboards scrawled with calculations and strategy diagrams. In the sketch titled "The Pow-Wow," writing takes center stage (Figure 1.3). The artist leaves the door on the right strategically ajar so that we can see the sign on the front: "lecture room." This alerts us to the fact that we aren't witnessing a friendly discussion among equals, as the title's use of "pow-wow" might suggest. Rather, the lecture room is structured by hierarchy, pitting military instructors against military trainees. The student soldiers, who face their teachers, are half turned away from the viewers of the cartoon. Their slouched bodies, indicating casual distraction, contrast sharply with the rigid, tense posture of their instructors. Prominent in the corner of the lecture room is a blackboard that indicates that this meeting is a debriefing exercise, a means of teaching soldiers how to develop foolproof strategies for war. In this particular case, the lessons to be learned derive from the "[m]istakes made Aug 9th." This day has apparently been disastrous for the soldiers, featuring all kinds of basic errors of judgment: "delay in firing," "wrong word of command," "wagons not sent away," and finally, "Batt[alion] Com[mander] left his Battery." The source of information about these errors is the sheaf of papers (a report of a training exercise? a newspaper article?) that the irate instructor clutches. He also holds a very small book—which fits perfectly in his hand—thrust forward with the threatening "[s]hew it me in the Book." The students respond with blank stares. If this is a book they're expected to have read, they clearly haven't done their homework. In the hands of their instructor, the "Book" is both a threatening presence and an empty object, a material constant and an unread presence in the military classroom.

The "Book" with a conveniently indecipherable title scrawled across its cover remains unnamed in "The Pow-Wow." But for its nineteenth-century audience, the "Book" and its scene of instruction would have immediately sparked recognition: the volume could only be Wolseley's *Pocket-book*. For twenty-first-century viewers like me, the sketch's inclusion in Wolseley's scrapbook locates it in the *Pocket-book*'s messy reception history, opening up questions on the value of bookish knowledge and inept military practice.[90]

"The Pow-Wow" is structured around the tension between the expectations of the instructors and the performance of the students. To read the sketch from the point of view of the instructors is to confront a fatal causation: soldiers don't read the *Pocket-book* and the result is basic military errors.

The failed training exercise or real-world example being dissected in the sketch then becomes a foretelling of what is to come on the field of actual war: clumsy and ignorant mismanagement. But to read the sketch through the eyes of the students leads us to a different conclusion. When we turn to the "mistakes of Aug 9th," we realize that these might not have been caused by a lack of reading or a lack of understanding. They could also have been the consequences of human error and, more crucially, human fear. A delay in firing is not necessarily the result of not knowing when to fire, but rather, it could be an automatic physical recoil from the possibility of taking another human life. A battalion commander's abandonment of their unit, bluntly dubbed "leaving it," might not have been a case of poor judgment but instead a complete loss of it. Taking the lessons of the lecture room into battle not only highlights their awkward fit with in-the-field situations, but also reminds us that soldiers-in-training have very little idea of the situation into which they are getting themselves. Texts like the *Pocket-book* might provide a set of instructions on how wars should be fought, but to soldiers, they are a poor guide to the realities of combat.

The *Pocket-book*'s circulation in "The Pow-Wow" suggests not just that no one actually reads such texts of instruction (remember how confused and bored the soldiers look), but that bookishness itself doesn't constitute adequate military training. But as readers of the *Pocket-book* will recognize, this was a sentiment also shared by Wolseley. In the preface to the 1869 edition, he pointed out that existing military manuals were authored by men who had "never seen a shot fired in anger."[91] The *Pocket-book* was not meant to displace battlefield experience, but rather, to supplement it. While the soldiers in "The Pow-Wow" don't read the *Pocket-book*, it is possible that its artist hadn't either. The sketch bears no recognition of the *Pocket-book*'s balanced aims and instead constructs for it a more straightforward narrative of soldierly rejection. Wolseley's text, in short, was willfully ignored, misread, and neglected. This fate was further consolidated by the efforts of Rudyard Kipling.

On the Frontier

The figure of the British soldier was an enduring source of interest to Rudyard Kipling. In his literary works, particularly *Soldiers Three* (1888) and *Barrack-Room Ballads* (1892), he sought to provide for the British and Anglo-Indian publics a new and unprecedented portrait of barracks life abroad, a life that was at once as exciting and dangerous as it was quotidian and boring. His writings about the British army's imperial presence frequently turn to Wolseley and his *Pocket-book*. Some of these are fleeting mentions; others show sustained engagement with specific statements from the text. Across this range of references, the *Pocket-book* serves as the locus for Kipling's trenchant critiques of military hierarchies and methods of training. In "The Taking of Lungtungpen" (1887) and "The Courting of Dinah Shadd" (1890), Kipling mobilizes the *Pocket-book* to categorize and dichotomize soldiers. There are those who unfailingly adhere to the book's prescriptions, often to the larger detriment of the army. And then, there are those who refuse to read the text or intentionally misuse it.[92]

Kipling's self-stylization as a competing authority to Wolseley on colonial war stemmed from sporadic brushes with military men. As David Gilmour points out in his biography of the writer, Kipling—unlike Wolseley—never saw a war fought in South Asia. He once visited the Khyber Pass, on the border between present-day Pakistan and Afghanistan, when he was working with *The Civil and Military Gazette*, and most of his descriptions of the North-West frontier are imaginative reconstructions of that visit.[93] He later made another visit to the barracks in Mian Mir, where he struck up a friendship with a lively and outgoing officer, Corporal MacNamara, the prototype for Private Mulvaney in his subsequent soldier stories.[94] Kipling, nevertheless, felt very strongly about the misrepresentation of "Tommy Atkins," the essential British soldier, whose life was as "hard as [his] own muscles, and [about whom] the papers never [said] anything."[95]

As a reporter for the *Gazette*, Kipling's own journalistic work at the time focused primarily on the social scene of Shimla. But the paper did play an important role in the development of the writer's representations of soldiers in colonial South Asia. Often his stories were first published in the paper, and they were also based on actual incidents it reported. Such was the case with "The Taking of Lungtungpen." On January 1, 1887, *The Civil and Military Gazette* ran a story about a group of British soldiers who stripped naked and swam across a river to burn down a Burmese village. Kipling's story based on the episode, "The Taking of Lungtungpen," was published in April the same year, albeit with gross exaggerations: the number of soldiers on the Burmese side is doubled, making cause for greater celebration, and the Burmese village is promoted to a town.[96] The story's description of unconventional military strategy and methods contests what constitutes knowledge in the context of the army, and it does so through a single reference to Wolseley. Military success, the story tells its readers, has very little to do with reading the *Pocket-book*.

"The Taking of Lungtungpen" is in the form of an exchange between an unnamed narrator and Mulvaney, a private in the British army, on the road to Dagshai, a cantonment town in Himachal Pradesh, North India. The context for the story is a conversation between the two about Mulvaney's military career: Mulvaney makes a case for drafting young, and therefore easily influenced, soldiers (they "av the surpassin' innocinse av the child") and regrets that if it were not for his love of drink, he "wud have been a hon'ry lift'nint by this time."[97] Nevertheless, he concludes with a nod to his own military expertise: "I know as much about the army as most men."[98] The narrator's response to Mulvaney's long declaration is slyly filtered out of the story and replaced by the noncommittal, "I said something here."[99] Mulvaney's reaction to this "something" is a violent outburst:

> Wolseley be shot! Betune you an' me an' that butterfly net, he's a ramblin', incoherint sort av a divil, wid wan oi on the quane an' the coort, an' the other on his blessed silf—everlastin'ly playing Saysar an Alexandrier rowled into a lump.[100]

Mulvaney's response to the narrator's unrevealed comment indicates that the narrator introduced Wolseley into the conversation as a person with an extensive knowledge of military strategy, and the aggression with which the occluded remark is met confirms that the narrator's words are complimentary. However, by concealing the comment from readers of the story, the narrator excludes the possibility of creating a balanced argument for and against Wolseley. Instead, he leaves them with a one-sided discussion, heavily weighted against the general.

The *Pocket-book* is not mentioned in the exchange between Mulvaney and the narrator, but the description of Wolseley as "ramblin'" and "incoherint" echoes his reputation as the author of the *Pocket-book*. Wolseley's loquacity was well-known and despised; one article even went so far as to declare: "Nor can it be said that mankind would lose much were the illustrious commander to practice taciturnity."[101] An 1886 review of the *Pocket-book* described him as "cocksure": a "glib master of frothy fustian, of flatulent high falutin', and of oratorical bombast."[102] Such critiques of the general's relentless self-aggrandizing spirit were mirrored in complaints about the *Pocket-book*. "Revised and enlarged"—the words printed on the title page of the *Pocket-book* from its second edition onward—did not gain praise from reviewers. At 551 pages, the 1886 fifth edition was exactly twice the length of the first, reflecting Wolseley's ongoing efforts at revisions and expansions.[103] Advertisements for rival military manuals in the 1880s often highlighted the brevity of those texts as opposed to Wolseley's increasingly voluminous tome.[104] Long, heavy, and containing incorrect information, the *Pocket-book* was perceived to be as rambling and incoherent as its author. If Wolseley's text was unread, Mulvaney's choice of adjectives tallies with, and reinforces, a popular consensus: it was so because it was unreadable.

Wolseley's *Pocket-book* may have been considered unreadable, but the volume of discussion about it meant that many soldiers and members of the general public had some knowledge of its contents, even if they had not read the manual themselves. An example can be found in "The Courting of Dinah Shadd." This story, put together as casual barrack-room talk, recounts the drunken exploits of Mulvaney and his marriage to Dinah Shadd, which is soured by his multiple adulteries with other women. The occasion for the story is the arrival of another unnamed narrator, who is a journalist embedded with a military unit in South Asia. The presence of the narrator provides the context for the first reference to Wolseley in the story. A major compliments the journalist, jovially stating that "Wolseley was quite wrong about special correspondents: they are the soldier's best friends."[105] Wolseley's hatred of journalists was legendary. His letters to his wife, Louisa, mention newspapers and correspondents who are particularly virulent in their attacks against him: *The Daily Telegraph* and W. H. Russell.[106] In a postscript to one such letter, he wrote about the constant anxiety he felt in the company of the journalists embedded with his battalion:

> I had those horrid newspaper correspondents round me . . . most of them were in a blue funk all day, and whenever the enemy approached very near us and the firing around us became very hot, I used to catch their eyes watching mine to see if I was in a funk.[107]

The major's comment refers directly to passages in the *Pocket-book* that labeled newspaper correspondents as a "newly-invented curse to armies."[108] Wolseley's dislike of journalists was so widely known that the section on journalists in the *Pocket-book* was regularly commented upon and cited in reviews of the book and in discussions of his views on military reform. Given the way the *Pocket-book*'s contents were distributed in and through the writings and conversations of others, the major in "The Courting of Dinah Shadd" is as likely to have heard about Wolseley's thoughts on journalists through a newspaper article or barrack-room talk as he is from having read the *Pocket-book* himself. What is at stake here is not so much whether or not he has read

Wolseley's text, but the realization that, at this point, it is impossible to tell. Working through a complex circulation of knowledge and ignorance of the *Pocket-book*, the major's offhand comment plunges us into a space in which various modes of reading and nonreading play with and against each other and become virtually indistinguishable. The *Pocket-book* may have been unreadable, but that did not mean readers did not know what it contained, even if they refused to read it.

When Mulvaney describes his encounters with women later in "The Courting of Dinah Shadd," he insists it is far more likely that a soldier has not read the *Pocket-book* than the converse:

> If you read the *Soldier's Pocket book* [sic], which niver any soldier reads . . . [109]

A review of Wolseley's autobiography, *The Story of a Soldier's Life*, repurposed these exact words. The reviewer noted that Wolseley's "most famous work, of course, is 'The Soldier's Pocket-Book for Field Service,' [sic] now in its fifth edition, which according to the scandalous Private Terence Mulvaney, 'niver any soldier reads.'"[110] A factual statement—the fame of the *Pocket-book*—is immediately undercut by the opinion of Mulvaney, Kipling's fictional mouthpiece. Mulvaney's denigrating comment functions as his own succinct and cutting review of the *Pocket-book*, both shaping and echoing popular opinion. Readers of the review are supplied with no additional information; they aren't told who Mulvaney is or given the original source of the lines.

It's worth stopping here to remind ourselves of the extraordinary influence Kipling's writings had on British colonial culture. His nickname, the "bard of empire," was a testament to his widespread popularity and readership. Most forcefully, his literary representations of soldiers had "a considerable impact on popular prejudices about the military," inculcating public sympathy and understanding for a disregarded class.[111] If the review provided no context for Mulvaney's comment, it's because context was moot. Kipling's views on the *Pocket-book*, embedded in his short stories, circulated as widely as the *Pocket-book* itself. Readers may not have read their *Pocket-book*s, but in 1904—the year the review was written—they knew their Kipling. They would have come to the review with their own priors about Wolseley, likely shaped by their familiarity with Kipling's insults leveled at the general.

The review of *The Story of a Soldier's Life* goes on to note that even if Mulvaney is correct, "if editions prove anything, the soldier buys it."[112] It is unclear if this is a defense or a neutral comment on the *Pocket-book*. Possession, after all, isn't tantamount to reading. Mulvaney knows this well. Let's return to his much-quoted comment:

> If you read the *Soldier's Pocket book* [*sic*], which niver any soldier reads . . . [113]

At first glance, Mulvaney's statement sounds like a lament that no one reads the *Pocket-book*, even though it is a useful source of information and advice. Placed, however, in the larger narrative of the *Pocket-book*'s reception and given the private's now established opinion of Wolseley, Mulvaney's comment can also be read otherwise. The conditional "if" with which the sentence begins, hurriedly followed by the qualification, "which niver any soldier reads," points instead to a guilty admission: to having actually read the maligned *Pocket-book*. Mulvaney's disavowals and disclaimers replay a history of the text: the *Pocket-book* is a book that everyone in the army knows about, is expected to read, may possess, but which everyone refuses to admit having read. If they happen to have read it (as Mulvaney hints he has, at least in part), they will either argue that everything it has to say is inept and ridiculous, or misappropriate what they have learnt to their own, often questionable, ends.

Against Mulvaney's denials and misappropriations in "The Courting of Dinah Shadd," "The Taking of Lungtungpen" presents us with a portrait of what sort of soldier Kipling thought a *Pocket-book* reader might be. In this story, Mulvaney, who cuts a dashing though clumsy figure, is placed in dialogue with his obstinate lieutenant, Brazenose, a man described as being "shtiff wid books an' the-ouries, an' all manner av thrimmin's no manner av use."[114] The reference to "books an' the-ouries" not only reminds us of the allusion to Wolseley and the implied gesture to the *Pocket-book* with which the story began, but also introduces a key argument against the *Pocket-book* that I discussed in the context of "The Pow-Wow": that reading about military strategy is inadequate preparation for war's unpredictability. Although Wolseley conceived of the *Pocket-book* as a corrective to books based on theory rather than practice, the effect, if not the intention, of the *Pocket-book* was to valorize reading over actual experience. "The Taking of Lungtungpen" also comes to this conclusion by pitting Mulvaney and Brazenose against each other in the lead-up to the siege. Both are eager to catch a group of dacoits (bandits) lurking around their camp in Burma, but Brazenose is uneasy, for "[a]ccordin' to the the-ouries av war, [they] shud wait for reinforcemints."[115] He finally gives in to Mulvaney's protestations and leads the charge to the dramatic siege of Lungtungpen. Their success, which demonstrates that "excepshin[s]" do indeed occur, culminates in an uncomfortable and naked, though comic, patrol of the town.[116] Such an odd juxtaposition of army rigor and low slapstick comedy shows how unpredictable combat can be and also how necessary it is to embrace that unpredictability with some good humor. Mulvaney's triumph, made possible by the belief that thinking on one's feet is much more effective than the lessons one learns in books, is relayed to the now compliant Brazenose, to whom he says, "You've the makin's in you av a great man; but, av you'll let an ould sodger spake, you're too fond of theourisin.'"[117] Brazenose's acquiescence confirms what "The Taking of Lungtungpen" has its readers work toward: those who refuse to read make for better and more effective soldiers.

The ludicrous nature of planned and studied strategy is also discussed in "The Courting of Dinah Shadd," through the conflation of war and sex. Military vocabulary and comparisons are continuously used to describe the acts of amatory conquest that form the core of the narrative.[118] Like the *Pocketbook*, Mulvaney's story provides his listeners with a "gin'ral theory of av the attack;" in his case, allowing him to devise a scheme by which to sustain multiple flirtations.[119] In all of these, he characterizes himself as a hapless victim. Mesmerized by Dinah Shadd, he nevertheless finds himself in the arms of the red-haired, green-cat-eyed Judy, who, along with her mother, later confronts him and accuses him of misleading her. Mulvaney's defense is a comparison:

> How does ut come about, sorr, that when a man has put the comether on wan woman, he's sure bound to put it on another? 'Tis the same thing at musketry. Wan day ivry shot goes wide or into the bank, an' the next, lay high lay low, sight or snap, ye can't get off the bull's eye for ten shots runnin'.[120]

Musketry and collecting women come together in a single paragraph, as women become targets to be shot or missed, and Mulvaney finds himself in a sticky situation in the middle of two equally fierce enemy camps. Further, throughout the story he exhibits the soldierly quality that Wolseley's text extols the most: resourcefulness as the key to success. Grotesquely distorted to suit his less noble pursuits, resourcefulness is translated into a less than pleasant statement, "I tuk whatever was within my reach an' digested ut."[121] Turning upside down the lofty connotations of both "courting" and the Mughal aristocratic notes of Dinah Shadd's name with this description of visceral sexual consumption, Mulvaney takes the core teachings of the *Pocket-book* and puts them to uses Wolseley would have had shuddered to have attributed to him. If for Wolseley the *Pocket-book* was a guide to self-help, for Mulvaney, too, it is exactly that: a lewd guide to sexual games for the bored soldier. The only way to deal with the *Pocket-book* is to distort it.

Sandhurst to West Point

The fifth and final edition of *The Soldier's Pocket-book for Field Service* was published in 1886; it was eventually replaced by a similar field service manual issued by the British War Office. In the two decades it remained in circulation, Wolseley's red handbook gained an unprecedented, if checkered, reputation as a text that was much talked about, but little read. The volume's unruly history, as this chapter has illustrated, includes a broad range of reception, from the indignant and self-righteous to the outrightly lampooning and irreverent. In each of these interactions, the *Pocket-book* is transformed into a completely different text, whether a guide to self-destruction in Wilson's account or a manual of mischief in Kipling's. The handbook, in short, was a mutable object, coming to life only in the misplaced transactions in which it participated. Ultimately, it was impossible to distinguish the *Pocket-book* from the critical readings it generated. A cloud of opinions, misreading, and obfuscations, the book became what its readers made it out to be.

The debate over how best to educate soldiers continues almost 150 years after the *Pocket-book* was first published, as armies around the world continue to rack up innumerable handbooks, guides, and training manuals. Military institutions struggle to convey technical information in a way that will ensure that soldiers actually read it. Much like Wolseley's attention to material detail—the size of the book, the pencil loop attached for easy notetaking—modern military commanders have grappled with how to optimize the delivery of information. In a bid to make instructional texts more accessible, the US Army announced in June 2019 that it would record two of its most important field manuals—Field Manual (FM) 3-0: Operations, and Army Doctrine Publication (ADP) 7-0: Training—as audiobooks. Steve Leonard, a military strategist, described this venture as an attempt to deliver military doctrine in more lucid, convenient ways: "Everything points back to a desire to get people reading and learning our playbook . . . because they don't."[122] The necessity of getting soldiers to read a military handbook, even in its digital, audio incarnation, hangs heavily on strategists. If soldiers can listen to the manuals on their morning commute, or while working out in the gym, perhaps they will embrace the precepts these texts set out. It remains to be seen whether soldiers are better listeners than readers.

2

Reading for the Record

Burn Without Reading

On August 20, 1909, Leonard Woolf, Assistant Government Agent of the Hambantota district in the Southern Province of Ceylon, future Bloomsbury intellectual, and author of the colonial novel, *The Village in the Jungle* (1913), confessed to having had a "most unpleasant experience." On his walk in search of peafowl the day before, he'd gotten lost in the jungle. Surrounded by the choking thick of the foliage on a moonless night, Woolf suddenly found himself plunged into complete darkness. Realizing that the possibility of finding a road out was slim, he resigned himself to spending the night in the jungle, clammy and wet from an afternoon of rain. Fortunately, as he wrote in the official diary he was required to maintain, he had two things to help him through the ordeal: matches, to light a fire, and a copy of the Rinderpest Regulations, for tinder.[1]

The papers Woolf used to feed his fire, the "Regulations relating to Rinderpest," were the imperial response to a cattle disease epidemic, a viral disease colloquially known as the "cattle plague." It had an alarmingly high fatality rate, wiping out entire domestic stock herds and ravaging populations of wild buffalo. In a bureaucratic fashion characteristic of the colonial government, the regulations put forward fourteen rules that dictated best practices for containing the spread of the disease. Infected cattle had to be shot; the humans who did the shooting needed to bathe in disinfectant. The regulations were published on July 2, 1909, in the *Ceylon Government Gazette*, the customary forum for government notices and draft ordinances, and Woolf's source for kindling, as well as rinderpest-related information (Figure 2.1).[2]

The "Regulations relating to Rinderpest" were disastrously ineffective. For ordinary people—nonelite colonial subjects, at best functionally literate—

IT is hereby notified that His Excellency the Officer Administering the Government, in exercise of the power vested in him by section 15 of the Cattle Disease Ordinance. No. 9 of 1891, and with the advice of the Executive Council, has been pleased to make the following regulations, and to substitute the same for the regulations dated June 30, 1892, and published in the *Government Gazette* of July 1, 1892, which are hereby revoked.

Colonial Secretary's Office,
Colombo. June 30, 1909.

By His Excellency's command,
H. L. CRAWFORD,
Acting Colonial Secretary.

Regulations relating to Rinderpest.

1. (a) It shall be the duty of all persons in charge of cattle which may die of disease in an infected area to burn or bury, or cause to be buried, within six hours after death, the carcasses of the cattle so dying in a grave at least six feet deep from the surface, and such carcasses shall be covered with quicklime, when procurable, before the grave is filled in.

(b) Every person who within an infected area finds the carcass of any cattle lying dead and unburied shall report the same to the nearest headman or police officer, who shall cause such carcass to be forthwith buried in manner aforesaid.

(c) The possessor or occupier of land within an infected area shall cause the fresh dung of all diseased cattle being upon such land, together with the litter (if any), to be burned, tar, when available, being sprinkled over them before the burning.

(d) It shall not be lawful for any person to preserve the hides, horns, hoofs, or other parts of the carcass of any cattle dying within an infected area without a permit in writing from the Government Agent of the Province or of the Assistant Government Agent of the district in which such area is situated, or from some person duly authorized by the Government Agent or Assistant Goverment Agent aforesaid to issue such permit. Every such permit shall contain the conditions under which such hides, horns, and hoofs may be preserved.

2. It shall be the duty of every person who buries or assists to bury the carcases of any cattle within an infected area, or is employed in tending diseased or suspected cattle either within or without an infected area, before he approaches healthy cattle to thoroughly bathe his body, and cause his clothes to be boiled in water containing a wine glass full of " kregaline," or " phenol," or " Jeye's disinfectant," or some similar preparation, or to be otherwise disinfected.

3. No person shall expose diseased or suspected cattle in any market, gala, garden, or other public or private place.

FIGURE 2.1. First page of the "Regulations relating to Rinderpest," *Ceylon Government Gazette*, July 2, 1909, 606, National Digital Library of Sri Lanka. Reproduced with permission of National Library and Documentation Services Board, Sri Lanka. The "Regulations" run from page 606 to 608.

the colonial government's response to a devastating epidemic that ravaged their livelihood suffered from unclear messaging. The measures ordered to control the disease were not only punishing; they were also lengthy and confusing. Each of the fourteen rules in the "Regulations" was replete with clauses and subclauses, absolutes and conditionals. Take, for example, rule 6 (a):

It shall not be lawful for any person to keep any diseased or suspected cattle in any chena or unenclosed land or field, or in any land or field immediately adjoining a thoroughfare or highway, without a permit from the Government Agent of the Province or the Assistant Government Agent of the district in which such person resides, or from some person duly authorized by the Government Agent or Assistant Government Agent aforesaid to issue such permit.[3]

Masquerading as a set of clear instructions, the rule nevertheless obfuscates. How could owners tell if their cattle were "suspected" to have contracted rinderpest? How close did a field have to be to be considered "immediately adjoining" a highway? Who would help owners fill out the necessary forms for a permit? How long would it take to obtain authorization? The rules presented uncertainties; uncertainties presented loopholes. This fact was mercilessly exploited by local headmen, officials, and clerks, who could choose to turn a blind eye to infractions in their villages (for a fee, of course). It is unsurprising, then, that Woolf reported that the regulations were pointless, generating useless work for him. In *Growing*, the volume of his autobiography describing his Ceylon years, he wrote of the disease outbreak:

> I felt acutely the failure and futility of what I was doing . . . I knew that the order to impound cattle was practically futile, because it would not be obeyed and could not be enforced. I knew that the villagers did not believe what I said to them; to them I was part of the white man's machine, which they did not understand. I stood to them [the villagers] in the relation of God to his victims: I was issuing from on high orders to their village which seemed arbitrary and resulted in the shooting of their cows.[4]

Woolf was correct. The rules did little to stymie the spread of the disease. Their instantiation did, however, mean that local cattle owners faced punitive consequences for noncompliance, ranging from paying fines to the threat of legal prosecution.

In this light, Woolf's burning the copy of the "Regulations relating to Rinderpest" in his bag is more than an innocuous detail in an amusing story. For one, Woolf had a deep-seated hatred of paperwork. In his letters home, he constantly grumbled about the mind-numbing nature of what he called the "daily tangle of red tape."[5] "*You* can't know how I hate the physical labour of sitting up & holding a pen," he wrote bitterly to Lytton Strachey, his primary correspondent while in Ceylon.[6] By describing the incident in the jungle in his official administrative diary—which, at the time, was read by other senior officials, and is now preserved for posterity as a manuscript in the Sri Lanka National Archives, as well as a cheap paperback available in local bookstores— Woolf was not just being cheeky. He was putting his grievance about empire's unhealthy entanglement with documents on the record. His concerns recall

Karl Marx's biting assessment in 1853: "No wonder, then, that there exists no government by which so much is written and so little done, as the Government of India."[7] Participating in an infrastructure of bureaucratic repetition, the "Regulations relating to Rinderpest" served as a stark reminder that the primary measure that the government had taken against the disease epidemic was to generate official papers about it, papers that lay around in offices and, occasionally, were set on fire.

Illiterate Readers, Illegible Documents, and a Novel

The British empire had always believed in the power of putting pen to paper. On the ground in Ceylon, the provincial *kachcheri* offices were its administrative hubs, comprising writers, receivers, and readers working in a continuous feedback loop. The "Regulations relating to Rinderpest" circulated in an avalanche of other forms of writing: licenses, forms, petitions, account books, official letters and reports, and gazettes. Intended as a surrogate for the colonial state, the bureaucratic document was the material appendage through which its presence was felt, whether in bustling urban centers or the deep recesses of remote villages.[8] While Woolf and his colleagues couldn't be everywhere at the same time, the "Regulations relating to Rinderpest" *could* be, as reproducible and portable specters of an absent government.

This chapter follows the trajectories of the bureaucratic document and its functional archive in late nineteenth- and early twentieth-century Ceylon. These texts circulated in colonial homes and colonial offices, were deployed as plot devices in literary texts, and were stored in the cupboards of archives till the present. As Cornelia Vismann points out, paperwork has the sneaky tendency of spawning more paperwork. Writing of files, she notes: "Their incessant proliferation seems a natural phenomenon. Masses of paper arise and merge into mountains that join to form entire mountain ranges. Floods of paper empty into oceans; ravines flanked by shelves cut through impassable terrain."[9] So while I aim to look at three paradigmatic examples—account books, licenses, and petitions—I inevitably stumble upon conduct registers, gazettes, ordinances, diaries, reports, newspapers, and even novels. These textual objects are bound together by the project of what ethnographers of the state have called *legibility*. In *Seeing Like a State* (1998), James Scott argues that the concept of legibility is a "central problem in statecraft," noting how states are driven by the need to carve out a disciplinary space within which their subjects can be made legible: categorized, regulated, and controlled. Key to these efforts to create a "legibility effect" are the empirical tools of data collection and bureaucratic standardization.[10] Their paper instruments and manifestations as forms and licenses, reports, census counts, and ethnographic surveys, advance a Weberian vision of bureaucracy in which empire's human subjects are transformed from unruly, slippery actors into depersonalized (that is, manageable) names on forms and statistics in reports.[11]

In what follows, I explore the ways in which bureaucratic forms of writing, designed as tools to assist in the project of legibility, came to be haunted by their murkier cousin: illegibility. Imagine a document in the hands of a reader in late nineteenth- and twentieth-century Ceylon. Is the document in English? In 1911, only 2.1 percent of the local male population of the Southern Province, where the district of Hambantota was located, could read and write in English.[12] The document is almost certainly handwritten, hastily scrawled with smudges obscuring important details. Beyond these immediate material barriers to reading, paperwork posed an ontological problem. In a world where counterfeits abounded, bureaucratic documents were often not what they said they were. Literally parsing a document was no guarantee of its accuracy or validity. Then, there was the question of volume. Every action in colonial life—from owning a gun to clearing agricultural land—required its subjects to draw up and file forms and requests. Local colonial offices were overburdened by the bulk of writing they both generated and demanded. Even if none of the impediments to reading I have listed here existed, the reader would still face the disjunction between the legible motives and illegible outcomes of bureaucratic empire.

In my exploration of bureaucracy and reading, I remain committed to the experiences of those who leave the fewest traces of their interactions with documents behind: the targets of the colonial legibility project, the nonelite populations of late nineteenth- and early twentieth-century Ceylon. They were illiterate Sinhala and Tamil speakers employed in subsistence farming, hunting and fishing, and manual labor. Despite the problems posed by illegibility, ignoring bureaucratic documents wasn't an option for these colonial subjects. An incorrect permit or unpaid dues came with punishing social and material costs.[13] The result was that day-to-day interactions with the colonial state, whether to obtain a permit or to file a complaint, relied on written documents that the vast majority of the population couldn't read. In the colonial archive, illiterate readers' brushes with illegible documents sit alongside other experiences of textual obstinance by readers of varying literacies: colonial administrators, clerks, local headmen and officials, and scribes. Collectively, these readers pose an important question: How do we read when we literally can't?

This chapter makes a case for the figure of the illiterate reader. The bureaucratic document, in all its maddening, frustrating illegibility, presents a uniquely level playing field, presenting barriers to reading across the literacy spectrum. It not only confused illiterate readers; it also tripped up highly trained, professional ones, as they struggled with its complex requirements and its ever-growing volume. The illegible bureaucratic document becomes the material site at which the distinctions between the illiterate and the literate fall apart. If the inability to read didn't prevent people from understanding bureaucratic documents, the ability to read provided few interpretive advantages and could even be actively misleading. Put boldly, when it came to the bureaucratic document, everyone in late nineteenth- and early twentieth-century Ceylon veered on the functionally illiterate.

In this light, illiterate readers did precisely what illiteracy is meant to preclude: they read. In moments in which content eluded them, they found alternative practices of meaning-making, ranging from the tactile, material feeling of paper to outsourcing their reading and writing to professionals. While divorced from the technical act of deciphering words on a page, their actions yielded the same interpretive outcomes as those of their more learned counterparts. Exceeding the demographic divisions of literate and illiterate, the aim of this chapter is to acknowledge the affective and intellectual force of a range of textual engagements.

The stakes and consequences of illiteracy varied dramatically across racial and occupational lines. For Leonard Woolf, illiteracy was part of the monotonous grind of everyday life in Ceylon, leaving him with mixed feelings of boredom and ambivalence about his role as an agent of empire. In an early letter from the island, he writes: "I have begun work already & very dull it is—every day to the Customs & the Kachcheri (the govt offices of the district) where I check the accounts of the province, test weights & measures, & issue orders which I hardly understand."[14] Existential angst, however, was the privilege of a colonial administrator. For the locals, moments of illiteracy cut closer to the bone, holding within them threats of punishment.

Foraging for bureaucratic documents and the fingerprints of their readers, I turn to late nineteenth- and early twentieth-century records from the Hambantota district, now housed in the Sri Lanka National Archives in the city of Colombo. As Nira Wickramasinghe writes, the "layered nature of the colonial archive" allows us to read "echoes and whispers and silences."[15] Even as it is created under the logics of colonialism, the official archive still has place for the voices of the illiterate if we look for them: through names on forms, thumbprints for signatures at the bottom of letters, and ventriloquized in the pleading tones of petitions. Further, as I will show, the history of reading bureaucratic documents is embedded in the bureaucratic documents themselves, whether through stories of paperwork havoc retold in reports and narratives, or through errors of use that point to confused understanding. I read deep into the archive, but I also skim along its grain, to borrow from Ann Stoler, revealing how material form and circulatory relationships tell us as much about a document as what it says.[16] Mining the archive for content and the *form* of that content, I argue that the bureaucratic document was not simply an empty vehicle for instruction, but rather an autonomous force, sometimes facilitating (though mostly impeding) the transmission of meaning.[17]

Alongside historical readers gleaned from the files of the official archive, I explore fictionalized, if realistic, scenes of reading from Leonard Woolf's ethnographic novel, *The Village in the Jungle* (1913).[18] Published two years after he resigned from the Ceylon Civil Service, the novel pulled extensively from Woolf's observations of local life in Ceylon to present an almost all-Sinhalese cast of characters.[19] Publicity materials for a 2006 edition of the novel proclaims that "it reads as if Thomas Hardy had been born among the heat, scent, sensuality, and pungent mystery of the tropics."[20] In reality, much of *The Village in the Jungle* details the banality of empire. Through a story about poverty, hunger, and loss, we witness the disintegration of Silindu, a hunter living in the fictional village of Beddagamma, as symptomatic of the crumbling of old, local ways of life under the pressures of the new colonial government. The novel's plot follows Silindu's skirmishes with local headmen and officials—his loans are denied, he is falsely implicated in a theft—which culminate in a violent act of revenge. He shoots his accusers and spends the rest of his life in prison. Entangled in these moments of drama is a steady stream of dull paperwork: petitions submitted to governmental authorities that are never answered, expired licenses that need to be renewed, unintelligible legal sentences that are read out in court.

My arguments are built around a conversation between my archival findings and *The Village in the Jungle*. In doing so, my aim is not to construct a historical narrative to support my literary readings, but to show how the novel and paperwork are interconnected and co-constitutive. Rather than representing distinct realms, they bleed into each other in surprising ways.[21] *The Village in the Jungle* is driven by a bureaucratic desire to hoard documents, binding them tightly into its plot like an official file. Sparks of the literary, in turn, flash across the bureaucratic archive, returning affect to a form traditionally geared toward blocking it out. While *The Village in the Jungle* is set in the world of Ceylon, the blurring between the functional archive and literature—and my observations about reading and the material document—is also a helpful way to understand texts circulating in other parts of South Asia, whether Bengal, Orissa, or the Deccan.

Greasy Notebooks and Crooked Moneylenders

Almost everyone in *The Village in the Jungle* is in debt. The novel's plot is driven by desperation, as its characters fight the perpetual scarcity of food and impending starvation. The narrator reminds us that whatever the season, or however much it rains, there are never enough crops to feed a family because there are always debts to be settled. Take this passage tucked away in the early pages of the novel:

> With the reaping of the chenas [plots of land cultivated using slash-and-burn techniques] came the settlement of debts. With their little greasy notebooks, full of unintelligible letters and figures, they [the moneylenders] descended upon the chenas; and after calculations, wranglings, and abuse, which lasted for hour after hour, the accounts were settled, and the strangers left the village, their carts loaded with pumpkins, sacks of grain . . . In the end the villager carried but little grain from his chena to his hut. Very soon after the reaping of the crop he was again at the headman's door, begging for a little kurakkan [finger millet] to be repaid at the next harvest, or tramping the thirty miles to Kamburupitiya to hang about the bazaar, until the Mudalali [moneylender and rich trader] agreed once more to enter his name in the greasy notebook.[22]

The harvest begins with the repayment of debts and ends with the renegotiation of new ones. Mirroring the cyclical nature of the agricultural seasons, cycles of debt can't be broken or challenged. In the parasitic world of *The Village in the Jungle*, debt is made to look like a natural occurrence. The locust-like descent of the moneylenders onto the village is like a natural disaster: foreseen, but unstoppable.

But the real problem that the characters face is not the inability to repay their debts (it is taken for granted they never will), but that their creditors will refuse to keep them *in* debt. The locus of this gnawing anxiety, as the passage above reminds us, is the Mudalalis' account books, their "little greasy notebooks." Introduced at the beginning of the passage and reappearing in its final line, the account book is at the center of the vicious cycle of debt and poverty in *The Village in the Jungle*. Representing the unequal exchange between debtor and creditor, the account book, with its characteristic bureaucratic efficiency, reduces the visceral bodily hunger that prompts seeking credit in the first place to a set of cold figures on a page. Unlike a bulky government file or ledger, it is unobtrusive and can be slipped into the moneylender's pocket and travel with him always, making the account book not just a potent instrument of domination but also a portable one. Its state—dirty, well-worn, and greasy—is a material attestation to the seasons, possibly years, of hunger and exploitation the villagers have faced, as well as to the duplicitous nature of the dealings to which it stands witness. Passing through the well-greased palms of its owners, the notebook is greasy by extension, documenting in bureaucratic disguise the informal networks of bribery, coercion, and corruption portrayed in *The Village in the Jungle*. Having one's name entered "once again" in the notebook provides momentary relief, but it also restarts the cycle of debt, hunger, and deferred payment that the passage above so poignantly describes.

Beyond *The Village in the Jungle*, the recurrence of the moneylender's account book in narratives from across colonial South Asia reinforces its centrality to histories of peasant societies. In Dinabandhu Mitra's Bengali-language play, *Nil Darpan* (1860) [The Mirror of the Indigo Revolt], an infamous retelling of peasant protests against the atrocities committed by indigo planters in 1860s Bengal, lawyers vociferously argue that farmers' debts never seem to be erased from the account books of local creditors, irrespective of the payments they make.[23] During the Deccan Riots of 1875—a series of incidents orchestrated against extortionary moneylending practices in the Pune and Ahmednagar districts—peasants seized account books and promissory bonds and burned them. These documents were not collateral damage in a moment of violent protest; they were the targets of the peasants' anger. As the commission instituted to investigate the Deccan Riots reported, the incidents were "not so much a rebellion against the oppressor, as an attempt to accomplish a very definite and practical object, namely, the disarming of the enemy by taking his weapons (bonds and accounts)."[24] Burning the books was an act of erasure, leaving no physical traces of the peasants' debts.

Filtered through the eyes of Silindu and the other villagers of Beddagamma in *The Village in the Jungle*, another detail about the account books stands out: their pages are "filled with unintelligible letters and figures." This descriptive detail reflected a broader historical problem. From the notebooks of local moneylenders to the ledgers of financial firms, the difficulties of reading another person's account books plagued Ceylon's bureaucratic system. In 1916, three years after *The Village in the Jungle* was published, the colonial government proposed a new ordinance to regulate moneylenders in Ceylon, which, among other things, targeted how moneylenders maintained their records, requiring them to "keep a regular account of each loan, stating in intelligible words, figures, and denominations the items and transactions incidental to the account."[25] By choosing the metric of intelligibility on which to assess account books, the vocabulary of which is an echo from *The Village in the Jungle*, the ordinance is an insistent reminder that account books were not simply private records. In their public circulation, they needed to be decipherable to multiple readers: borrowers, lenders, government clerks, and legal officials. Bureaucracy relied on transparency, clarity, and accuracy. A properly maintained account book, a declaration of honest dealings, was an indispensable part of the authority of empire.[26]

By telling moneylenders what to do, the ordinance's prescriptions hint at what they *didn't* do. While the ordinance insisted on "*intelligible* words, figures, and denominations," Silindu stares at a page of "*unintelligible* letters and figures." The report written by the commission tasked to investigate the Deccan Riots raises similar concerns about the messiness of the moneylender's account book as a universal problem in precisely the same terms: "Many *sowkars* [moneylenders] do not keep such accounts as would be *intelligible* to a *ryot* [peasant], but none ever do more than come to a rough settlement at long intervals, usually when some new form is to be given to the debt."[27] But, barring deliberate obfuscations by the moneylenders—tampering with documents, refusing to give debtors receipts—there is another reason for Silindu's befuddlement. He, as most of the other characters in *The Village in the Jungle*, is illiterate. Even Babehami, the village headman, can only barely write his name, and this distinction is what leads to his being appointed to his role. The account book's impenetrability, coupled with Silindu's inability to read it, force us to think about literacy in a more expansive manner. Mark Amsler's work on the European Middle Ages presents the useful framework of what he calls "affective literacy," responses and practices that challenge the belief that "reading is unilateral consumption and the text is a discrete object."[28] At the heart of Amsler's theorization is the acknowledgment that we do many things with books, not all of which are contingent on what is written in them. We touch them and are scared to touch them. We are saddened and amused by them. If conventional theories of literacy demand access to the page or book, affective literacy is an evocative reminder of how somatic, physical, and emotive responses to writing exist alongside textual ones, even independently of them.[29] Literacy isn't just decoding words; it is decoding the material worlds that enclose them.

For Silindu in *The Village in the Jungle*, while the account book's content is unintelligible, the significance of the book itself is not. As other incidents in the novel demonstrate, debts and repayments permeate all aspects of Silindu's life beyond his interactions with the colonial bureaucracy. Indeed, the phrase "something must be given" is something of a refrain in the novel.[30] Take, for example, an episode in which Silindu goes on a pilgrimage to heal an ailment he has contracted, accompanied by a witch doctor named Punchirala. After Silindu prays to the shrine's deity, Punchirala produces a rupee to give as an offering, saying, "Even the gods require payment."[31] Punchirala's comment introduces the notion of a ritualistic pledge, of asking the gods for something but having to repay the favor in money or in kind. If the promise is not kept and the debt not paid, consequences are inevitable. In return, the successful completion of this divine transaction is sealed with a sign of fulfillment acting as a spiritual receipt; in the case of the novel, the birth of a child to Silindu's daughter, Hinnihami. To reiterate: what confuses Silindu isn't debt, but the material document recording it.

Eliciting more than just the confusion of the illiterate, the account book, too, is invested with sacred powers. The book is transformed in the villagers' imaginations into a referent of power with magical effects: the promise of putting an end to their hunger. In fact, by not fulfilling its intended purpose—to be intelligible, *legible*—the account book perfectly performs another role. It prompts feelings of terror, followed by memories of hunger and desperation that give way, finally, to resignation, in full recognition of the ways in which the book circulates and participates in their world. This is as much as could be expected from a literate reader. Indeed, the report of the Deccan Riots Commission notes that accounts and records of monetary transactions were notoriously difficult to track and read and would even "baffle an intelligent accountant."[32] In this snapshot of a reception history, illiteracy allows the reader to bypass the technical act of deciphering words on a page and get down to the real work of reading: interpretation. It is just that the words themselves have little to do with this.

But while Silindu is shrewd enough to grasp the power of the account book and the importance of having one's name written down in it, he often forgets that documentary evidence is intractable.[33] Begging for loans from Babehami the headman, more often than not he slips into exaggerated declarations, promising to repay him "twofold" or "threefold."[34] These are momentary enunciations, not binding promises to which he expects to be held. He fails to realize that once words are on paper, they cannot be taken back. Headmen, as we will see, are as unforgiving as the gods.

Dubious Licenses and Annoyed Bureaucrats

The Village in the Jungle culminates in Silindu shooting Babehami, the village headman, and Fernando, a local moneylender. When he goes to the Ratemahatmaya with the story of how his actions, compounded by anger and desperation, were a long time coming, the Ratemahatmaya coldly interrupts him with a pressing question.[35] "Was it [the gun] licensed?"[36] You might balk at this as a response to a confession of murder, but readers of *The Village in the Jungle* will smile wryly. For implied in the Ratemahatmaya's response is the uncertainty of what the crime before him really is: Murdering village officials, or doing so with an unlicensed gun? In this world in which actions are guaranteed by documents, if you're going to murder someone, you have to do it by the book.

Gun licenses were just one of the many kinds of permits that colonial subjects were required to hold in Ceylon. Permits were needed to farm chena, sell salt, trap elephants, and transport cattle. They were customarily issued on an annual basis for a fee and needed to be renewed on expiration.[37] The licensing office kept a record of the documents issued in a register, against which a holder's document could be checked and verified, if necessary.[38] Beyond their bureaucratic function of surveillance, licenses reminded colonial subjects that even their everyday actions were possible only because they were authorized by the state. This realization dawns on Silindu through a series of episodes involving his gun license. For him, a gun is not merely a tool of his profession— he is, after all, a hunter—or even a means of protection against the unknown horrors of the jungle. Occupationally linking generation after generation, it stands for family longevity and perpetuation. So when Silindu's wife gives birth to twin daughters, he laments: "Where is the son who is to carry my gun into the jungle, and who will clear the chena for me?"[39] Just as the account book puts traditional networks of borrowing and lending into documentary form, Silindu's hereditary right to hunt is undermined by colonial bureaucracy: he is told that to practice the only trade he knows, he needs a special gun license.

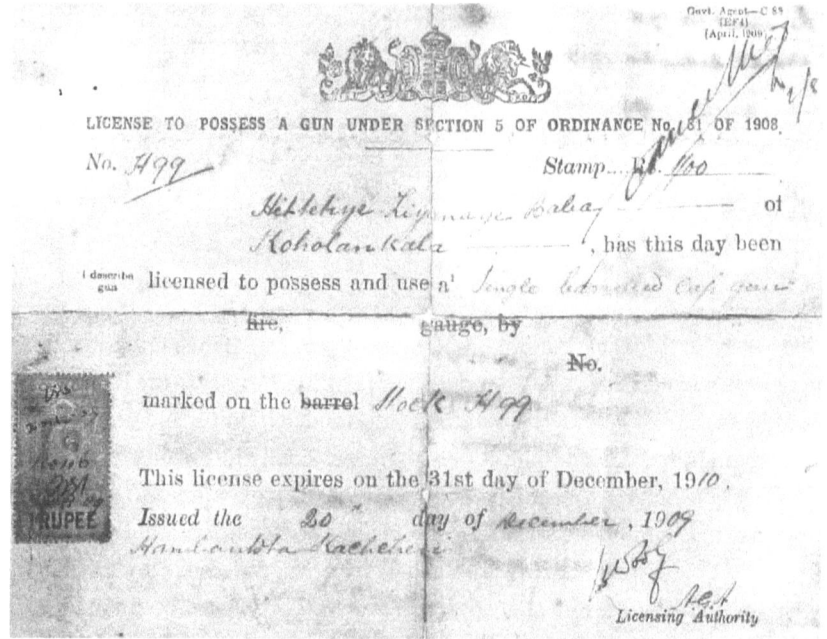

FIGURE 2.2. A gun license counterfoil signed by Leonard Woolf, December 20, 1909, "Petitions addressed to the AGA Hamb[antota] (reports annexed, nos. 600–797)," Lot 27 / 399, Records of the Hambantota Kachcheri. Reproduced with permission of Sri Lanka National Archives, Colombo.
Note the attested stamp in the bottom left-hand corner.

The regulatory function of licenses was evident even in their documentary forms, to which groups of readers would respond differently. Issued in foil and counterfoil, otherwise plain-looking gun licenses were emblazoned with the royal insignia, an elaborate header and the authority it represented announcing themselves boldly before the menial bureaucratic details followed (Figure 2.2). For license-holders who were English-illiterate, the header was intended to be a recognizable visual cue that the piece of paper they had been given was an official government-certified document. The counterfoil, the shadow copy of the license retained by the local colonial office, had in its left-hand corner a revenue stamp, a sticky label that confirmed that the fees for the license had been collected. A government official signed across the stamp to confirm the transaction, as well as to prevent the stamp from being reused.

The information the license contained, however, opened itself up to multiple readings. Though at first glance deeply depersonalized, a gun license was by necessity unique, imbricating person to document (license) and object (gun). While its details would be scrutinized for accuracy by government officials, this imbrication would be lost on someone who couldn't read English, making each license interchangeable for them. Similarly, the identity of the licensing authority presented in the signature in the bottom-right corner would be parsed differently by different groups of readers. In a bureaucratic universe, Woolf's signature on the document is an embodiment of the colonial state and serves the twin purposes of authorizing permission and attesting to documentary authenticity. For illiterate licensees, Woolf's neat signature is moot, nothing more than an indecipherable scrawl. But for scholars like myself, Woolf's name on the license marks him as its author: as the creator of a text-object that circulated beyond him, being read, misread, and not read, in ways that were often out of his control. Evinced by special collections holdings, writers often leave behind extensive traces of their ordinary lives beyond drafts and manuscripts, ranging from personal income tax returns to shopping lists. For contemporary researchers, these are precious, fetishized peeks into their private worlds, made relevant by the writer's celebrity. The gun license signed by Woolf, along with the scores of other bureaucratic documents to which he put his pen in Ceylon, form a dispersed archive of private papers, preserved not because of his identity as a writer and intellectual, but irrespective of it.

A license marks a transaction between the colonial state (the licenser) and the colonial subject (the licensee). But between the two entities lay a series of crucial intermediaries: local headmen and officials. These individuals, colonized subjects themselves, represented an extended network of the state's native employees. A Sinhalese peasant might not ever meet the Assistant Government Agent of their district, but the village headman was a familiar face. Coordinating between the rulers and the ruled, headmen operated in the murky zone between regulation and reality. They coerced and bullied those over whom they had power, taking advantage of their vulnerabilities. But they also provided villagers with loopholes and ways out of bureaucratic demands, if at a high cost.

Such petty dramas around bureaucracy provide the building blocks for the plot of *The Village in the Jungle*. Take, for instance, the figure of Babehami, the villainous headman of the novel. Like others in his position, his power is personalized, consolidated by the solicitation of favors and the acceptance of bribes.[40] A representative of the shadowy state, he arbitrarily vacillates between the legal and the extralegal, the official and the unofficial, as it suits him.[41] The villagers astutely surmise that while "[with] the traders in Kamburupitiya the transactions were purely matters of business . . . with the headman . . . they were something more."[42] The "something more" is what confuses them. It represents Babehami's continuous dance between benevolence and harshness, duty and favor.

Babehami shields the villagers from bureaucratic demands, protecting them from the vagaries of the colonial state. While this protection come at a price, it still isn't guaranteed. Each favor he grants comes with a threat of the withdrawal of the headman's support in the future. While, for example, he is usually happy to take advantage of the penniless villagers by offering to pay their taxes for them and then demanding repayment with exorbitant interest, a shift comes about when he uncharacteristically refuses to provide Silindu with any kind of assistance. This becomes an increasingly common occurrence, best portrayed in the novel in a moment when Babehami presses him to get a license for his gun. Silindu's solution to the problem is this: "I will hide the gun in a place that only I know of and if it be taken or question be made, is it not easy to say that the stock was broken, and it was not considered necessary to take a permit for a broken gun?"[43] This argument, we are told by the narrator, had swayed Babehami in the past, but in this instance, he is obstinate in his refusal to help: "It is the order of Government."[44]

Silindu ultimately acquiesces, making the trip to Kamburupitiya to obtain a new license. The gun license's presence, legitimizing Silindu's possession of a weapon, thus stands as a material reminder not only of the colonial attempt to categorize and codify. Rather, within the logic of the novel, the piece of paper—affirming what Silindu takes as a given, his right to bear arms—becomes indicative of his fast-failing relationship with Babehami. While having his name reentered in the Mudalali's account book represents an uncertain victory, the gun license marks favor lost.

While I have highlighted the rigid material infrastructure of blanks, stamps, and signatures, in practice, licenses were more flexible documents than they seemed. One reason for this was the role that intermediaries like Babehami played in their acquisition. Indeed, at the level of material document, licenses were open to all kinds of manipulation by headmen. A case in point is recorded in a file from the Hambantota district, labeled "Missing Stamps on Gun Licenses Issued by AGA [Assistant Government Agent] on Circuit."[45] Officials were alerted to the fact that a large number of gun licenses issued in the district hadn't been properly validated: their counterfoils in the colonial office were missing the necessary revenue stamps.[46] The error suggested that the correct fees for the licenses hadn't been collected, and by extension, that the licenses hadn't been issued according to guidelines. Orders were circulated, calling for a systematic examination of all the licenses in the district, but these efforts were quickly foiled by the noncooperation of the village headmen, who claimed that the villagers had gone for chena cultivation and taken their licenses with them. Over a year later, further investigation in East Giruwa Pattu, a region in the district, revealed a second twist to the problem: the revenue stamps had, in some cases, been accidently affixed to the licenses instead of the counterfoils.[47] Despite the careful paper trail of empire, the situation was neither helped by the fact that everyone involved claimed not to remember exactly what had happened in their districts, nor by the fact that the stamps that were alleged to be on the licenses didn't appear to be so.[48] The file also contains a letter from G. F. Roberts, the Assistant Government Agent at the time the licenses in question were issued. In this, he summarized the complexities of the situation, two years after the investigation had been opened:

> In view, however, of the fact that the kachcheri Mudaliyar [native headman] stated definitely that the stamps were affixed to the licenses, whereas the investigation revealed that they were not so affixed, I am not at all satisfied with the decision [to simply recall the faulty licenses]. The stamps were issued by me and were affixed to the licenses by the kachcheri Mudaliyar, yet are not to be found on the licenses. It would not appear to be a difficult task to trace exactly why the stamps do not appear on the licenses, and what became of them.[49]

Despite the headman's vociferous defense of a simple error of confusing foil for counterfoil, Roberts not-too-subtly implies that the headman has perpetrated bureaucratic theft: pocketing the stamps for his personal use and authorizing illicit documents without having to pay the associated fee.

That headmen were both lax and corrupt when it came to documentation is hardly a surprise. But the case of the missing stamps does tell us things about the relationship between reading and material form and between the license and authenticity. At the heart of this is the question of verification. The gun license's authenticity can only be verified by matching it with the corresponding counterfoil, which was kept safely in the local kachcheri office. To read the gun license is to read at a distance, to read it in relation to the absent counterfoil. As Roberts quickly discovers, without a proper counterfoil, the license is incidental. It's little more than a piece of paper. The faulty licenses also pose questions about validity. The validity of a license was separate from its accuracy. A valid and an invalid license could both hold the same correct information about the license holder and their weapon. Without a counterfoil, valid and invalid licenses were indistinguishable, even to literate and discerning readers. The headmen's machinations highlight this crucial connection, dissociating the truth claims of a document from its validity.

In this light, the incident with the missing stamps isn't merely a story about bureaucratic malleability. It's a story about false legibility. Bearing accurate information even as they're invalid, the gun licenses circulating in West Giruwa Pattu present a facade of a smoothly functioning bureaucracy. The invalid license—masquerading as a valid one—is a testament to the inconsistencies that surround the document. It's these inconsistencies that the headmen exploit, even blatantly parody, in their scheme. More importantly, the case of the invalid gun license presents us with a situation in which reading isn't just irrelevant; it is also misleading. As a meaning-making practice, it can actively deceive its practitioners into making faulty judgments and assessments.

Anthropologists such as Akhil Gupta and Veena Das explore the valences of forged documents and suggest that the production and circulation of unauthorized duplications challenges authoritarian state practices.[50] While not quite a forgery, the case of the missing stamps has a similar effect: questioning the state-given right to collect fees and attest documents. But it's crucial to remember that while the theft of the revenue stamps may undermine colonial authority, it does consequently lead to the construction of an alternative power hierarchy. For the aim of the headmen's subversion is personal gain rather than antigovernmental protest. Questioning the power of the state is only a means of consolidating local power and directing it toward the unsuspecting and helpless inhabitants of their villages, creating, in the process, new spaces and subjects of domination. In an unusually sensitive passage about chena permits and bureaucratic callousness, Leonard Woolf registered just this in an entry in his administrative diary:

> For instance, when a headman is slack in this way the headmen under him become slack and the sins of the headmen are frequently and unfortunately necessarily visited upon the villages, e.g. in East Giruwa pattu last year one vidane arachchi [high-ranking village headman] failed to send in his list of chena applications by the due date—consequently in that VA's [vidane arachchi's] division no chena permits were issued. The result is that a villager in that division must either lose all opportunity of a chena crop or chena illicitly and pay double rent. Of course, one is told at once that the villagers did not apply in time: but it is the V.A. who knows the date by which ap-

plications should be in and if he does his work properly the villager will apply in time. This is a case of "the house that jack built." The villager does not apply because the V. A. is slack and the V. A. is slack because the Mudaliyar is slack.[51]

Not only is laziness reinforced by a hierarchical chain of commands (villager to vidane arachchi to mudaliyar), one must make do with the "official" reasons provided for various inconsistencies. "The villagers did not apply in time" is clearly not the whole story. Woolf's comment reminds us that the errors, missteps, and intentional manipulations of headmen had real consequences for villagers, who would face serious financial hardship due to their inability to get a chena permit. In the next section, I move to the question of how these subjects—with the help of another document, the petition—worked to overcome these challenges.

Plots and Petitions

In *The Village in the Jungle*, when Babehami's growing animosity toward Silindu and his son-in-law, Babun, leads to the confiscation of their chena, they go to the nearby town of Kamburupitiya to register a complaint against the headman and his accomplice, Fernando. There, they meet an intermediary, a Moorman, who helps them draw up an official petition to submit to the relevant government office. He is, however, skeptical that it will have the desired outcome:

> I should like to stop that swine's [Fernando's] game. But it is difficult. One wants time. We must send a petition; the Agent Hamadoru [Assistant Government Agent] would stop it if he knew. But there are always peons and clerks and headmen in the way before you can get to him. Cents here and cents there, and delays and inquiries! You want time, and we haven't got it. But there is nothing for it but a petition.[52]

Bureaucracy's primary mode, as the Moorman wearily declares, is delay. Between Silindu and the Assistant Government Agent are obstacles and roadblocks to be mollified, bribed, or overcome: the "peons and clerks and headmen in the way," nodes in a vast circuit of circulation and reading. Each stage in the bureaucratic process spawns more investigations and inquiries, drawing the wheels of the colonial office to a sluggish lurch, if not a complete halt. Silindu has no option but to wait patiently for his petition against Babehami to make its gradual progress through tiers of readers, even while he can ill afford to.

"You want time," the Moorman reminds him, but the colonial office, chockful of petitions like Silindu's, has no time to give him.

We never see Silindu's petition in *The Village in the Jungle*, but there is no dearth of similar documents in the Sri Lanka National Archives. Routinized and ordinary, petitions are among the most common bureaucratic forms encountered in archives of the colonial world and beyond. Addressed to local British colonial authorities (in Silindu's case, the Assistant Government Agent), petitions were how ordinary people sought to have their grievances heard, whether through channels of complaint or by asking for special dispensations. As a universal tool, petitioning is the "indisputable right of the meanest subject."[53] Anyone can file one, and in Ceylon, everyone did, for all sorts of reasons: to protest the illegal seizure of their agricultural land, to request permission to play tambourines in public spaces, to complain about the bad luck associated with meteorological phenomena, to name just a few.[54]

Underlying each complaint is a fundamental acknowledgment that the state has failed to protect the interests of its subjects. Petitions were intended to bring this to the notice of the authorities, in the hope that this failure would be satisfactorily addressed.[55] In Ceylon, as Nira Wickramasinghe notes, the British would "artfully display their sense of justice and fair play in unimportant incidents, thereby giving the local people the impression that the colonial government was defending their interests."[56]

Unlike other examples I have discussed in this chapter—spare, bare-bones account books and gun licenses—petitions are meaty units of bureaucratic writing. Rather than the efficient system of filling-in-the-blanks we associate with official paperwork, colonial petitions were convoluted narratives that often ran several pages long in their attempts to present a convincing case to the reader. For this reason, beyond their role of redressal, petitions are narratives of the self, rehumanizing—rather than dehumanizing—modes of bureaucracy. Foregrounding the "I" of individual complaint, petitions prioritize the perspectives of colonial subjects over agents, the small voice of history, to borrow Ranajit Guha's phrase.[57] They are not just stories of people's everyday problems—broken amenities, high taxes, cruel headmen—but a unique window into the micro-negotiations endemic to imperial belonging.

Drawing on examples preserved in the Sri Lanka National Archives, I ask what the material form and the textual content of the petition might tell us about the entanglement of reading and writing in the colonial bureaucracy.[58] Petitions were premised on the good-faith assumption that one's complaint would at least be read, if not addressed. If and when they were taken up by the state, petitions led to investigations and consequences. They circulated through the bureaucratic office, acquiring more readers along the way: magistrates, government officials, clerks, not to mention the peons who would have carried the files from office to office, and from person to person. Each time a document passed through the hands of another, it came to bear the marks of this event. Notes and queries, or simply a dated signature as an acknowledgment of perusal were the paratexts to the text of the petition.

For the petitioners, these documents, which represented them in absentia, embodied something of a disjunction. Given low literary levels in Ceylon, the majority of petitions couldn't be read by those in whose names they were filed. Ceylon, like other parts of South Asia, had a long-standing, robust culture of scribes who, like the intermediary in *The Village in the Jungle*, drew up petitions for the illiterate and vernacular-literate in English.[59] Petitioners attested to the content of the petition with their signatures: in a vernacular scrawl for the literate, with a thumbprint or a cross for the illiterate. The scribe's signature is often at the bottom of petitions, too, tying them to the document. One commentator referred to the "industry" of producing petitions in colonial South Asia, sketching a scene of mutual collaboration:

> In the market places and street corners the ingenious scribe may be seen with his legs tucked under him, a rude writing pad on his knee, laboriously writing out, with the aid of a native reed pen about the thickness of a walking stick, the communication which his humble patron, who squats placidly by his side, pours into his ear.[60]

The social relationship between the scribe and the petitioner, the writer and the written, is emblematic of the distinction between literacy and what C. A. Bayly has called "literacy awareness." As he notes, both precolonial and colonial South Asia were societies "acutely aware of literacy, where even the poor could gain access to writers and readers at a cost."[61] That said, once their petitions were drawn up, the petitioners were hardly silent observers, waiting for their fates to be sealed. The written version of their appeals provided them with props in the performance of their grievances and granted them the possibility of access to the Assistant Government Agent of their village. Woolf's diary describes the "usual vast crowd who always come ... with a varied quantity of petitions and requests," supplementing the documents they carried with vocal protestations.[62] Allowing the illiterate to participate in a system that rested on written complaints, the reliance on scribal networks and the incorporation of text and performance breaks the causal relationship between illiteracy and domination.[63] The very act of having petitions drawn up and submitted is a startling reminder that neither a lack of English-language skills nor illiteracy prevented colonial subjects from harnessing writing as a tool aimed to solve their grievances. Put another way, one of the affordances of writing is that it can have effects that are independent of its writer. In this context, petitions are exercises in irony, representing people to whom they are illegible, but nevertheless accomplishing their tasks.

One of my concerns in this chapter is paperwork's organicity, its ability to grow and multiply. Delving into the archives of petitions from the Hambantota district of Ceylon, I immediately noticed that most of the paperwork I was sifting through recorded people's struggles *with* paperwork. In these archives, the crimes of paperwork are numerous. They range from failing to obtain licenses to carry guns and trap elephants to being unable to produce titles and deeds to land. In one petition, four men claimed that their land had been confiscated by their local headman on the grounds that they had not paid their grain commutation taxes for the year. The headman sold the land to a friend and pocketed the profits.[64] Land disputes of this sort are unexceptional and clutter the Ceylon archive. What is curious is how paperwork forms the crux of their dispute, comprising both the impetus for the land seizure and the means by which the villagers contest this seizure as illegal. The plot is convoluted: the villagers cited their names being listed in the records of the grain commutation register as proof that they had paid their taxes. As evidence of misconduct, the villagers further gesture to the absence of paperwork and the failure of the headman to announce the sale of their land according to official guidelines. Finally, the petition to the Assistant Government Agent is the medium by which the land dispute is narrativized and brought to the attention of the state.

Now, to see how paperwork's interlocking functions of creating and resolving tension cultivate specific practices of reading, let's turn to another example. The story goes like this. On July 6, 1906, a petition was received by the Assistant Government Agent's office. According to the two petitioners, Palawinnege Babun Appu and Manage Babehami (not to be confused with the characters in *The Village in the Jungle*), on June 22, three government officials—the head constable, a police officer, and an acting police officer—"wrongfully unlawfully and maliciously with intent to cause wrongful loss and damage to the petitioners and without any just and reasonable cause" seized and took into custody the 103 buffalo that they were driving back from muddying paddy fields in nearby Tihawa. The officials claimed, while giving no evidence, that eleven of these were stolen. The cattle were ultimately released, but to their owners' dismay, the headman not only charged them for the upkeep of their cattle while the animals were in custody (a regular practice), but also confiscated five of the buffalo, presumably for himself. With the hope that "justice may be administered," the wronged men had a petition drawn up and submitted to the Assistant Government Agent.[65] The claim was successful. Government officials concluded that the headman had overcharged the petitioners, an appropriate sum was returned to them, and the headman chastised.

That a headman had taken something to which he had no right is unsurprising. After all, this very premise is the driving point of *The Village in the Jungle*. What jumps off the page in the headman's official account of the incident, also submitted to the Assistant Government Agent as part of the investigation, is how he uses paperwork to justify his actions. Cattle drivers needed permits to take their animals out to graze. The petitioners claimed that despite having the correct permits, the headman told them that their papers were "irregular" and "incorrect" since they were not signed by the correct government authority. The men avowed to have amended their mistake. This claim, however, is completely dismissed in the headman's version of events. According to him, the cattle drivers had a report—not a permit—granting them the transport of 41 cattle, a number much lower than their estimated herd of 103. He said that the men were notified, and told to rectify their mistake in a stipulated period of time. When they failed to do so, their lack of compliance resulted in a fine.[66]

The conflicting accounts we have here pit documents against each other: regular against "irregular," signed against unsigned, permits against reports. In turn, they reveal different relationships to, and uses for, bureaucratic documents. Take, for one, the petitioners' relative indifference to the distinction between the documentary forms that permission can take. What at first seems like a simple misunderstanding—or a pretense of innocence by the petitioners to avoid punishment—is also a problem of recognition. In part a product of their likely inability to read English, a permit and a report become indistinguishable, both pieces of paper bearing an elaborate header, a couple of signatures, and an illegible script. By contrast, the headman floods his defense with a careful accounting of all the bureaucratic errors of which the petitioners are guilty. Irregular paperwork is his excuse to detain the cattle owners, but it is also his cover. Minor bureaucratic infractions to which most headmen turned a blind eye in return for favors become opportunities to confiscate private property under the guise of legitimacy, that the petitioners didn't have the "right papers."

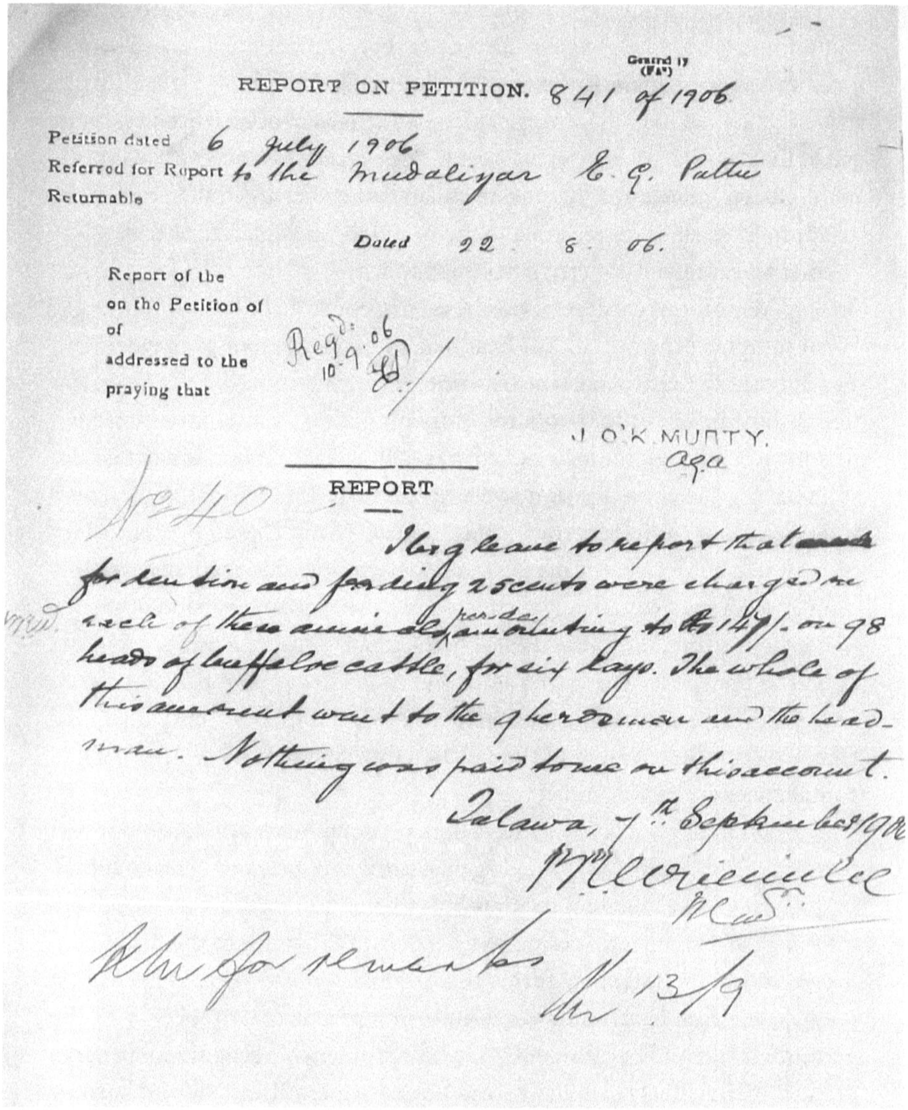

REPORT ON PETITION. 841 of 1906.

Petition dated 6 July 1906
Referred for Report to the Mudaliyar E. G. Pattu
Returnable

Dated 22. 8. 06.

Report of the
on the Petition of
of
addressed to the
praying that

Reg'd: 06
10-9

J. O'K MURTY.
aga

No 40

REPORT

I beg leave to report that ~~such~~
for detention and feeding 25 cents were charged on
each of these animals per day amounting to Rs 147/- on 98
heads of buffaloe cattle, for six days. The whole of
this amount went to the gherraman and the headman. Nothing was paid to me on this account.

Talawa, 7th September 1906
M L Orieuiulee
MC__

Rtn for [?] [?]
[?] 13/9

FIGURE 2.3. "Report on Petition," August 22, 1906, "Petitions to A.G.A. reg[arding]: Buffaloes seized by the Headmen and Corr[espondence] between A.G.A. Hamb[antota]: and Mudaliyar E.G.P [East Giruwa Pattu] reg[arding]: the Recovery of Irregular Fees," Lot 27/745 G 32, Records of the Hambantota Kachcheri. Reproduced with permission of Sri Lanka National Archives, Colombo.

The petitioners may not have had permits for their buffalo. But in a way, they did have the "right" papers: a petition meant to argue their case and convince the reader. Petitions were something like unfinished stories, as their endings were written by the bureaucrat-readers for whom they were intended. Petitioners and scribes crafted elaborate plots of dispossession and befuddlement using stock characters: the helpless peasant, the greedy landlord, the cruel headman, and the all-powerful white colonial officer to whom flamboyant appeals were made. In an article on the emotional life of public forms of expression, Arjun Appadurai writes about what he calls "coercive subordination," describing how supplicants use modes of flattery and praise to force their superiors into generosity. This oral strategy, as histories of petitioning cultures have noted, translated onto the page, with colonial petitions presenting petitioners in such positions of inferiority that the government would be obliged to address their needs.[67] The conclusions of petitions were often written in the tone of a petulant child, not only begging a higher authority to take seriously their claims but also speaking to the heart of what constituted fair rule. The men who filed the petition about the misappropriated buffalo ended it with the hope that "justice may be administered" and that they be compensated for their loss. Another petitioner, claiming that his gun was confiscated on false grounds (he didn't renew his gun license on time as he wasn't aware of the final date by which he had to), asked plaintively, "And honoured Sir, the poor petitioner makes to ask whether this is British Justice."[68]

Many of the narrative poses and strategies that went into the making of colonial petitions were the historical debris of early modern practices of appealing to leaders and benefactors. Since Natalie Zemon Davis's *Fiction in the Archives* (1987), a study of pardon tales from sixteenth-century France, it has become a truism to say that petitions have literary elements.[69] That said, the literary aspects of the genre of the petition—its modes of address, rhetoric of persuasion, and emotional appeals—were an embedded part of its functional apparatus. They were part of a ritual of paying obeisance to authority, and for this reason, routinized and repetitive. In a sense, they constituted a preconstructed skeleton of affective appeal that held together the unique aspects of a petitioner's story. Every petition I consulted claimed extreme deference to the colonial authorities. The petitions I cited above railed about "British Justice," as did almost every petition I encountered. To make a comparison to a bureaucratic form: the literary flourishes constituted the preprinted portion of the form; the nuts and bolts of the story went into the blanks.

From the viewpoint of the history of reading, the articulations and verbal excesses of the colonial petition aren't just pro forma enactments of coercive subordination, performed by a scribe on behalf of a petitioner. Take, for example, how the petition about the seized buffalo describes the act as "wrongfully unlawfully and maliciously with intent to cause wrongful loss and damage to the petitioners and without any just and reasonable cause." On the face of it, this awkward, if pseudo-official, mouthful ventriloquizes the petitioners as too upset to be economical in their choice of words, blubbering and terrified, overwhelmed and tripping over the unfamiliar terms. But the vocabulary the petition employs isn't simply affect-driven; it suggests a society coming into both English-language literacy and bureaucratic-speak. It's easy to imagine a scribe cutting and pasting these words and phrases from a legal manual or report, strung together here as a mark of officialese. Unable to decide which word was the correct or most effective one, he perhaps would have opted for all of them.

If the petitioners were overwhelmed by the demands of the colonial bureaucratic process, so were colonial bureaucrats. Petitions flooded offices on a daily basis, piling up on desks, often left unread. Getting the reply you wanted was like a winning lottery ticket; it was not unheard of, but it was unlikely. Julia Stephens has suggested that to file a petition in colonial India was to participate in a "bureaucracy of rejection": to witness continuously the failures of the state to fulfill the promises of paternal care it made to its subjects.[70] Scribes, like the intermediary in *The Village in the Jungle*, knew that when bureaucrats read petitions, they were tired, distracted, and resentful. Woolf wrote to Lytton Strachey of how "sick" he was of "Salt and Relief works, of the births of illegitimate children, the deaths of venereal old men," all of which increased his burden of paperwork.[71]

What could petitioners and scribes do to maximize the odds that their requests and complaints would be heard? Examined in this light, "wrongfully unlawfully and maliciously with intent to cause wrongful loss and damage to the petitioners and without any just and reasonable cause" is not just evidence of the colonial subject's feeling overwhelmed; it is an acknowledgment of how overwhelmed bureaucrats were, too.[72] The phrasing of the petition about the misappropriated buffalo anticipated economical reading, skimming for the basic contours of the case at hand. Excesses and repetitions were cues and tags, signposts in a long document. The bureaucrat reader didn't need to read the whole phrase to understand what had happened to the buffalo owners; any one word would do. That scribes had the ability to showcase the petitioner's concerns in the most advantageous manner led even literate subjects to seek their guidance and services.

Further, coercive subordination sits in the archive alongside a whole range of other strategies of self-determination and representation. Returning to the example of the stolen buffalo and the mis-signed paperwork: in addition to the original petition, the headman's reports, and documents detailing the administration's deliberations, the case file holds a second follow-up petition, submitted by one of the original two petitioners. Petulance and self-abasement quickly give way to open boldness, as he cheekily suggests that

> with the greatest deference ... your Honor [the Assistant Government Agent] will not be able to hit at the truth by an inquiry from the Mudaliyar alone. If the constable Arachchy [Arachchi] of Kanukitigama and acting Police commissioner of Batatta are examined on a day to be appointed for their examination, and the Vidane Arachchy [Arachchi] of Modanagama division and the police officer of Lumana are examined on a different day[,] giving no room for the two sets of headmen to arrange among themselves the replies they should give at their examination, [the] whole truth is sure to come out ... the petitioner also being willing to attend such inquiry if his presence is wanted.[73]

The statement opens with a double take that quickly puts aside niceties about the Assistant Government Agent's standing ("with the greatest deference") and declares that the plan simply to interrogate the headman may not be the best plan to "hit at the truth." At the heart of his own hypothetical plan—interrogating everyone implicated in person—is the issue of credibility. Whose story do we believe? The petitioner's anxiety that the officials involved might try to "arrange among themselves" a convenient version of events is an acute reminder that stories can appear true even when they aren't. Hoping to denigrate the opposition, the petitioner bolsters his own trustworthiness. By attempting to inject himself into the investigation, the petitioner attempts to control a well-worn narrative: the clichéd and overplayed one in which he is the helpless colonial subject in a perpetual pose of supplication. Instead, he places himself alongside the Assistant Government Agent (rather than at his feet), taking on the role of trusted adviser, whispering suggestions in his ear, standing on the same side of a two-way mirror with him. This is a claim on intimacy that operates not along the gradient of the weak and the powerful, but rather by dissolving the gradient to create a playing field of equals. This dissolution, of course, was nothing more than a fantasy. There's nothing further in the correspondence to suggest that the petitioner's suggestion was considered.

A lack of reciprocation with which their suggestions were received didn't stop petitioners from claiming intimacy with colonial administrators, reminding them how to do their jobs, or filing petitions documenting fabricated violations. A petition submitted by a villager from Tissamaharama accused the headman of carrying a gun without a license and then burying it to hide it. This isn't an implausible scenario; recall from earlier in this chapter that this is exactly the series of events that Silindu proposes to Babehami when trying to avoid renewing his own gun license. The petition concludes with the loaded "I therefore beg that you may be pleased to enquire into the above matter and though he being a headman, I am of the opinion that he has no right to use a firearm without a license, if I am not mistaken."[74] The petitioner draws attention to the immutability of colonial law, applicable to everyone, at least on paper.

The Affordances of Bad Handwriting

Let's return to the petition about the cattle-holding fees. In his report to the Assistant Government Agent, the headman casually drops in this piece of information: when he sends for the cattle drivers to check their permits, he notices that the documents have not only been signed by the wrong official, but that the signature on the paper is completely "illegible." Though this is never explicitly stated, by highlighting the mismatch of legible name and illegible signature, the headman's intention is to cast doubt on the authenticity of the documents. It may not have mattered. If you remember, the petitioners present him with a report instead of a permit, anyway. But what was coded as cunning on the part of the petitioners could just have easily been their bad luck. As archival scholars globally will attest, that a bureaucratic document might be covered in unreadable scrawl seems entirely reasonable. Serendipitous archival discoveries are contingent on their being decipherable. Colonial archival holdings from the late nineteenth and early twentieth century are filled with documents written by hand, some practiced and well-formed, but more often than not, careless, hurried, and shaky.

Bad handwriting doesn't just pose scholarly obstacles in the present. From across colonial South Asia, there were complaints about the practical problems—and the dangers—of being unable to read someone else's hand. These ranged from the routine to the sensational. An article in *Kalapataru*, a Bombay newspaper, reported that a local government official had presented the Bombay High Court with papers written in such illegible hand that they were completely unreadable to the judges. New, clear copies were requested, the official was chastised, and a circular was issued reminding magistrates that they wrote for others, not themselves.[75] A story in *Sanjivani*, a Bengali newspaper, suggested that the consequences of unreadability might well be fatal. In the newspaper's account, a doctor "hastily" wrote a prescription for a patient with a headache; his poor handwriting led to the pharmacist giving the patient the incorrect drug, resulting in his death.[76] Such stories were so pervasive that when it was rumored that illegible handwriting had been made a criminal offense in Germany, the *Dabdaba-i-Qasari*, a Bareilly-based Urdu newspaper, urged the colonial government to do the same.[77]

Could writing illegibly have been a deliberate bureaucratic strategy to obscure details and mislead readers? I turn to H. E. Beal's *Indian Ink* to describe at least one instance in which it was.[78] Beal, a colonial administrator about whom little is known, published his novel in 1954, but he set it in early-twentieth-century Orissa in India. Unlike *The Village in the Jungle*, which portrays a rather pitiful view of Silindu and his family, *Indian Ink* gives us a view of the colonial bureaucratic system from the perspective of Krupa, a conniving Indian clerk working in the Balasore district. Krupa spends his time like Babehami and Fernando in *The Village in the Jungle*, jettisoning gun license applications and blackmailing others with no consequences, as he sets up a network of bribery and corruption in the colonial office where he works. Through his hands pass innumerable reports, petitions, and applications.

The problems posed by bad handwriting became less urgent when typewriters appeared in colonial offices in the final years of the nineteenth century.[79] Against the backdrop of this historical juncture, illegible handwriting makes a loaded, if unexpected, appearance in *Indian Ink*. A man called Rai Gopal Krishna Mahanty comes to Krupa with a problem of some seriousness. The daughter of the magistrate of his village has given birth, and since her husband died some time ago, there are suspicions regarding the legitimacy of the child. Concealing a birth, particularly an illegitimate one, is a punishable offense. Asked to investigate the matter, Mahanty's fears are confirmed, yet he dares not submit a false report concealing the magistrate's misdemeanor. Krupa's advice is simple:

> You will write a report, and you will not have it fair-copied or typed by one of the clerks, but you will submit it to the Sahib in your own handwriting, which is exceedingly bad. And when the Sahib sees it, he will call me, and he will say, "Babu, I can't read this muck. Take it away and type a copy." And in typing a copy I shall change the name of the month in which the lady's

husband died, so as to make it appear that he might have been the father of the child. And if the change is found out, I shall take the blame on myself and say that I made a mistake in copying, because your handwriting is so exceedingly bad.[80]

Readers will be struck by how effortlessly Krupa devises this solution to Mahanty's problem. It comes to him without hesitation, and all the parts of this complicated scheme come together without a hitch, as the novel proves. He even has an infallible backup plan should he be discovered: he wouldn't be the first clerk to make a typographical error.

More striking are the underlying assumptions of Krupa's scheme, both the elasticity and unreadability of bureaucracy. Key here is the relationship between Mahanty's report in his "exceedingly bad handwriting" and the typewritten version Krupa will produce. Krupa's formulation assumes that the magistrate will read the two documents as opposites, which he indeed does. The handwritten version will present as "muck": smudged, confused, and unreadable, its content impenetrable. The typewritten version, by contrast, promises a crisp accuracy, unmoored from the unreliability of a quirky hand. Indeed, this was the hope with which typewriters were introduced into the colonial office, replacing the painstaking and error-making tasks of writing, rewriting, and making copies with the guarantee of speed and efficiency, but also uniform readability.[81] Krupa's plan reverses these associations by disassociating the material form of the documents from their truth values. By pretending that the handwritten word will translate accurately into the typewritten word, Krupa uses unreadability both as a strategy (to have to provide a typed version) and an opportunity (to emend the date on the report). When the report is made readable, it is no longer the same report. It is a palimpsest on which different versions of his story are written, erased, and rewritten and become, ultimately, indistinguishable from each other. If handwriting can be illegible, error-ridden, and inefficient, *Indian Ink* reminds us that the typewriter's promise of legibility is often not more than a loophole through which to subvert the bureaucratic process.

Dirty Newspapers, Ink Blots, and Jungles

Returning to *The Village in the Jungle*, the failure of Silindu's bureaucratic negotiations culminates in his shooting Babehami and Fernando. After he confesses to the murders, he is escorted to prison to await trial. En route, he meets a Buddhist mendicant, the novel's proverbial madman. While their conversation focuses on a complex cosmology of sin and merit, it is oddly prefaced by the appearance of an unlikely object, an English newspaper that the beggar carries around with him. The paper is old and dirty, marked perhaps by signs of touch and fingerprint smudges, but the man admits as he shows it to Silindu that he cannot "read writing or letters."[82] The newspaper is, however, preserved because it cannot be read. Gaining a power like that of the account book, the lure of the exotic here translates the dirty paper into a sentimental fetish object.

But the newspaper, unreadable as it is, opens alternative possibilities of legibility for the old man. The newspaper is a curious object; the mendicant's relationship with it equally eccentric:

> "I will look at it like this afterwards, for some short time—staring hard—then I shall see things on the paper, not the writing— ... —but I shall see things themselves, a little hut up there in the jungle, if you desire it—your hut, my son—and I'll tell you what is doing there, that the woman is lying in the hut, crying perhaps ... before I could only see what was doing in this country; but now, by its help, I can see over the sea, to the white Mahatmaya's country. Then they say this is a mad old man."[83]

This description is much like that of a favorite book. The newspaper, too, is overread and overused, dirty and thumbed through. The mendicant returns to it time and time again, even if only to "star[e] hard" at it (instead of reading it closely). But it is this form of intense scrutiny that transforms the newspaper for him, from a mundane piece of paper to a vibrant document. His inability to "read writing or letters" is not a barrier to meaning, but rather, allows him to transcend the fixity of writing. Instead, he can "see things on the paper": an imaginative act that exceeds the material document and collapses time and distance, "this country" and the "white Mahatmaya's country." While the Victorians believed that reading could transport one to other worlds (hence the excitement and danger associated with the act), the mendicant's relationship with the unreadable newspaper tells us otherwise. The imaginative potential of writing often has less to do with what we read than what we do not.[84]

In the very first pages of *The Village in the Jungle*, the narrator describes the village's relationship with the encroaching jungle:

> The jungle surrounded it [the village], overhung it, continually pressed in upon it. It stood at the door of the houses, always ready to press in upon the compounds and open spaces, to break through the mud huts, and to

choke up the tracks and paths. It was only by yearly clearing with axe and katty that it could be kept out. It was a living wall about the village, a wall which, if the axe were spared, would creep in and smother and blot out the village itself.[85]

The village is not only *in* the jungle; daily existence pivots on the constant necessity to fight its oppressive presence. So integral to the life of the Sinhalese and yet so life-denying in its cruelty and power, it is a zone of reference that remains inexplicable to every character in the novel, even to Silindu and his daughters. The jungle may "choke," "creep in," and "smother" the village, but it cannot be coincidental that it is also described as having the power to "blot [it] out." A careless drop of ink from a leaky pen can render a document unreadable, just as human error can misaddress envelopes and mis-number petitions. The jungle's final inky threat is that bureaucracy, just like anything else, is answerable to the vicissitudes of that which can't be read.

Coda: File Strings, Card Catalogues, and a Book Historian

This chapter, like the mendicant's newspaper, has argued that we take seriously the limits of reading. Tracking bureaucratic documents as they circulate in the colonial village, the bureaucratic office, and the literary imagination, I contend their histories of reading are inextricable from the histories of their illegibility. The bureaucrat and the peasant represent two sides to this story. In the face of masses of paperwork and the incomprehensibility of bureaucratese, Leonard Woolf's Cambridge education provides few tools to tackle problems of volume or alienation. On the other end of the spectrum is the peasant, whose illiteracy doesn't eliminate understanding. The difficulties of reading provide their own interpretive and affective possibilities, spawning networks of bribery, duplicity, and subterfuge. If bureaucracy was the colonial state's attempt to negate the "wilderness, the lawlessness, and savagery" of unreadable colonial outposts, I have pointed out the ways in which this attempt is constantly thwarted from within, not just by the restraints of procedure but also by the very fragility of writing.[86] The literate and illiterate populations of Ceylon who inhabit both Woolf's novel and the historical archive enter this history of reading to circumscribe the practices that we call reading. From them, we learn about the eccentric ways in which texts were circulated and received in the colonial world. From them, we can also learn the epistemic power of the illegibility of books, documents, and spaces.

I began with Leonard Woolf burning the pages of the "Regulations relating to Rinderpest," a symptom of his antipathy toward an empire of paperwork. Across the chapter, I have assembled a range of readers whose lives were entangled with bureaucratic documents: illiterate peasants, colonial administrators, clerks and typists, peons, and scribes. But scholars like myself are also readers of paperwork. We order files from archives, we read what they contain, we make notes on our laptops. Where Woolf was at best, indifferent, and at worst, annoyed, I arrived at the Sri Lanka National Archives, the country's primary repository for historical documents and government records no longer in use, propelled by curiosity. When I'd read *The Village in the Jungle*, it struck me that for a novel whose main characters are illiterate, there was an awful lot of reading and writing going on in its plot. I had wondered what everyday encounters with bureaucratic documents outside the novel's universe looked like. How did colonial subjects with little to no literacy skills use the medium of paper to communicate with the colonial state? What traces, if any, had these interactions left in the official archives of colonial rule? Where Woolf would have gladly never looked at an account book or a report again, I hungrily searched through the physical card catalogue at the National Archives, hunting for files that might tell me something about the imbrication of reading, writing, and bureaucracy in this colonial world.

In the process of my archival research, I began to realize that scholarly modes of reading, like the other nonacademic forms I explore, are wrapped up in questions of illegibility.[87] I mean *illegibility* here quite literally: the inability to find, access, and read records. The history of archival collections in the postcolonial world is inextricably tied up in acts of material inaccessibility and wanton erasure that have their roots in the colonial period. In the wake of decolonization, the material destruction of archives was rampant in South Asia. In the weeks leading up to Indian Independence in 1947, a haze of smoke hung over the city of Delhi. The smoke was generated from the troves of documents British officials incinerated, documents that contained evidence of colonial biases, political cover-ups, and horrific events of state-sponsored violence. This story repeated itself across the British empire. In 2011, the British government admitted to Operation Legacy, a covert attempt at document disposal during the decolonization process across the African continent, Jamaica, and Cyprus. According to the plan, the ash that resulted from burning the documents was packed up in crates, taken out to sea, and dumped a safe distance from the coast. The government sneaked out other documents from the colonies as part of "migrated archives," which were then hidden in lots and basements outside of the public eye.[88] As Maya Jasanoff writes, Operation Legacy was forward-looking: "By eliminating written evidence of their actions from the archival record, British officials sought to manipulate the kinds of histories that future generations would be able to produce."[89]

Even unspectacular colonial documents that didn't contain the type of sensitive information that would mark them out for "special handling" under programs of violent deaccessioning have disappeared. But the loss of these documents bears less the mark of an insidious government than the slow violence of neglect that can be tracked back to the colonial office in the nineteenth century. As Sarath Wickramanayaka has noted, it was only in the early 1900s that the colonial government in Ceylon began to address the question of what to do with files no longer in use.[90] Confusion over mandates of destruction and preservation ensued. Files dealing with "routine" matters could be shredded. Those that held information that might turn out to be useful in the future were archived. Junior staff members—departmental clerks and record keepers—were responsible for making that determination, which often led to dubious decisions.[91] Files weren't safe even after being officially archived. They could be misplaced and mis-shelved. Precisely because of their unsensational content, such documents' status as "missing" regularly goes unnoticed in the postcolonial archive. It is only made apparent when the file is requested by a reader and can't be found.

Beneath the steadily eroded archives of the postcolonial world is the long history of their reception that renders them unreadable for the present. In them, we see sedimented instances of careless handling, poor storage conditions, lack of organization, and administrative chaos. The weather is a major contributing factor to archival disintegration. An increase in ten degrees Celsius (50 degrees Fahrenheit) drastically halves the lifespan of a book. In the hot, humid, and dusty tropical conditions of South Asia, preservation is a race against inevitable decay. Untying the fraying strings holding a file together is almost guaranteed to reveal dog-eared and brittle pages cracking along the lines where the paper is folded, the musty smell of old age, and a cloud of paper fragments. Temperatures and lighting in archives can now be controlled, but the documents held in archives bear the cumulative weight and damage of their histories of mishandling and mis-storage. Before being bound or boxed up to be put away as a "non-current record," bureaucratic records of all descriptions would have passed through the hands of multiple clerks and readers, stored recklessly in drawers and cupboards, exposed on shelves and tables to the torrents of winds created by electric pedestal fans.

Insects are another force with which archives have had to contend. After all, entities other than human readers also have uses for books and records. For termites and silverfish that breed in dark, damp spaces like storage rooms, the cellulose in paper and the glue holding books together are food. These nonreaders leave traces of their interactions in the form of damage, eating through words, phrases, and other relevant details on the page. While the archive's tussle with pests continues in the present, this isn't a new problem. As Rohan Deb Roy notes, termites were an issue in the nineteenth century, too, causing problems in the colonial office and adding to the disorder of empire. Visible only through the traces they left behind, the insects indiscriminately attacked and destroyed the textual spine of empire: currency, promissory notes, bureaucratic records, dictionaries.[92]

When a staff member at the National Archives told me that some of the files I wanted to consult had been "destroyed," he was referring to the state to which they'd been reduced by the forces of weather, termites, and history: too fragile to be used. To open an old file or ledger that hasn't been touched for a while is to guarantee their disintegration. Against the imperial fantasy of archival permanence is the irony of its ephemerality. To open a fragile nineteenth-century file in the twenty-first century is to render it illegible.

3

Reading for Time

Out of Time

In July 2014, I was working in a damp, hot room on the second floor of the administrative offices of the Gupta Press, a publishing house in South Kolkata. The Gupta Press began as an all-purpose printing company in 1861. In the years that followed, it became one of the major players in the burgeoning market for *panjika*s (Bengali Hindu almanacs). Panjikas were compendia designed to structure everyday life by providing readers with quick, portable access to a variety of essential information to organize their time efficiently. Each volume contained astrological charts and tables that allowed readers to find auspicious times for rituals and domestic events. Prior to the nineteenth century, such information was accessed exclusively in handwritten manuscripts or oral form via expert astrologers. The almanacs also functioned as directories, collating information about bureaucratic and infrastructural timings, including railway schedules and government holidays. By the end of the nineteenth century, as demand for these books escalated, Bengal witnessed an almanac printing boom, with hundreds of thousands of copies produced annually by different publishing houses. The Gupta Press published its very first panjika in 1869. Today, it continues to publish a new edition every year, claiming readers from rural households in remote villages to the "highest echelons of society": politicians, industrialists, and administrators.[1] These texts also circulate in a global network of digitized versions in the form of CDs and DVDs. You can even call a telephone hotline to make your astrological inquiries.

I discovered the Gupta Press on a hunt for traces of reading in nineteenth-century panjikas. Searching for panjikas in the Bodleian Library in Oxford, the British Library in London, and the National Library in Kolkata had turned up books that appeared to have never been read at all. Most of these library copies

FIGURE 3.1. Cover of *Nutan Panjika* [New Almanac], 1861–62 (Calcutta: Cones and Co., 1861), Offices of the Gupta Press, Kolkata.
This copy has been rebound.

were disappointingly pristine, held only in the careful hands of scholars and deposited into these collections in immaculate condition.[2] Counterintuitively, the fact that they were exquisitely preserved and sparingly consulted made my task of uncovering traces of readership all the more difficult. By contrast, I now stood in front of a very different, makeshift archive in the offices of the Gupta Press. These panjikas bore marks of intensive engagement: notes hastily scrawled in the margins, bored doodles on the back flaps, and self-inserted errata and emendations to the printed text. These signs of reading spoke to how important panjikas were to the lives of nineteenth-century Bengali Hindus, who searched for all kinds of information in their pages. This extraordinary collection is the work of a single individual, Arijit Roy Chowdhury, the current head of the Gupta Press and a fourth-generation panjika publisher. A sense of historical obligation and a desire to document the history of the company drove Roy Chowdhury to assemble and preserve some of the earliest

FIGURE 3.2. A storage shelf in the offices of the Gupta Press, Kolkata. Author's photograph.
Note that the panjikas are double-stacked and are of different sizes.

mass-printed books that circulated in Bengal. Comprising copies of panjikas donated by Bengali families living across North Kolkata, the bookshelf represented a microhistory of the genre. It showcased a range of publishers who were known for their nineteenth- and twentieth-century panjikas: Cones and Co.; Day, Law, and Co.; and, of course, the Gupta Press.

My time in the Gupta Press offices contrasted sharply with the sanitized, silent space of the institutional archives in which I was used to working. Around me, business continued as per usual, with people rushing in and out with invoices, order forms, and copies of the latest edition of the panjika. During one of my visits, a staff astrologer, employed to draw up the astrological charts the volumes contain, dropped by briefly and offered a prediction about the upcoming local elections (His prediction was correct.). The panjikas themselves were rapidly decaying artifacts. Double-stacked in a massive wooden cupboard, they were wrapped in paper repurposed from other ephemeral genres (sheets of newspaper, pages from arithmetic workbooks, covers of examination answer booklets). Time, heat, and humidity hadn't been kind to these books. The frayed pages were difficult to handle, threatening to disintegrate when turned. The annotations, made in ink, were beginning to fade. The endless attack of insects had left webs and tracks of holes across the pages of almost every copy. Historically, these were books readers wanted to rush through, dipping in and out for salient pieces of information. Like my nineteenth-century counterparts, I was attempting to read them quickly and selectively. Like those historical readers, I was forced to return to the panjikas time and time again.

The Timely Reader

Panjikas were books made for a single year. Their entries started on the first day of the Bengali new year, in mid-April.[3] Each day was presented as a series of astrological phenomena, listing auspicious and inauspicious times. A panjika could tell a reader, for example, whether December 5 was a good day to get married. It could even indicate the precise window of time in which the ceremony would have to be performed to ward off bad luck and ensure the longevity of the union. Armed with this information, readers could tailor the prescriptions of the volumes to their own specific needs.

Panjikas were ubiquitous. Every Bengali Hindu family bought a copy; each copy in a family attracted multiple readers, all of whom found different uses for the volume. The texts were produced alongside literary pamphlets, chapbooks of popular songs, and thrilling detective stories: all part of the "small book" trade of the Battala publishing circuit of nineteenth-century Calcutta.[4] While I examine only Bengali-language versions, astrological almanacs in different languages and under different names mushroomed across colonial South Asia: the Hindi *panchang*, for example, or the Telegu *panchangam*.

This chapter is a reader's history of the panjika. Many of the reading practices that the genre cultivated were directly connected to the formal innovations it underwent over the course of the nineteenth century. Printed panjikas were produced in Bengal as early as 1818.[5] From the mid-century onward, panjikas began to expand their designated briefs as astrological compendia to include large amounts of paratextual material. At first, this meant bureaucratic information such as railway timetables, postal rates, and lists of government holidays. Then, from the 1880s, the volumes were flooded with advertisements. A reader opening an almanac in this period would first encounter a series of advertisements, followed by the core astrological information, and finally, the bureaucratic portion.[6] The panjika in its new *dairektari panjika* or almanac-cum-directory form, evolved into a functional archive in miniature, holding together a network of different print objects within the covers of the book.

The panjika's new and improved form—part astrological guide, part advertising billboard, part Yellow Pages directory—acquired a secondary function in this period. If its astrological prescriptions could assist Bengali Hindus in living auspicious lives, its miscellaneous advertisements and timetables provided another kind of self-help, offering readers the tools to grapple with the unreadability of empire's new infrastructures and the transformations of capitalist modernity. As a guide to a world in flux, it helped readers navigate a confusing landscape of government offices, railway stations, and consumer goods. While the future under the British looked uncertain and terrifying, a panjika gave its readers the comfort of finding agency in how they anticipated and orchestrated their own lives. The expanded volumes quickly rose to the status of required reading, a necessary companion to all sections of Bengali Hindu society. Without one, accomplishing basic tasks wasn't just ill advised; it was virtually impossible.

Scholars of early modern Britain have scoured the pages of old almanacs, excavating marginalia in search of forms of life-writing.[7] I push this idea a step further to suggest that the margins and blank pages of panjikas didn't merely provide a convenient space in which to document the fragments of one's notes and thoughts. The texts proffered templates on which readers could construct their own lives, whether in consultation with a railway timetable or an astrological chart. The form of the panjika not only documented lives; it provided readers with the means to write their own.

I explore how, for Bengali Hindus, the three-part panjika became a conduit between two forms of time. On the one hand, there was local, astrological time. On the other, there was imperial, bureaucratic time. Panjikas invited colonial subjects to participate in an act of temporal oscillation that obviated a choice between traditional, religious obligations and the demands of a modern bureaucratic world. For these readers, astrological auguries pertained as much to train travel as to religious rituals. To own a panjika was emblematic, then, of living a life between two worlds, the local and the colonial. In a more literal sense, the volumes enacted this oscillation as a matter of reading. They allowed readers to flip between astrological and bureaucratic content, just as they could fold the traditional into the modern. Learning how to read *for* time was tightly bound up with learning how to move *between* times.

This chapter builds out a profile of the panjika reader as a selective reader. While readers oscillated between different kinds of time, their relationships with their panjikas were routinely timebound. As compendia of disparate forms of reference information, panjikas weren't meant to be read from cover to cover in a sustained manner. Readers dipped in and out of their volumes in search of time-sensitive information. Always in a hurry and overwhelmed by the amount of information that the books could provide, readers skimmed and skipped through the pages of their copies. Unlike the soldiers we encountered in chapter 1, who refused to read their military manuals, the readers I present here were willing and eager participants, actively embracing the possibilities their volumes provided.

Alongside the selective reader, my exploration of nineteenth-century panjikas identifies a countervailing presence: the *corrective reader*. Opting for comprehensiveness, not readability, each page of a panjika was composed of a mix of cramped layouts, small fonts, and typographical errors. These obstacles slowed down readers and made selective reading a complicated fantasy. While selective readers were quick and careless, corrective readers were slow and deliberate. Their reading practices were marked by the great deal of time they spent with their panjikas, manually editing and repairing their copies of the incalcitrant volumes. The corrective reader's careful labor transformed their panjikas into more accessible texts that were easier to consult. Put another way, they retooled the volumes to enable future acts of selective reading. That corrective and selective reading were inseparable and mutually reinforcing complicates well-worn narratives about the kinds of relationships that readers develop with ephemeral genres. The fact that most people threw away their panjikas at the end of the calendar year confirms scholarly beliefs about the almanac as a disposable genre. But the care the corrective reader showed toward these volumes demonstrates to us how disposability can sit alongside intense and meaningful readerly relationships.

The capacious mandates of nineteenth-century panjikas have left a productive archive for twenty-first-century scholars, who have found in these texts evidence for all kinds of historical inquiry. Projit Mukharji's history of medicine in nineteenth-century colonial Bengal turns to panjikas in search of advertisements for supplements, tonics, and other touted cures.[8] Debjani Bhattacharyya urges us to "think through the almanac," finding in the volumes' entangled spatio-temporal regimes methodological inspiration for her environmental history of the Bengal Delta and its surrounding city of colonial Calcutta.[9]

My own approach to the panjika is less about the information it contained, and more about the history of the form itself. I draw inspiration from Gautam Bhadra, who uses the many woodcut illustrations that fill the printed volumes as a lens through which to think about the panjika's relationship to the shifting temporal landscape of colonial Bengal.[10] But for me, the ties between the panjika and time open up different questions about reading practices, reception, and circulation. The history I write brings together enumerative bibliographies, publishing records, and literary representation. At its core is a close examination of copies of nineteenth- and early-twentieth-century panjikas that I have found in cupboards in the twenty-first-century offices of the Gupta Press and other publishers, and in institutional libraries in Kolkata, London, and Oxford. These copies allow me to recover readers' affective relationships with the volumes, whether evident in the design of the page or notes in its margins.

A Brief History of the *Dairektari Panjika*

James Long, an Anglican missionary, arrived in Calcutta in 1840. Long was deeply invested in educational institutions (such as the Calcutta School-Book Society and the Bethune College) and Bengali literary culture, which led him to compile three catalogues on the state of the vernacular press in the Bengal Presidency.[11] Based on his interviews and conversations with readers, booksellers, and printers in Calcutta and its surrounding provinces, the catalogues systematically organized print into genre, listing the names of presses and collating difficult-to-obtain print run figures of their publications. Long's efforts represent an extraordinary example of enumerative bibliography, providing us with invaluable information about print production in nineteenth-century Bengal.

Long's third catalogue, published in 1859, discussed almanacs at length. He noted that in 1857, nineteen different kinds were in print by ten presses, with at least 135,000 copies in circulation. However, in Long's opinion, this number was seriously undercounted. A more accurate number, he suggested, was 250,000.[12] Precise publication figures aside, the report also gives us poignant (if tongue-in-cheek) ethnographic descriptions of the role of panjikas in everyday Bengali Hindu life:

> Almanacs circulate where few other Bengali books reach; just previous to the beginning of the Bengali year is a busy season with the Native Almanac sellers of Calcutta; book-hawkers in numbers may be seen issuing from the printing presses, freighted with the store of Almanacs which they carry far and wide some of which they sell at the low rate of 80 pages for one anna. The Bengali Almanac is as necessary for the Bengali as his hooka or his *pan* [stuffed betel leaf], without it he cannot determine the auspicious days for marrying (22 in the year), for first feeding an infant with rice (27 days in the year), the feeding the mother with rice in the fifth month of gestation (12 days), for commencing the building of a house, for boring the ears, putting the chalk into the hands of a boy to teach him to write, when a journey is to be begun, or the calculating the duration and malignity of a fever.[13]

Long not only reinforces the indispensability of the panjika to everyday Bengali Hindu life; he also points out the defining characteristics of the panjika market. A mass-produced genre fueled by quick production, panjikas were portable and affordable. These characteristics continued to shape the demand for the volumes through the nineteenth century. Panjikas were most frequently pocket-sized and could be left at home or carried around by their owners. Printed on cheap paper, they have, even today, a newspaper-like quality, with delicate, transparent pages that are easily torn or bent. Bound together with thread between soft paper covers, panjikas were available at astonishingly low prices, a key reason for the large number sold each year. A typical copy cost a mere six or seven annas and, despite some changes in size and paper quality because of paper shortages during the world wars, prices remained consistent for a thirty-year period. Given its low quality as well as its prescribed shelf life of a single calendar year, the panjika soon became associated with disposability. Though family priests might have kept old copies in their personal libraries for future reference, most other readers threw their volumes away at the end of the Bengali calendar year (April 13 or 14).

Long's catalogue documented and lamented the popularity of "native almanacs." In his mind, as in the minds of most Christian missionaries in South Asia, the obsessive desire to know the future that the panjika represented was evidence of the irrationality of Hindus. Organizations such as the Vernacular Literature Committee attempted to popularize almanacs that replaced astrological predictions with "valuable" information about medicines, plants, court fees, directions, and police stations, among other things. These proposed additions, we are told, were emphatically rejected by Bengali readers.[14] The content, if not the spirit, of these innovations would later reemerge in the printed panjikas of the late nineteenth century.

Alongside Long's catalogues, another source for the history of panjikas emerged. In 1867, the colonial government passed an act "for the regulation of printing-presses and Newspapers, for the preservation of copies of books printed in British India, and for the registration of such books."[15] Subsequently, the government began to publish the Bengal Library Catalogues, quarterly reports listing all the books, pamphlets, newspapers, and periodicals published in the presidency.[16] These give us a substantial sense of the almanac market into the mid-twentieth century. For one, they tell us about the different kinds available for purchase (financial, astrological); their size (single sheets hung on walls like calendars, expanded exhaustive volumes of typically three hundred to six hundred pages, and smaller portable ones of a hundred pages or less); the different languages in which they were printed (Bengali, Oriya, Persian, and English, among others); their prices; and, in the case of astrological almanacs, the different religious traditions and calendars they followed (the Islamic *jantri*, the Christian daily prayer book, or the Bengali Hindu panjika).

By the late nineteenth century, there was a well-established readership and demand for printed panjikas. Against this backdrop, two clear controllers of the market emerged in Bengal: the Gupta Press, established in 1861, and P. M. Bagchi and Co., established in 1883. Both presses had convoluted, itinerant histories. The Gupta Press, started by Durga Charan Gupta, began as an all-purpose printing company, not only producing pocket dictionaries, political histories, and Bengali language primers, but also seeking, as advertisements in their almanacs indicate, private print jobs for wedding invitations and self-financed pamphlets. They published their first panjika in 1869.[17]

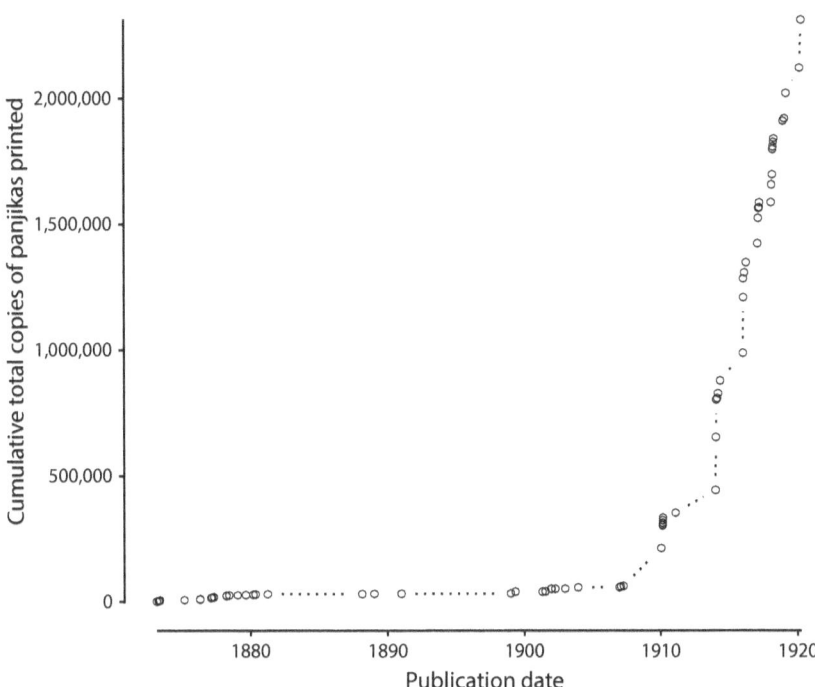

FIGURE 3.3. Graph depicting the cumulative number of panjikas printed from 1871 to 1920.
Many panjika publishers didn't follow the legal requirement to register their volumes, making the Bengali Library catalogue numbers significantly lower than historical circulation. For this reason, this estimate is likely an undercount of the cumulative number of panjikas printed in this period.
Source: Compiled using data from the Bengal Library Catalogue of Books (1871–1920).
Image courtesy: Zachary Barnett-Howell.

P. M. Bagchi began as a company that produced commodities as varied as ink and perfume.[18] The earliest recorded dairektari panjika published by the firm is *The Illustrated Directory of India*, published in 1899.[19] *The Illustrated Directory of India* and its subsequent versions were modeled on the format of English-language publications such as the magisterial Thacker's *Indian Directory*. Thacker's directory was produced annually between 1885 and 1960 by Thacker, Spink and Co., a Calcutta-based, British-run publishing house.[20] Including, among other information, a list of employees of colonial administrative offices and street directories, the volume soon became a central reference

FIGURE 3.4. Historical locations of panjika publishers, P.M. Bagchi and the Gupta Press, on a map of present-day Kolkata.
Image courtesy: Zachary Barnett-Howell.

point for Anglo-Indian society and remains a valuable resource for trade and family historians of South Asia. Thacker's directory, however, had a clear Anglo-Indian bias. Not only did it contain basic introductory information about South Asia, such as charts of seasonal vegetables and local temperatures, suggesting a readership of newly arrived Britons, but it also managed, through its advertisements and street directories, to create the illusion of a British South Asia with practically no South Asian subjects in it. Coupled with its high price of twenty-six rupees—an annual expense—the directory remained out of the reach and realm of usefulness to most of the South Asian population. The dairektari panjika more than compensated for these deficiencies.

The Gupta Press and P. M. Bagchi's panjikas followed the same astrological school, the *Odriksiddhanta*, which draws on a sixteenth-century revision of a 500 AD Hindu astronomical text, the *Suryasiddhanta*. As a result, the two catered to the same Bengali Hindu community of readers. By the second decade

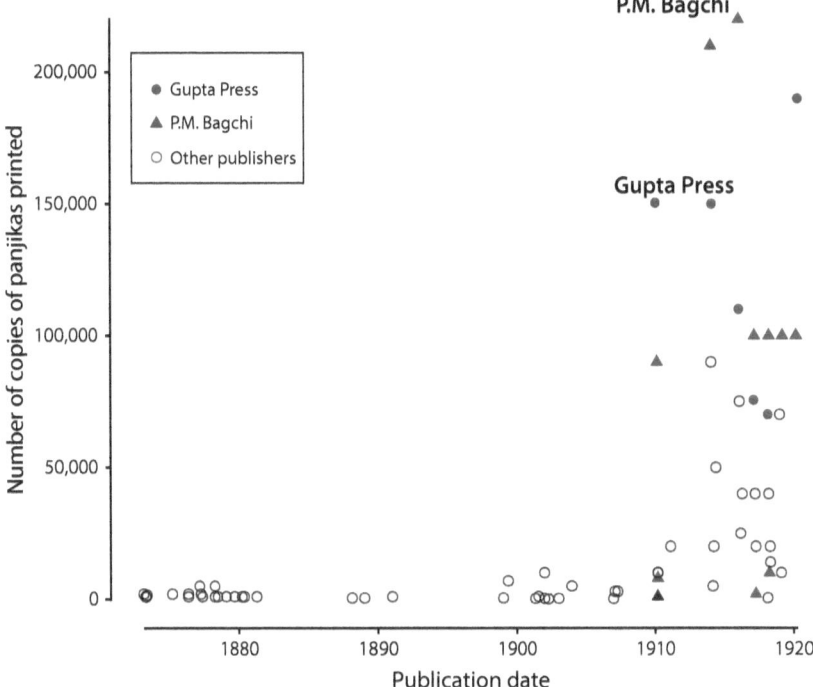

FIGURE 3.5. Graph showing the print runs of different panjika publishers (1871–1920).
The earliest record in the Bengal Library catalogues for a Gupta Press panjika is 1910.
Source: Compiled using data from the Bengal Library Catalogue of Books (1871–1920).
Image courtesy: Zachary Barnett-Howell.

of the twentieth century, however, the Gupta Press had outstripped the sale and production of P. M. Bagchi's panjikas by a huge margin. In 1920, the Gupta Press produced 190,000—as opposed to P. M. Bagchi's 100,000—as can be seen in the Bengal Library catalogues of that year (Figure 3.5).[21] To stress the magnitude of these numbers: the average print of a contemporary novel, even a successful one, was around a thousand copies.

The mass-produced, printed panjika marked a crucial shift in astrological practice. Across early modern South Asia, traditions of learning were "anthropocentric" rather than "bibliocentric."[22] That is, as Nile Green puts it, "knowledge was located in persons rather than in books."[23] Prior to the arrival of the printed book in South Asia, reading and writing (including the calculation of astrological charts) in the Hindu community was the caste prerogative of a handful of male Brahmin priests and astrologers. While they produced manuscript items like horoscope scrolls, their orientation to learning de-centered the written text. Instead, their studies relied on and led to their being able to commit vast amounts of knowledge to memory.

Astrologers in early modern South Asia were diviners and interpreters, helping individuals make sense of events in their lives and map out their futures. As the primary source of this knowledge, astrologers wielded significant power, charging exorbitant amounts of money for their services. Despite their centrality to daily religious life, depictions of astrologers in literary texts across the nineteenth century were far from laudatory. Take the example of Lal Behari Day's English-language novel, *Bengal Peasant Life* (1878). *Bengal Peasant Life* was written as an entry for a literary competition seeking a novel depicting the "Social and Domestic life of the Rural Population and Working Classes of Bengal."[24] The role of the astrologer in Bengali society was so integral that Day spends an entire chapter on the character of Surya Kanta, the village astrologer.[25] The portrait of Surya Kanta is shot through with skepticism about his powers. He boasts of being able to predict famines and help villagers track down their lost possessions. The novel's narrator, however, is quick to set the record straight. Surya Kanta's success at recovering the stray cows and diamond rings of his clients suggests his own nefarious involvement in their initial disappearances. And for what it's worth, it didn't take an astrologer to predict famines. They were terrifyingly widespread and frequent in South Asia under British rule.

The rise of the mass-produced panjika in the mid-nineteenth century didn't completely displace the historical monopoly that astrologers had held over forecasting the future. Many individuals still sought the advice of astrologers; even panjika publishers needed their services to perform the calculations that went into the volumes.[26] But the printed book definitely loosened the hold of astrologers over local communities, a fact that Long noted in his 1859 catalogue:

> We have seen Almanacs 135 years old in MSS. In former days a rupee a copy was paid for printed Almanacs; now the same kind are to be had for 2 annas, this cheapness has greatly reduced the profits to the old *daivajyas* or astrologers, who, like a Doctor in Europe, has in various cases the right of *entre* into the female apartments. Messrs Cones and Co. have got up an Almanac profusely illustrated containing 304 pages and sold wholesale for 7 annas—20,000 copies were purchased by natives last year.[27]

By the late nineteenth century, the printed panjika had been absorbed into the industries of astrology and religion. It was used as both a reference book and a prop of erudition by priests and astrologers alike. But just as a priest could consult a copy, so could anyone else. The mass-produced panjika may not have erased the cultural standing of traditional figures of astral knowledge, but it did fundamentally alter how readers viewed the content of their panjikas. They viewed them not as repositories of arcane knowledge, but as sources of accessible information. You needn't be a scholar to read through a printed panjika; it could be negotiated with even a basic knowledge of letters, a characteristic emphasized by publishers targeting functionally literate women readers.[28]

The Time of the Future

For the Hindu population of colonial South Asia, time meant many things. Time could be read philosophically as "an eternal substance, as the concrete becoming of matter, as instantaneous being, as a philosophical transcendent or even as an indeterminate entity." It could be read politically through the *purana–itihas*, "a technique of narrating past regimes with hindsight but in the form of future prophecies."[29] Time could follow the natural or seasonal cycles, or the astrological calculations of the almanac that allowed one to live from one appropriate moment to another.[30] It could be measured in all kinds of ways: "as *nimesha* (the twinkling of the eye), as *matra* (metres and rhythms of utterance), as *prana* (a full breath), or as the subtlest moment of piercing a single lotus leaf with a needle."[31]

Well before the arrival of the printed panjika, debates and discussions about South Asian notions of time structured the colonial encounter. European and British philosophers and Orientalists, from Hegel to William Jones, suggested that South Asians experienced time as cyclical, pointing to the simultaneously destructive and regenerative cycles of 432,000 years they encountered in ancient Hindu scriptures.[32] Cycles of time presented a problem: you go round and round in circles and end up in the same place. The British harnessed cyclicity to support their argument that South Asians had no sense of forward movement and, therefore, of history.[33] Western temporality, by contrast, was a straight line. This teleology was overladen with meaning, connoting historical consciousness and an investment in modern progress. Their South Asian counterparts were destined to be banished, in Dipesh Chakrabarty's evocative phrase, to the "waiting rooms of history."[34]

So for the British, questions of temporality in South Asia were at the heart of the colonial project, explaining South Asian underdevelopment and justifying British interventions in the region. On a day-to-day basis, time also posed more practical problems. In the mid-nineteenth century, India operated according to independent time zones at the local, presidential, and national levels. The establishment of national railway systems in India and other parts of the world made a standardized system of time imperative. Measured against the Greenwich Mean, this would allow for an easier coordination of train schedules across regions.[35] In the run-up to the adoption of Indian Standard time (five and a half hours ahead of Greenwich Mean), Calcutta, like many other cities in India, became a muddle of different measures. While by 1905, the railways and telegraph network were following the new standardized system of time, clocks in offices across the city continued to use local time, in protest against the imposed temporal shift. In 1919, a journalist wryly commented that "Calcutta is already possessed of more times than she knows what to do with."[36] With the imposition of infrastructural and bureaucratic changes that created the need for such measures, South Asians found that they had been incorporated into the temporality of the British empire.

Whether in early modern Britain or nineteenth-century Bengal, almanacs have always responded to humankind's fear of being unable to control worldly and extra-worldly forces.[37] Through their claims to prediction, these texts encouraged their readers to believe that they could determine personal outcomes through foresight. In the case of the panjika, readers used this knowledge to choose when or when not to perform certain actions. The future, it would seem, could thus unravel in a series of self-determined moments, neatly woven together to create the texture of one's life. The new changes in temporal organization reminded panjika readers that their futures were precariously double. In addition to the usual astral phenomena, they also had to deal with empire's shifting horizons. Readers required methods to allow themselves to control this growing, unknown portion of their everyday lives. They needed to know auspicious and inauspicious times for rituals, but they also needed to plan railway journeys and decide when to visit their local post office. If a vast unknowable future lay before them as vague and undetermined, mastering the mechanics of daily colonial life provided some reassurance.

The mass-produced panjika's arrival was auspiciously timed in the middle of the temporal reorganization of India under the British. As a repository of astrological information, it was the very embodiment of "nonstandard" time. But over the second half of the nineteenth century and into the twentieth, the panjika evolved into a tool that allowed its readers to articulate both critical and conciliatory stances toward the disruption of everyday life by the colonial regime. Several panjika publishers named their volumes after imperial authority figures, such as Lord Ripon, the viceroy of India (1880–84), or even Queen Victoria herself.[38] These gestures signaled an acknowledgment of the pervasive influence of British rule across all sections of Bengali society. So, with colonialism's new time-sense, adopting the Gregorian calendar in the panjika seemed like an unavoidable step. However, the fact that this system measured time relative to the sun, a moving point, as opposed to Hinduism's reliance on a fixed star, the *dhruva*, made it potentially difficult to shift from the one system to the other. Some astrologers suggested using the representational apparatus of the Christian calendar—days, months, clock-time—not its ideological precepts.[39] Twenty-first century panjikas continue the compromise made in the nineteenth century, placing the Bengali and Gregorian calendars side by side. This was an important step toward the standardization of domestic ritual practice. Disparate readers from around the Bengal Presidency came together as an invisible community by reading the same instructions and performing the same rituals in auspicious synchrony, no longer disjointed by the idiosyncratic calculations of individual astrologers. Panjikas were hardly a secular enterprise, but their readers did bear resemblance to Benedict Anderson's newspaper readers, joined together in simultaneous, if anonymous, community.[40]

The presence of the new imperial regime left its mark on other parts of the nonastrological sections of the panjika, too. From the late nineteenth century on, panjikas began to include advertisements for watches and clocks, the mechanical instruments of imperial time.[41] By the early twentieth century, these timepieces had been transformed into necessary—if expensive—items, initiating the upwardly mobile journeys of those who could afford to possess them.[42] The different kinds of timekeeping devices advertised in the panjikas indicate how every member of the family's daily patterns had been reorganized by colonial intervention. A popular choice was a watch called "The Railway Regulator," whose advertised advantages included its precision and that it could run without being wound for three days at a stretch.[43]

Time didn't just structure the railways, though. It was also an indelible part of the experience of working in an office. In Sumit Sarkar's influential account, Bengali middle-class men working clerical jobs (*chakri*) were resentful of the "new rigorous discipline of work regulated by clock-time."[44] A contemporary play even featured disgruntled clerks complaining about their salaries being docked for tardiness.[45] An alarm clock was potentially pitched

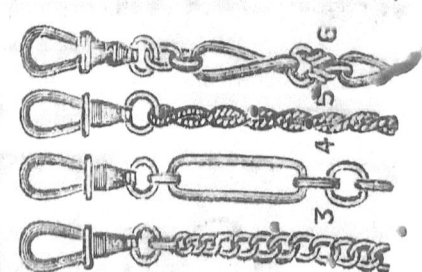

FIGURE 3.6. Advertisement for West Watch Co., in *Panjika*, 1914–15 (Calcutta: Gupta Press, 1914), Offices of the Gupta Press, Kolkata.
Clockwise, from the top right, the six kinds of clocks and accessories depicted are: table clock, alarm clock, white metal chain, courtesan timepiece, Courvoisier Frere's watch, and a ladies size watch.

at this demographic of professional men, who had to wake up at a fixed time every day to reach their offices at the appointed hour. With the daily rhythms of the household restructured by the comings and goings of its male members, women entered the market as buyers, too. A ladies size watch, described as extremely small, beautiful, and accurate, was also regularly advertised in panjikas (Figure 3.6).[46] A watch provided new sensory experiences that were auditory (the ticking of the hands) and tactile (worn on the wrist or on a chain attached to a pocket or around one's neck).[47] Crucially, it gave the experience of time a personal dimension, allowing watch-wearers to measure it for themselves. With the time discipline of the office firmly entrenched in the life of a working man, the watch was an instrument of agency. It was a small way of reminding yourself that, even if your time was chained to the bureaucratic regime of the British empire, you had the fantasy of organizing your hours, minutes, and seconds, just by consulting your wristwatch. A particularly racy advertisement for a "courtesan watch," suggestively named for an image of a smiling courtesan engraved onto its dial, promised to "seduce" men into buying one for themselves. Even time could come with its guilty pleasures.[48]

The information included in the bureaucratic sections of the panjika also routinely dealt with questions of time, listing the hours of operation of local businesses and offices, railway schedules, and postal rates. The panjika's presentation of this information allowed readers to oscillate expediently between astral and imperial time. Take, for example, a list of Hindu festivals on which offices were closed (Figure 3.7 and Table 3.1).[49] From left to right, the columns of the table present: (1) dates according to the Bengali calendar, (2) dates according to the English calendar, (3) the day of the week, (4) the name of the festival, and (5) number of days for which offices would be closed. Looking across row seven, for example, a reader could tell that on the eighth day of the Bengali month of *Aashin*, which was September 23 and a Tuesday, offices would be closed for *Mahalaya* (the first day of the festival of Durga Puja), for the length of a day. Where Bengalis felt adrift, accosted by new rules, timetables, and calendars, the table was a helping hand. How we read the table is structured by the Bengali calendar, represented in the very first column, and indicative of the preferences of panjika readers in the nineteenth century. Rather than collapsing the Bengali and Gregorian calendars and, by extension, two senses of time, the format of the table is crucial in holding them together in an unresolved tension. But the format of the table provides an opportunity to calculate equivalencies, effectively allowing its readers to translate between the Bengali and Christian calendars, moving nimbly from one column to another.

এতদ্দেশীয় পর্ব্বদিন যাহাতে কোম্পানির আফিস বন্ধ হয়।

বাং তারিখ	ইং তারিখ	বার	পর্ব্ব	দিন
২৫ জৈষ্ঠ	৭ জুন	শনিবার	দশহরা	১
৩০ জৈষ্ঠ	১২ জুন	বৃহস্পতিবার	স্নানযাত্রা	১
১৬ আষাঢ়	২৯ জুন	রবিবার	রথযাত্রা	১
২৪ অষাঢ়	৭ জুলাই	সোমবার	পুনর্যাত্রা	১
২৫ শ্রাবণ	৯ আগষ্ট	শনিবার	রাখীপূর্ণিমা	১
২।৩ ভাদ্র	১৭।১৮ আগষ্ট	রবি সোমবার	জন্মাষ্টমী	২
৮ আশ্বিন	২৩ সেপ্টেম্বর	মঙ্গলবার	মহালয়া	১
১৩ আশ্বিন	২৮ সেপ্টেম্বর	রবিবারাবধি	দুর্গোৎসব	৮
২২।২৩ আশ্বিন	৭।৮ অক্টোবর	মঙ্গল বুধবার	লক্ষ্মীপূজা	২

FIGURE 3.7. Table depicting Local Festivals and Company Office Closures, in *Nutan Panjika*, 1862–63 (Calcutta: Cones and Co., 1862), Offices of the Gupta Press, Kolkata.

The table shows the correspondence between the Bengali and the English calendar. The column headings from left to right read: date (according to the Bengali calendar), date (according to the English calendar), day of the week, name of the festival, number of days of vacation. The entry for *Mahalaya*, the first day of the Hindu festival of Durga Puja, is seventh from the top.

Local Festivals and Company Office Closures

Bengali Date	English Date	Day of the Week	Festival Name	Number of Days Off
25 Jaishtha	7 June	Saturday	Dasahara	1
30 Jaishtha	12 June	Thursday	Snan jatra	1
16 Aashaar	29 June	Sunday	Rath jatra	1
24 Aashaar	7 July	Monday	Purna jatra	1
25 Sraaban	9 August	Saturday	Rakhi	1
2/3 Bhaadra	17/18 August	Sunday/Monday	Janmaashtami	1
8 Aashin	23 September	Tuesday	Mahalaya	1
13 Aashin	28 September	Till Sunday	Durga Puja	8
22/23 Aashin	7/8 October	Tuesday/Wednesday	Lakshmi Puja	2

TABLE 3.1. English Translation of Figure 3.7: Table depicting Local Festivals and Company Office Closures. Translation by author.

The Promises and Perils of Selective Reading

The temporal lessons of the panjika were also lessons in reading. The panjika not only changed how readers positioned themselves in time; it also initiated a temporal shift in how they read. In the world of the panjika, there was never enough time for anything. Bengali middle-class men employed as clerks in colonial offices complained endlessly about working long hours for little pay. Their wives, depicted in these accounts as haranguing shrews, complained that they were never at home for any length of time.[50] The nineteenth-century Bengali was constantly in a rush, flipping through their panjika to retrieve the information they needed: say, the price of a train ticket or the date of the next full moon. Such hurried relationships with reading material, panjikas and beyond, spurred on formulations of "slow reading," most famously, Gandhi's articulation of the practice. Isabel Hofmeyr traces this experiment back to the years Gandhi spent in South Africa editing the newspaper *Indian Opinion*.[51] Gandhi's newspaper, appearing in a different part of the British empire, existed in a world similar to the mass-produced panjika, a world inundated by new industrial developments and an overwhelming quantity of printed text. For Gandhi, slow reading was a means of slowing down life itself, stopping to pay attention and lingering with words. For this reason, he styled *Indian Opinion* as what Hofmeyr calls an "anti-commodity, copyright-free, slow-motion newspaper."[52]

By contrast, panjika publishers, unmotivated by moral ideology, worked toward creating commodity-filled, revenue-building almanacs that could boast of being exhaustive compendiums of information. They saturated their readers with advertisements for jewelry and dubious medicines, tables of bureaucratic information, and pages of astrological calculations. The assumption—which was correct—was that readers would always be short on time, and their engagement with their panjikas would be necessarily interrupted, discontinuous, and selective. Even the astrological section, which unfolded in chronological order, would not be read as an uninterrupted narrative. Rather, the panjika was a text to which readers returned repeatedly throughout the year, whenever they felt the need to consult it. In this manner, the genre initiated both an expansion and contraction in reading time. Readers might spend less time engaging with the textual content of the volumes, but it was guaranteed that they would refer to them more frequently over a given period.

This contrast between the contracted nature of reading and the rising frequency of the act itself was a mounting concern for panjika printers. If readers were to construct their own narratives from almanacs, choosing what they thought was necessary for themselves, how would compilers go about putting together a volume that could address the needs of everyone?

In their prefatory comments, panjika publishers repeatedly emphasized how easy it was to find information in their volumes:

> There will be *no difficulty*. This almanac *contains everything. Consult it when you want to.*[53]
>
> An almanac is a most essential book. In fact, one has to consult this book every day for conducting daily domestic affairs. I have worked hard to add to it a variety of necessary details with great care. I present this almanac and directory to the general public at a very cheap price so that everyone can use it *without difficulty*.[54]
>
> To let you find days, dates, etc. *easily*, we had to print each day's information on a separate page.[55]

These quotations reiterate that these texts anticipated selective consumption in bits and pieces from their readers. Read alongside each other, the quotations also highlight what the nineteenth-century reader expected of an almanac or directory: consultation without any "difficulty." The measure of a panjika was determined by whether it could anticipate every reader's varying demands.

Even literary portraits of panjika publishers reflect these anxieties. Shashishekar Chattopadhyay, a character in Saswati Sengupta's family saga, *The Song Seekers* (2011), aspires to produce a panjika.[56] His volume, *Chatto's Panjika*, enters an overcrowded market but is an immediate success, fulfilling the fantasies of wealth that drew many young men in the nineteenth century to the publishing business. Like other compilers, Shashishekar is confronted with the problem of selection. What festivals or information should he include in his edition? The narrator comments wryly, "Indeed, many said that if the deity did not make it to *Chatto's Full Panjika* then he—or she—was not worth it." There was no end to the scale of information a panjika could include: the "immortal pantheon was vast." But "mortal needs varied" and were difficult to anticipate. Shashishekar's solution is to produce two versions of the yearly almanac: a "Full Panjika" crammed with all possible information and an abridged version, a "Half Panjika."[57]

The railway timetable provides an object-lesson in how a nineteenth-century reader might have approached their panjika selectively. With the establishment of the Indian railways in 1854, travel by train steadily increased through the latter half of the nineteenth century. The railway timetable, providing information about train timings, routes, and fares, became an indispensable companion to any frequent traveler. Like the panjika, it was a print object that aided in the construction of an imagined community, ensuring that groups of disparate, unrelated people came together at a particular time through the shared necessity of travel. Beyond its immediate practical value, British colonial officials touted the secondary advantages of this printed item: it forced South Asians to take punctuality seriously.[58] The timetable was, in effect, thought to discipline travelers, reminding them that the train wouldn't, in fact, wait for them if they were late to the station. Trains *and* people nevertheless continued to be late.[59]

Most early timetables were published in English in newspapers (like *The Friend of India*) or in popular travel guides such as Newman's and Bradshaw's.[60] This posed a significant obstacle to many South Asians who, despite their lack of English-language proficiency, might still want to travel by train. From the 1860s on, several panjikas included railway timetables in Bengali, providing some of the earliest examples of non-English-language railway timetables in South Asia.[61] A panjika published by Cones and Co. for the year 1861–62, for example, listed routes and fares for the train service between Calcutta and Rajmahal, a city in the present-day state of Jharkhand (Figure 3.8 and Table 3.2). Timetables like these were included in the directory section of the panjika, embedded alongside a range of other railway-related information, including charts of ticket prices, pages of railway regulations, and woodcuts depicting train travel.

Beyond the historical insights a timetable can provide (how many trains, what destinations, what ticket prices), it can also allow us to reconstruct how its nineteenth-century readers might have approached it. Let's look more closely at the timetable published in a Cones and Co. panjika for 1861–62 (Figure 3.8 and Table 3.2). The information that it contains is presented in a grid, a form that gained popularity in the nineteenth century but was still confusing to many readers.[62] A reader would have had to parse the grid in multiple directions: horizontally along rows, vertically down columns, only finding what they were looking for at the intersection of the two. Different parts of the timetable would take on significance or recede into the background depending on the reader and why they'd picked up the timetable in the first place. For a poor traveler looking for a cheap fare, the columns of ticket prices would be paramount. It's worth noting that the column listing prices for first class tickets was irrelevant to many Bengali readers, for whom the tickets would have been too expensive. For a person selling goods to travelers at railway stations, the

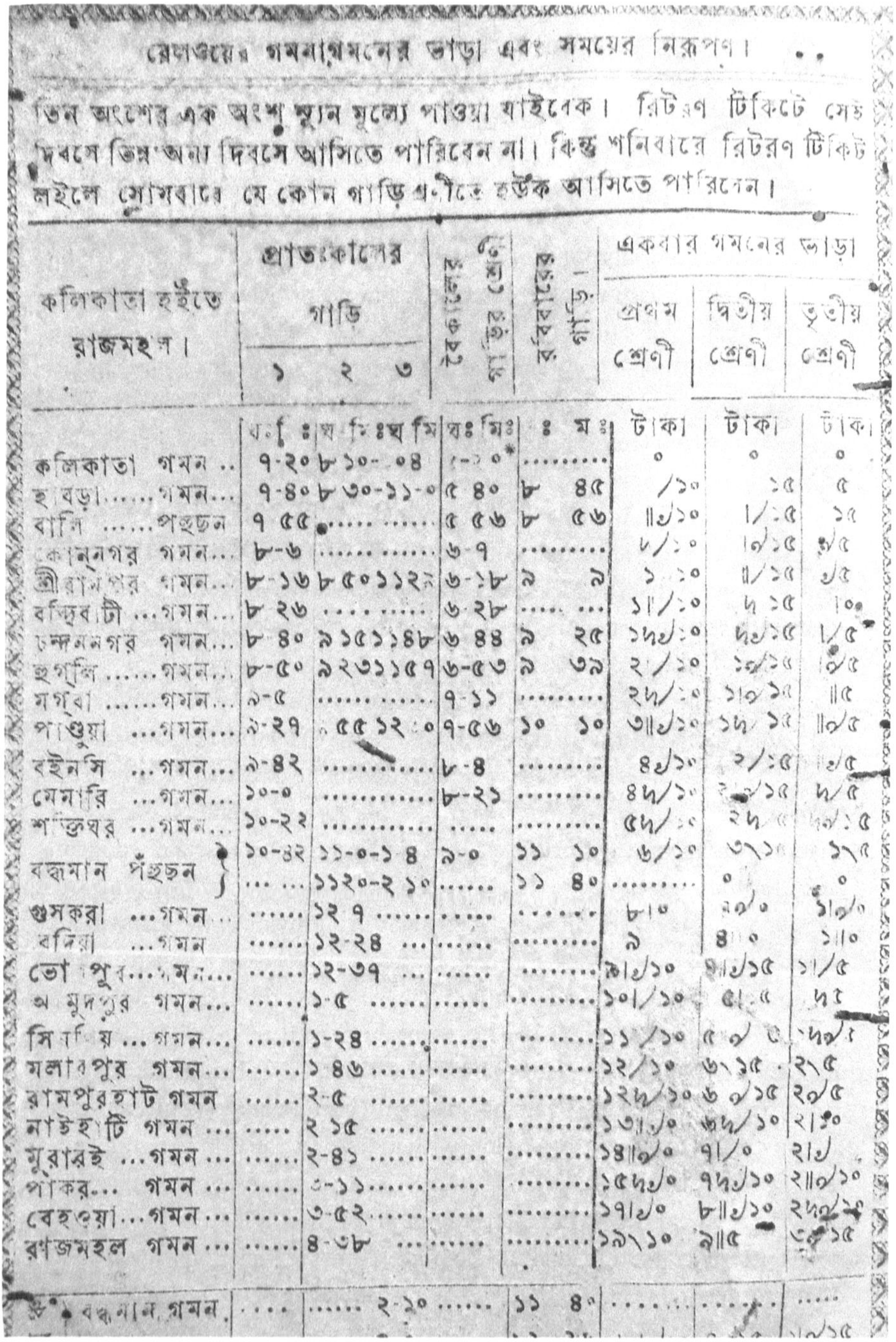

FIGURE 3.8. Railway timetable for trains running between Calcutta and Rajmahal, in *Nutan Panjika*, 1861–62 (Calcutta: Cones and Co., 1861), Offices of the Gupta Press, Kolkata.

Railway Timetable Indicating Ticket Prices and Train Timings							
Stops on the Route between Kolkata and Rajmahal	Morning Trains			Evening Train	Sunday Train	Price of a Single Ticket		
	1	2	3			First Class	Second Class	Third Class

A third of the tickets will be sold at a discounted rate. Return tickets are nontransferable. However, a Saturday return ticket can be used to travel on any train on Monday, regardless of the class of the ticket.

TABLE 3.2. English Translation of column headings of Figure 3.8: Railway timetable for trains running between Calcutta and Rajmahal. Translation by author.

columns denoting the timings of the morning, evening, and Sunday trains would be crucial, the columns for ticket prices less so.

Readers who traveled on a few routes regularly found simple ways of making these tables easier to negotiate, either by circling or underlining the information, or, in the rarer case of a narrative timetable (with destinations, and the trains that would pass through them listed in paragraph form), by writing the relevant details in the margins for future consultation. But it's worth remembering that a railway timetable is never read in full. It's designed to be read selectively, with readers dipping in and out of it to obtain a specific piece of information. Having no need to read it in its entirety—let alone remember its content—a reader must once again turn to the timetable to plan future journeys. Readers would consult this page briefly, but repeatedly, transforming it into a well-worn section of the family almanac.

The railway timetable brings together questions about the urgency of reading, inhabiting different modes of time, and the need for selective perusal. It elicits a dizzying range of reading practices: casual glancing, targeted and selective reading, repeated consultation. But even as it provided its readers with an avalanche of information, it also exceeded this informational role. By allowing readers to consider the multiple possibilities of travel before them, the timetable showed them how they might construct and control their own futures in a time of colonial precarity. It was more than an instrument of colonial discipline. Like the wristwatch or the list of office holidays, it was a tool for planning a life, even if within the limits of imperial time.

While the railway timetable embodied such utopian desires, the format of the timetable and the manner of its presentation often brought readers back to earth with a rude jolt. Let's look at the example printed in the Cones and Co. panjika in Figure 3.8. It, like the rest of the panjika, is printed on cheap paper liable to tearing. Large amounts of information are crammed into the restricted space of a single page. To save space, the headings of columns three and four (the Evening Service and the Sunday Service, respectively) jarringly flip to a vertical format, demanding that the reader repeatedly reorient themselves to the page. Dashes are used to fill up empty spaces in rows, but they clutter the table to produce an impenetrable wall of text that defies easy separation. The entire effect of how the table is constructed could lead to information from one row being attributed to another row, potentially throwing well-designed plans into disarray. This railway timetable isn't an isolated example. The good intentions of panjika publishers were often undercut by the format and layout of the volumes they produced.

The Corrective Reader

The example of the railway timetable and the reading practices it elicited confirms that panjikas were meant to be read selectively. Nineteenth-century publishers were eager to emphasize that their volumes were easy to consult. Even today, the Gupta Press's website describes their editions as being "simple reference book[s]" and "handy reckoner[s]."[63] In reality, opening up a nineteenth-century panjika reveals exactly how overwhelming one of the volumes could be. In the battle between optimizing comprehensiveness versus accessibility, comprehensiveness won. Over the mid-nineteenth century and into the early twentieth, panjikas steadily increased in length, with even their pocket-sized or "half" versions running well over six hundred pages.

Remember the panjika publisher who initially declared that they'd opted for a well spaced-out format to aid readers' searches for information? Such good intentions soon petered out. To keep both production costs and the length of the volumes down, panjika publishers resorted to material tactics to accommodate the information they wanted to include. As more and more information came to be included in panjikas, the layout of their pages came to be more and more cramped. Printed cheaply on small pages with narrow margins (if any), tables and charts on a single page often ran into each other, making them indistinguishable to the selective reader. As in the case of the railway timetable, this messy organization was prevalent even within a printed table, with readers being unable to differentiate between the rows. Inadvertently, panjika publishers were slowing their readers down with material obstacles.

The material and paratextual apparatus of the panjika not only shaped the ways in which readers approached their volumes. It actively impeded their selective readings of it, often confusing and misleading them. In the hands of its Bengali readers, the panjika embodied an irony that lay at the heart of empire, print, and reading in late nineteenth-century South Asia. It was an instrument created and circulated by Bengali Hindus to make sense of the new and unreadable infrastructures of British imperial rule. But as a textual object that was often difficult to read and sometimes even completely incomprehensible, it came to embody the very unreadability it was designed to overcome.

Industrious and frustrated readers deployed numerous tactics to overcome the limits of the printed text. Some of the most fundamental tools that aid selective reading across genres are indexes and page numbers. Panjikas commonly used an alphabetical index or a table of contents to guide their readers, pointing them to where they needed to go. Yet the publishers often failed to provide a complete index for the volumes, curtailing the scope and usefulness of this guiding apparatus. While the astrological section was paginated, the paratexts—the advertisements and the bureaucratic information—were only erratically so. The absence of consistent page numbering in the advertisements is understandable, given that they were not consulted in the same way as the astrological section.[64] But given that the bureaucratic information was practically guaranteed to be read selectively, the absence of consistent pagination from this section of the text is puzzling. If readers wanted to check train timings quickly, they would have to leaf through the entire section page by page to find the pertinent schedule. Barring the separation of the astrological section from the opening advertisements (by the placement of the index), the sections run neatly into each other like a continuous text. The fact that the index was dominated by astrological topics indicates what panjika compilers, if not readers, still considered to be of paramount importance: ritual. In doing so, the volumes were structured around an informational hierarchy that resisted the imposition of colonial habits over traditional practice.

Where page numbers did exist, there was no guarantee they were correct. The index of a copy of an 1895–96 Gupta Press panjika had no less than fifteen misnumbered sections (Figure 3.9). Handwritten emendations alerted me to this fact. As you can see, a careful reader has compensated for these errors, neatly striking out the incorrect page number in pen and substituting it with the accurate one. In sharp contrast to narratives of ephemerality that surround panjikas, this exercise embodies a deep sense of care for the text. It also points us toward the counterintuitive reading practices that went into the process of

সূচীপত্র।

বিষয়	পৃষ্ঠা	বিষয়	পৃষ্ঠা
পর্ব্বদিন ও আফিস বন্ধ	১১০	অক্ষয়তৃতীয়া ব্রত	১২৭
পাষাণ চতুর্দ্দশী	৩৩৬	রাখী পূর্ণিমা	২০৭
পিপিতকী দ্বাদশী ব্রত	১০৩	রামনবমী	৪৭৪
ফুলদোল	১০৬	রাজাদ্যানয়ন	৪
পীরাষ্টমী ব্রত	২৬৬	রাধাষ্টমী ব্রত	২৩৪
বাসন্তী পূজা	৪৬৮	রামযাত্রা	৩৪
বামন দ্বাদশী শক্রোথান	২৩৭	রটষ্ঠী পূজা	৪১
ব্রাহ্মোৎসব	৪১৪	রেজেষ্ট্রি খরচা	৫০৪
বরাহ দ্বাদশী	৪৯৫	রেলগুয়ের ভাড়া ৫১৮ হইতে ৫৩৫	
বৃহস্পতির গোচর	১৯৭	রক্ষা পঞ্চমী	২৩১
বিষহরা সপ্তমী ব্রত	১৬৫	ললিতা সপ্তমী কুকুটী ব্রত	২৩২
বিষ্ণু দিগের পর্ব্বদিন	৪২৭	লাইসেন্স ট্যাক্‌স	৫১১
বন্দা চতুর্থী (৬ মাঘ হইবে)	৪২৩	শীতল ষষ্ঠী	
বিধান সপ্তমী	৪২৭	শিবরাত্রি	
ভূত চতুর্দ্দশী	২৯২	শীতলাষ্টমী	৪৮
ভাতৃদ্বিতীয়া	২৯৬	ষট্ পঞ্চমী ব্রত	১২৯
ভীমাষ্টমী	৪২৮	ষ্ট্যাম্পের নিয়ম	৫০০
ভৈষ্মী একাদশী	৪৩৪	সীতানবমী ব্রত	৯৯
মধ্যাষ্টরোদশী	২৫৬	সাবিত্রী ব্রত	১২২
মধুকৃষ্ণা ত্রয়োদশী	...	স্নানযাত্রা	১৪০
মদন ত্রয়োদশী	৪১৭	অক্ষয়ষষ্ঠী	৪১
মদনভঞ্জি	৪৮০	সৌভাগ্য চতুর্থী ব্রত	২৭০
মহানন্দা	৪৩১	হরিতালিকা ব্রত	২২৮
মহানবমী	২৩১	হাইকোর্ট	৪০৯
মনোরথ দ্বিতীয়া ব্রত	১৫৯	ঘোড়াপঞ্চমী লক্ষ্মী বিজয়	১৬৩
মিত্রসপ্তমী	৩৬৫		

FIGURE 3.9. Handwritten emendments to an index, in *Panjika*, 1895–96 (Calcutta: Gupta Press, 1895), Offices of the Gupta Press, Kolkata. There are fifteen emendments on the page.

making the corrections to the page numbers. After detecting a mismatch between a listed page number and its content, the reader would have had to work their way through the volume, search for where the items listed in the index appear in the text, and then note the correct page numbers. While panjikas were designed for selective reading, the misleading index opens this copy to an intensive engagement, start to end. This exhaustive read is meant to eliminate the need for repeat performances, restoring the text to its intended status as selective reading material. By investing a few hours in renumbering the table of contents, the reader saves future minutes and seconds.

The corrections made by readers to their panjikas vary from the extreme (the renumbered pages of the index) to the commonplace (emending dates in the astrological sections or typographical errors in the body of the text). We might call this kind of reader a *corrective reader*, one who puts time and effort into preparing a text for future readings, whether by themselves or by others. After all, panjikas were books that, even if read selectively, were consulted repeatedly. The copies I consulted in my research in the Gupta Press offices were frayed and bent, bearing marks not just of their age but also of being read and reread. I imagine the corrective reader thumbing hurriedly through the volumes—as other readers would have, too—often damaging the pages in the process.

Another example of readers' feelings of impatience and frustration, coupled with care and patience, can be found in a copy of a Gupta Press panjika for 1888–89 (Figure 3.10). Four printed pages from the astrological section, presumably torn or damaged, are missing.[65] Taking their place in the volume are handwritten replacements. A reader has neatly copied by hand the information on the four pages, format and all, onto blank sheets and placed them in the copy. The mended book is, as a result, a patchwork combination of print and manuscript. Here, the reader is thinking like a panjika publisher: What if, one day, the information they were looking for was on one of the four missing pages? The reader's act acknowledges the fragility of the text and the short lifespan of its pages. In doing so, it reclaims it as an object that can now be read again, if only selectively. Why, given that panjikas were cheap and widely available, didn't the reader replace their damaged copy with a new one? It is possible that the evidence of care that we find in these panjikas points to some readers saving their copies for retrospective consultation, instead of just throwing them away at the end of the calendar year. Given the rapid turnaround rates of panjika production, it would have been extraordinarily difficult to track down and buy a copy of a panjika from some years ago.

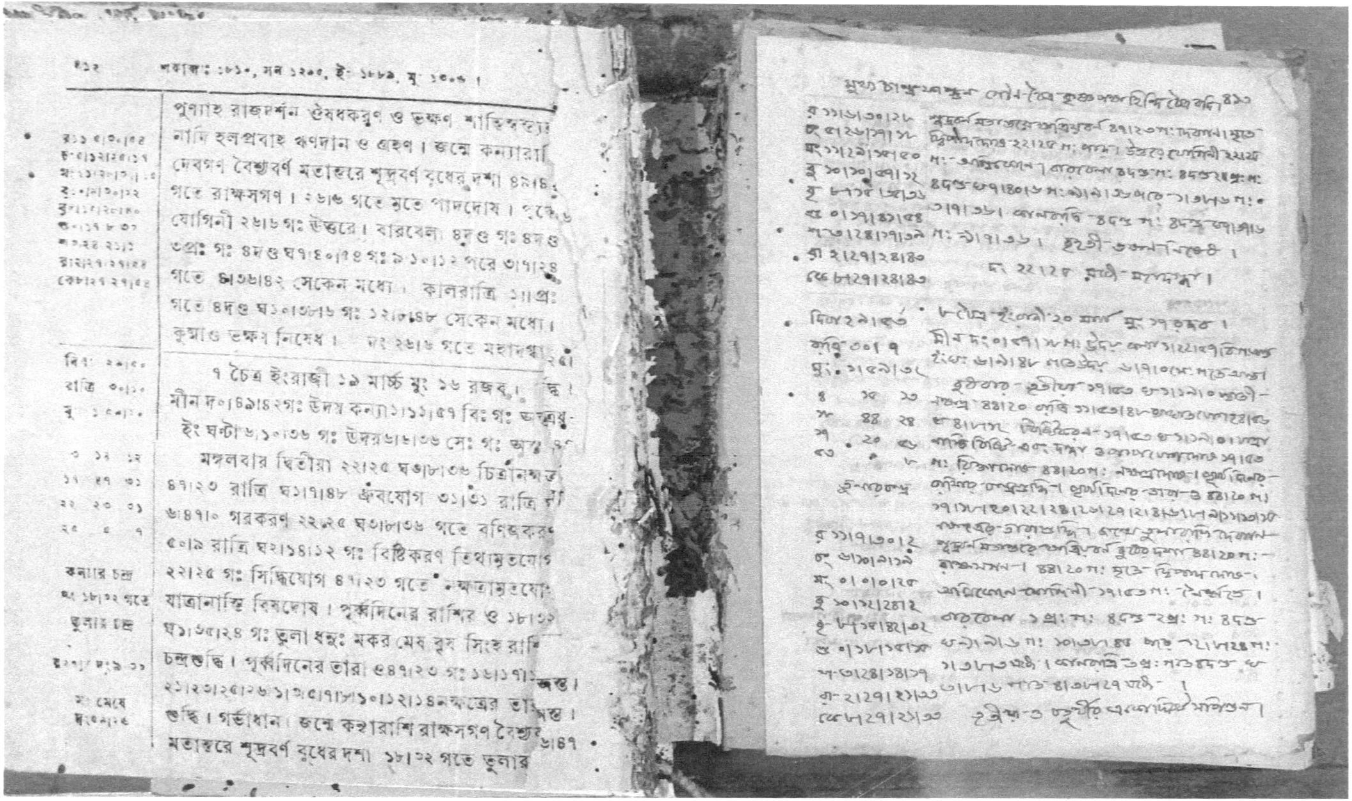

FIGURE 3.10. Handwritten pages replacing missing printed pages in a panjika, in *Panjika*, 1888–89 (Calcutta: Gupta Press, 1888), Offices of the Gupta Press, Kolkata.
Pages 413–16 were missing from the panjika.

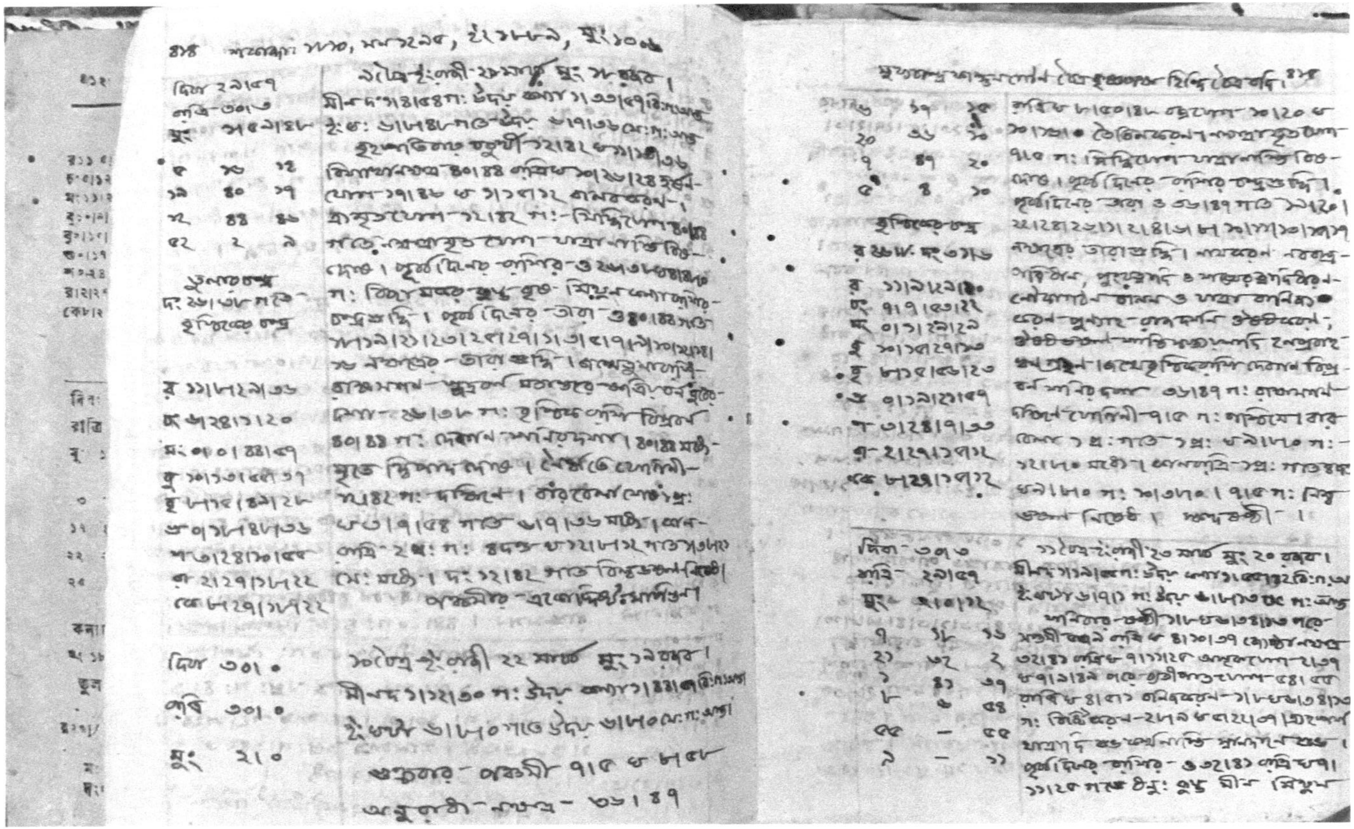

FIGURE 3.10. (continued)

Bengali Readers, English Writers

As I combed through dozens of copies in the Gupta Press offices and other repositories, I was surprised by the number of marginal notes in English I found in the panjikas. It's worth pointing out that English appears sparsely and erratically in panjikas beyond the readerly annotation, often as part of advertisements or in the bureaucratic sections. As I've mentioned, advertisements were an increasingly prominent part of panjikas from the 1880s onward. The volumes would generally open with details of a variety of products. Hair curlers, cures (real and imagined) for sexually transmitted infections, detective novels, and watches were just some of the commodities peddled to the Bengali middle class from the pages of its almanacs. The number of advertisements increased with each year, a testament to the acknowledged popularity of the almanac, which made it an excellent vehicle for capitalist aspirations. The exact number of advertisements depended on the popularity of the edition. Panjikas produced by the Gupta Press and P. M. Bagchi carried more advertisements, often accounting for close to 30 percent of the volume's page count. A less popular panjika named after Lord Ripon, of which I have only located a single issue, had no more than five to six pages of advertisements.

Look at the advertisement for H. Dey's Wonderful Gonorrhoea Mixture in a panjika published by Day and Brothers for the year 1885–86 (Figure 3.11). What draws the eye of the reader to this advertisement for the "cure" is the striking image of a scantily clad man, probably an ascetic, facing us and propped up seductively on his left arm, his legs coyly crossed. The titillating possibilities of this image—and the clash between the expectations associated with an ascetic and the image itself—are immediately compounded by what is written across his torso: gonorrhea. While the text of the advertisement is in wordy Bengali prose, it's only the advertising caption that's in English. There's a cheeky double play here, created by the placement of the words. Is the mixture "wonderful"? Or is it a reference to the illicit sexual activities that presumably led to the infection? To what does "success" refer: the (infected) man's sexual conquests or his attempts to get cured? This double play is only intelligible to users of the panjika who could read English. The readers who would be excluded from the advertisement and, by extension, the joke, would be women readers, the vast majority of whom had little to no knowledge of English. The seemingly innocuous caption of the gonorrhea advertisement targets the male, English-literate Bengali to create a shared homosocial com-

FIGURE 3.11. Image from an advertisement for H. Dey's Wonderful Gonorrhoea Mixture, in *Nutan Panjika*, 1885–86 (Calcutta: Day and Brothers, 1885), Offices of the Gupta Press, Kolkata.

munity of readability that excludes women readers, or, rather, their wives, who are kept in the dark about their extramarital escapades.

Zooming out from the advertisement, the presence of English words in panjikas testifies to growing English literacy rates in late nineteenth-century Bengal. As a community, Bengalis were among the first to embrace Macaulay's call for a class of native informants, "a class of persons, Indian in blood and colour, but English in taste, in opinions, in morals, and in intellect."[66] English literacy was a prerequisite for the many clerical jobs open to Bengali men, whose aspirations to Englishness and affluence were mercilessly mocked in the popular imagination. Jokes aside, the presence of English in the nineteenth-century panjika, whether printed as part of an advertisement or scribbled in a margin, points us in the direction of one section of the panjika's readership: middle-class, English-literate Bengali men.

We can surmise that the English annotations in Bengali-language panjikas are the handiwork of this group of readers, too. While the astrological sections held Bengali-language annotations and calculations on their pages, English annotations roamed across the volumes. The scale and complexity of the English-language annotations I encountered varied. Sometimes they were related to the content of the panjikas; at other times, a blank page or a margin was simply a space for scribbling.[67] As Adam Smyth's examination of seventeenth-century English almanacs reminds us, often the lone note in a copy can generate a "somewhat ghostly significance, their presence suggesting how much is left unrecorded."⁶⁸ It imbues the annotation with a significance that is strengthened by the absence of other annotations, giving us a sense of what was important to a reader.

Unlike the practical annotations of the corrective reader, English annotations operated as signs of other kinds of textual engagement that exceeded the informational role of these astrological compendia-cum-directories-cum-advertising catalogues. The most common examples of notes that I found in panjikas were marks of ownership. The names of readers were written across the soft paper covers of the panjikas and sometimes on the inner flyleaves, often several times. Similar evidence can be found in the volumes' margins. In a panjika published by the Gupta Press for the year 1902–3, the owner has written the year twice, in Bengali and English, in what appears to be nothing more than an exercise in boredom, just as one would doodle on a newspaper.⁶⁹ Scholars of the early modern book in Europe have suggested we think of these as graffiti: exercises in establishing presence as well as displaying literacy.⁷⁰ This takes on particular resonance in the context of colonial Bengal. The owners of panjikas wrote their names on them in English and Bengali not only to demonstrate that they could. In their doodling, they also enacted the oscillation between the modern and the traditional. They move between two different selves, articulated in English and then in Bengali.

More "serious" notes qualifying as annotations—in the sense of demonstrating a direct engagement with the printed text on the page—can also be found in panjikas. In one case a conscientious reader has even transliterated into Roman script the titles of the books in a publishing house's advertisement (Figure 3.12). No translation from Bengali (*Upakhyan Manjari*) to English (Garland of Stories) accompanies it. The absence of a translation marks the absence of a second reader, someone else at whom the annotation is directed. The annotator and reader, we can assume, are one and the same.

Transliterations of this kind were a common archival practice. Many copies of South Asian-language books in the British Library, for instance, yield such examples.⁷¹ But this copy of the panjika has never been housed in an institutional repository and has passed through the hands of no professional readers (or the kinds of professional readers who would write in historical books, at any rate). As a book that was read and circulated among everyday Bengali readers for its content, not for its historical or archival value, we can assume that the transliteration is the work of a reader literate in Bengali and English. It's difficult to say what the point of the transliteration was. Whether for pen practice or out of sheer boredom, what we can do is surmise the effect of the

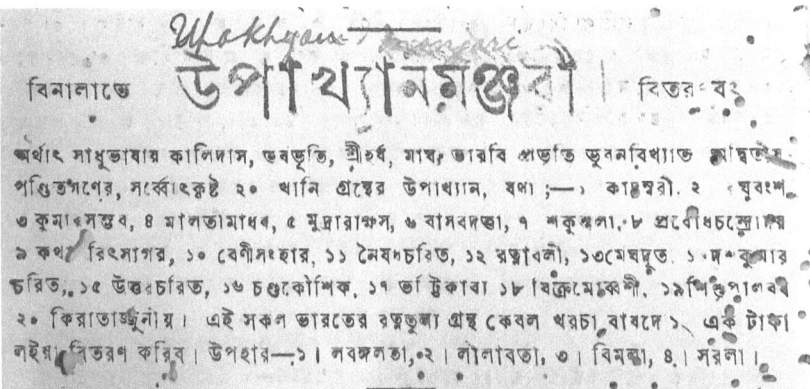

FIGURE 3.12. Bookseller's advertisement depicting Bengali book title with English transliteration, in *Panjika*, 1896–97 (Calcutta: Day and Brothers, 1896), Offices of the Gupta Press, Kolkata. The title of the book, *Upakhyan Manjari* [Garland of Stories], appears above the Bengali title in Roman script.

transliterated title in a nineteenth-century panjika. Hanging above the Bengali title, the foreign English note defamiliarizes the familiar Bengali. With neither glossing the other, their juxtaposition replays the tension of the English and the Bengali, the colonial and the local.

Late nineteenth-century panjikas often came with blank pages included in them, inviting readers to use them to record personal information of their own in the book, making each copy of an almanac unique.[72] This impulse possibly drew from the form of the pocket almanac, such as Tilt's Almanack and, subsequently, the Brahmo Pocket Diary and Almanack. These examples contained pages alongside the usual calendar to allow readers to record events of personal importance. But readers also wrote all over their almanacs and not just in the margins or in designated blank spaces. The astrological section of a Day, Law, and Co. panjika for 1871–72 reveals a note across the astral chart for 29 Chaitra (April 10 in the Gregorian calendar) that reads "[a]t ten minutes past nine in the morning J. N. Sen got a son" (Figure 3.13).

Panjikas were not customarily used to record significant events such as births, deaths, and marriages, unlike family bibles. This was because of their disposable nature and also because writing has little place in Hindu ritual. A sacred text may exist in print or manuscript but gains power only in the act of recitation. On its own, the text is not much more than an ordinary object. But unpacking the annotation itself—the language, the invocation of a time and date, and the

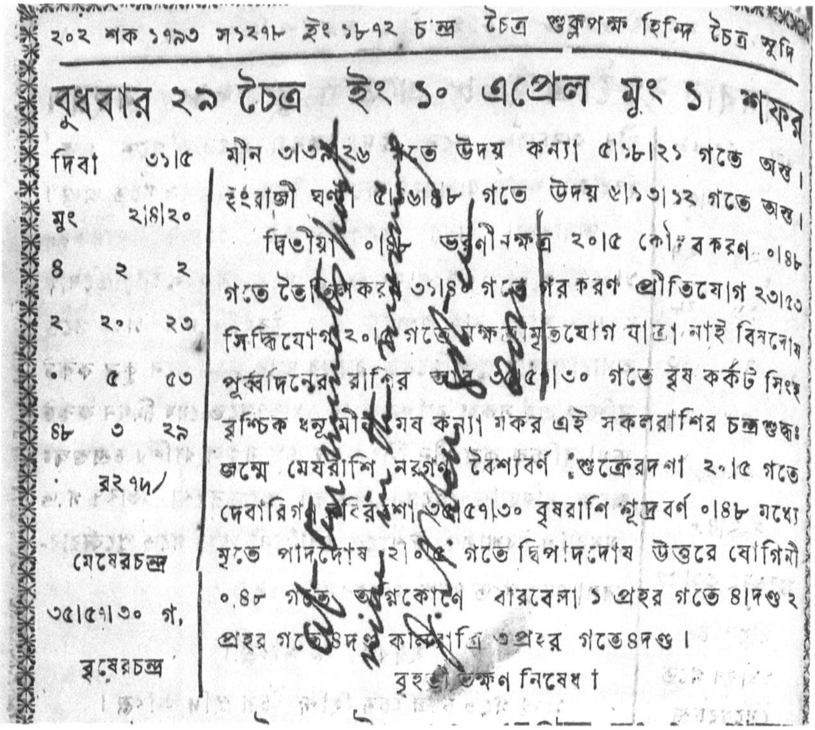

FIGURE 3.13. The astrological section for the 29 Chaitra (10 April), in *Panjika*, 1871–72 (Calcutta: Day, Law and Co., 1871), Offices of the Gupta Press, Kolkata. The note reads, "At ten minutes past nine in the morning J. N. Sen got a son."

placement—can reveal the oscillation between the astral and the imperial. Look, for example, at the detail "at ten minutes past nine in the morning," an unambiguous allusion to the dreaded "clock time" that was beginning to overtake homes and offices across colonial India. There's also the placement of the annotation, superimposing the English note on the Bengali text. The margins of this panjika were nonexistent; the reader may have had no choice but to write across the page and over the printed text. The Bengali text beneath is eclipsed by the inked English handwritten note over it, but it can still be read. What this does is create the effect of a palimpsest, of notes on top of notes, of languages layered on top of languages, and returns us to the question of readability. The example of this annotation, like other English-language annotations in Bengali-language panjikas, allows us to unpack how Bengali readers located themselves in their almanacs and, by extension, within the unyielding structures of the

British empire. The English note and the Bengali text is a clash, but it is one in which they are both readable and meaningful, both referencing and reinforcing each other. In doing so, the note opens onto the possibility of a new world that the panjika is working toward, a world in which the English and Bengali, the imperial and the astral, coexist, neither more familiar nor foreign than the other.

The Panjika, Then and Now

Every April around the Bengali New Year, articles appear in newspapers and magazines that predict the end of the Gupta Press.[73] A 2017 newspaper article bore the headline: "A Bengali almanac that's survived 150 years of history is now counting its last days." Panjika publishing is no longer the lucrative business it used to be in the nineteenth, even early twentieth, century. The article tracks the transformation of the panjika from a living artifact, deeply entangled in people's lives, into an ossified piece of decaying history, removed from the social, political, and cultural concerns of Bengali society today. It concludes that the iconic Gupta Press panjika "survived World Wars, the Partition of India, floods and famine, but may not survive smartphones."[74] In the struggle to survive, panjika publishers—the Gupta Press included—have turned to diversifying their businesses, providing services ranging from wedding planning to religious training, a throwback to the early days of the business. Nineteenth-century panjika publishers, after all, started out as multipurpose enterprises, publishing panjikas alongside many other kinds of books, even producing other less-bookish things like soap and perfume.

For me, the "death of the panjika" lamentations feel a lot like "death of the book" lamentations: that digital technology has fundamentally changed our need and desire for print and paper. Rather than a simple narrative of decline, what I see instead is history repeating itself. Now as then, panjikas face the same problems: the struggle to be relevant in a rapidly changing world, a floundering and confused readership, the limited attention spans of readers.

This chapter has charted how nineteenth-century panjikas navigated the social and cultural shifts of their originary moment. These texts, inextricable from the fabric of daily life, highlighted a challenge that faced Bengali Hindus: making sense of a confusing and convoluted world reshaped by colonial rule. By presenting readers with railway timetables, astrological information, and advertisements, the panjika was a reassuring voice. It showed its readers how to live a double life, seamlessly oscillating between two temporal regimes: one bound by the astral order, the other bound by the colonial order.

This oscillation shaped how Bengali Hindus read and responded to their panjikas. Through a close examination of these volumes, I have unpacked the different ways in which readers responded to them: they read them selectively, they expressed frustrations at the typographical errors and unyielding layout. Navigating the Indian railways took more than just a panjika; it necessitated close and careful reading to parse, correct, and annotate the text. Despite the frequent errors found and corrected within each book, people still bought them. They were a necessary starting place, after all. Better to fix an existing timetable than do without one altogether. The content of the pages moved between the traditional and the modern, just as the readers were forced to navigate both worlds. The issue of time was omnipresent; scrambling to find information, the readers constantly found themselves out of time. In theory, the right annotation or emendation might save them precious minutes, hours, even days.

The Gupta Press isn't the only nineteenth-century publisher to have survived to the present day. P. M. Bagchi, one of its most prominent rivals, has also continued to put out a yearly panjika since its very first one in 1899. While the Gupta Press's offices have been relocated to South Kolkata, the newer part of the city, P. M. Bagchi has remained entrenched at its original nineteenth-century location. As I was scouring Kolkata in search of more and more panjikas in the summer of 2019, I walked into the offices of P. M. Bagchi at 38A Masjid Bari Street. When I arrived, I was instantly disappointed. Although they maintained a sizable archive, they hadn't kept any panjikas published before 1914, the period of my study. However, having made the journey, I stayed to look through them. I still wanted to make the visit worth my time.

P. M. Bagchi's twentieth-century panjikas had much in common with their nineteenth-century antecedents: advertisements for health tonics and dubious supplements, postal information, tidal charts. Most of all, I was struck by how the authority panjikas commanded and the essential role they played in daily life continued well into the twentieth century. Nestled between the usual advertisements in a P. M. Bagchi panjika for 1943–44, I came across a public service announcement. In the thick of World War II and the Nationalist Movement in India, a railway company published a full-page plea to travelers, which I translate from Bengali here:

> Even if your panjika tells you that it's an auspicious time to travel
> Unless you absolutely need to
> Don't take the train.
> By letting only those who have no recourse to delay their journeys travel
> Contribute to the war effort.[75]

The announcement highlights a sequence of actions we have come to associate with the panjika. Readers would check the astrological section for auspicious times to travel, followed by checking the directory section for a train that suited their needs. Mutually supporting each other, these two sections of the panjika dramatized the demands of the imperial time of bureaucracy and the astral time of tradition, showing readers a way forward between the two. The announcement is evidence of the enormous sway that these volumes continued to hold in Bengali Hindu society in 1943. By begging its readers not to travel, whatever their panjikas might tell them, the announcement asks individuals to unlearn the lessons of the nineteenth-century volumes. It asks them to, even if momentarily, let their astral demands be subsumed by the demands not of empire, but of the nation.

4

Reading for Company

The Lonely Reader

The protagonist of Krupabai Satthianadhan's semiautobiographical novel, *Saguna: A Story of Native Christian Life* (1887–88), recounts visiting an English missionary's family with her mother.[1] Born to a family of Brahmin converts to Christianity, the precocious Saguna is always reading. The novel is filled with traces of her encounters with English literature, which range from a rapturous reception of Milton's *Paradise Lost* to encounters with Spenser's *The Faerie Queene*. She brims with excitement at the prospect of meeting the missionary family's young daughter, fantasizing about the possibility of borrowing books and learning about English girls from her new friend. Her overtures, however, aren't entertained. The English girl doesn't even have to say anything for Saguna to feel her judgment: she smiles "faintly" as she eyes Saguna's worn clothes with a dismissive "slight shrug of her shoulders."[2] When Saguna musters up the courage to blurt out her request—does the girl have any books to lend her—she immediately feels its "audacity and awkwardness." The English girl retorts scornfully: "*You* read? You can't read what I read. You won't understand."[3]

Saguna's embarrassment captures something of the difficulties of being an English-literate, South Asian woman at the end of the nineteenth century. It also identifies English literature as an object of anxiety. While the earlier chapters of this book explore how readers' efforts were hindered by their lack of desire (chapter 1) or ability (chapter 2) or the inhospitable trappings of the material text itself (chapter 3), Saguna lacks for neither willingness nor skill. She enthusiastically embraces English literature, committing verses of poetry to memory and hungrily tearing through any book she can get her hands on. Throughout the novel, she's also unsure of herself. Is she reading the right books? Is she reading them "correctly"? Saguna is confused by the complexities of *The Faerie Queene*, of which she confesses to only "guess the meaning."[4] She tells us that as a young girl, she mistakenly identifies Satan as the hero of *Paradise Lost* (arguably, the correct reading). As Priya Joshi notes, these moments of confusion point to the "considerable gulf between the British literary texts she consumes and her uncooperative social world."[5] But as Saguna's encounter with the English girl reveals, irrespective of the quality of her interpretation and the level of her skill, she's never considered an equal reader because of her race. Literacy is no guarantee of understanding, and education alone can't confer the status of "reader" on Saguna.

The desire and need to read English literature, and the sense of inadequacy that this object generated in its colonial subjects, were inseparable. This mixed set of feelings is what Saguna experiences as she shuffles awkwardly in front of the condescending English girl. I use the term *provincial* to describe this peculiar strain of anxiety. The word finds a corollary in the Anglo-Indian lexicon: *mofussil*. The term mofussil refers to small towns and villages outside of the urban centers of the imperial presidencies. According to the *Hobson-Jobson* glossary (1886), a compendium of Anglo-Indian words, the term was deployed always in relation to a metropolitan center: "Thus if, in Calcutta, one talks of the *Mofussil*, he means anywhere in Bengal outside of Calcutta; if one at Benares talks of going into the *Mofussil*, he means going anywhere in the Benares division or district (as the case might be) out of the city and station of Benares. And so over India."[6] In Britain, the provincial connoted any place outside of London, whether elsewhere in England, Scotland, Ireland, or the colonies.[7] The sharp collision of the elite status of English-educated South Asian women at home and their peripheral status in the wider anglophone world led to a confused sense of place. As they discovered, South Asia was always in a relationship of provinciality to the hallowed halls of the imperial metropolis, London.

The spatial separation of the province and the metropole implies a temporal separation, too. The provincial is always out of step with the arbiters of cultural authority. Removed from the anglophone cultural center of empire, everything about Saguna is off-center and out of fashion; the belief that she can read on a par with the English girl is both quaint and ignorant. For Sumana Roy, this feeling is characterized by an irrevocable "sense of belatedness," "the awareness of having been born at the wrong time in history."[8] This was particularly true when it came to reading. Books, magazines, and newspapers published in England had to make the journey across the Suez Canal to reach their South Asian audiences. As a result, colonial readers were always reading a few weeks, if not months, behind their English counterparts. Central to the experience of a provincial reader is this perpetual condition of catching up, of struggling to grasp at what comes naturally to readers in the metropolis. No level of achievement could erase this sense of being left behind. Even when *Saguna*—a novel written in English by a South Asian woman—was published to acclaim, a reviewer remarked: "Where, the European reader will ask himself, did an Indian lady get hold of such a sweet, tender style? As we read, we fancy it is some English lady who has written the book, so charming it is to us."⁹ Explicit in this compliment is a sense of disbelief: How could Satthianadhan have closed the gulf between South Asia and England, the province and the metropole?

Reading Together

Krupabai Satthianadhan died suddenly in 1894. Her husband's second wife, Kamala, also had intellectual ambitions. In July 1901, she started *The Indian Ladies' Magazine*, an English-language monthly in Madras. From its very first issue, the magazine boldly declared its political aim to "advance the cause of the women of India."¹⁰ To this end, it presented its readers with a range of articles curated for an audience of English-educated South Asian women. But for a publication with ostensibly political goals, *The Indian Ladies' Magazine* included a lot of content about English literature. Throughout its print life, this content took on different forms: curated collections of quotations by famous writers such as Wordsworth and Shakespeare, literary puzzles to challenge the reader's mind and memory, columns listing must-read books, and essays discussing the merits of well-known literary works. As I show in this chapter, for Kamala Satthianadhan, English literature—and how to read it—was inextricable from the political project of her magazine. By offering readers opportunities to learn more about English literature or, alternatively, confirm what they already knew, I argue that the magazine presented itself as something that could alleviate the duress of being a woman reader in the shifting social and cultural terrain of colonial South Asia. It created a space in which women read as part of a community, against the alienating feeling of being provincial.

The readership of *The Indian Ladies' Magazine* emerged at the intersection of two colonial projects: a state mandate for women's education and the institutionalization of English studies in British India. In 1854, a dispatch from Charles Wood, then president of the Board of Control of the East India Company, declared that the "importance of female education [could not] be overrated," reversing the colonial government's long-standing silence on the matter.[11] Wood's statements turned women's education and literacy into a demographic marker of progress. Over the second half of the nineteenth century, the colonial state established schools for girls, developed grant-in-aid schemes to support existing networks of missionary and native-run schools, and periodically commissioned official reports that reiterated that "something" must be done about the state of women's education.[12] The readers of *The Indian Ladies' Magazine* were among the earliest generations of women who were recipients of this expanded access to education.

The readers of *The Indian Ladies' Magazine* further inherited a nineteenth-century debate about the value of reading English literature in colonial South Asia. As Gauri Viswanathan's *Masks of Conquest* (1989) notes, British colonizers encouraged the study of English literature as a means of shoring up imperial power in South Asia. Imperial administrators were eager to harness literature's "character-building" aspects, a euphemism for what they saw as its civilizing potential. Their goal was to use the study of English literature to create obedient, pliant colonial subjects.[13] To tie a national literary tradition to political goals in the imperial world was to cast even private acts of reading into the shadow of the colonial state. For colonized readers, English literature persistently held connotations of status, class, and learning. In the world of *The Indian Ladies' Magazine*, to read Milton was no neutral act of edification. It was freighted with the baggage of racial hierarchies and state policies.

Despite the widespread circulation of pro-education arguments made by the colonial government and local reformers, the actual number of girls receiving some semblance of formal education was exceedingly low.[14] In 1882, twenty-eight years after the release of the Wood Dispatch, there were a total of only six girls in college across British India, about two thousand in secondary schools, and 124,000 in primary schools.[15] The very first issue of *The Indian Ladies' Magazine* countered its readers' "cheery optimism" about the strides taken in the field of women's education with cold, hard numbers taken from J. S. Cotton's *Report on the Progress of Education in India* (1898): "Out of every 100 girls of school-going age not even three are receiving instruction."[16] Soon after, the census of 1901 for the Madras Presidency found that 9.1 percent of Christian women were "not illiterate" in at least one language, a low but significantly higher figure than the 0.7 percent for Hindu women.[17] The census of 1901 specifically describes English literacy in the Madras Presidency as "microscopic," with only 0.1 percent of women claiming knowledge of the language, most of them Christian.[18]

The women readers of *The Indian Ladies' Magazine* were, in short, a statistical improbability. That they could read—let alone read complex works of literature in any language—made them elite and exceptional. It also meant that, for the most part, they read alone. Prejudices and superstitions about the dire consequences of women's literacy competed with educational imperatives.[19] Among Hindus, women were told that if they learned how to read, they would lose their eyesight or their husbands would die.[20] Older women in the family tended to be illiterate, and they even actively opposed the acquisition of literacy by younger members.[21] And while English women were happy to see their South Asian counterparts as recipients of their charity and goodwill, as the story of Saguna's snub highlights, they were reluctant to see them as equal discussants.[22]

Historians of gender have turned to *The Indian Ladies' Magazine* as a repository of valuable historical sources: the minutes of committee meetings, reprinted lectures on the role of the "new Indian woman," and debates between prominent activists of the early twentieth century.[23] To literary scholars, the magazine was an incubator that encouraged the literary talents of its anglophone South Asian readers. Sarojini Naidu, the politician dubbed the "Nightingale of India," contributed poetry to the magazine. Rokeya Sakhawat Hossain's "Sultana's Dream," a sci-fi short story depicting a world founded on the reversal of gender roles, was first published in the magazine's September 1905 issue.[24] *The Indian Ladies' Magazine*, in short, has been a springboard for all kinds of interesting cultural and literary histories of colonial South Asia without becoming an object of inquiry itself.[25]

Reorienting attention to the publication and its readers, this chapter frames the magazine as *scaffolding*. The book reviews and literary essays included in *The Indian Ladies' Magazine* formed a textual apparatus that accompanied, complemented, and assisted South Asian women in their individual acts of reading English literature. Mediating between a reader and her relationship with a novel or a volume of poetry, *The Indian Ladies' Magazine* worked to provide readers with important lessons in what to read, how to read, and what to feel after reading it. This supportive structure broke "English literature" down into manageable pieces: a book recommendation here, a literary essay there. In doing so, it transformed the act of "understanding" English literature into a practical process. You didn't need to be English or have grown up reading English books to claim proficiency. English literature was something that could be mastered with the right direction and the right set of skills.

At the heart of *The Indian Ladies' Magazine* was the belief that reading was an activity that was meant to be shared. Where readers had few peers in their proximity, the magazine stepped in as a substitute. To this end, it presented English literature as composed of texts that were meant to be *read together*. For historians of South Asia, reading together conjures up scenes of oral performance and reading aloud. James Long's 1859 report on native publishing, which we encountered in chapter 3, paints a striking image of such a scene:

> With orientals it is a common practice to be read to, and hence numbers who cannot read themselves listen to those who can . . . We know a native who has for years employed a rich Babu to read 2 hours daily to 40 or 50 females in his house. This has been a practice from time immemorial in Bengal—where "readings" as in all Eastern countries have been so popular, and where intonation, gesture, &c., make a book listened to more telling, than when simply read. Women sometimes sit in a circle round a woman, who reads a book to them. Allowing them an average of 10 hearers or readers to each book, we calculate that these 600,000 Bengali books [the total number Long's report documents] have 2,000,000 [6,000,000?] readers or hearers.[26]

The figure of the reader/listener was definitely a part of the audience of *The Indian Ladies' Magazine*. But my use of "reading together" defies the logics of proximity to encompass a much broader sense of reading companionship. I track how the magazine's content—the reprinted article and the "News and Notes" column, the reading suggestion, and the literary essay—recreated the otherwise inaccessible experience of reading in the company of others, whether in the friendly space of a literary group or the daunting space of the colonial classroom. By placing themselves in a larger network of the magazine's other readers, South Asian women felt like they were participants in, not just provincial witnesses to, the cultural and literary discussions of their time. Crucially, the magazine allowed women to construct intellectual and affective relationships with other readers through the shared consumption of its printed pages, often against racial and geographical limits. At times, the magazine itself emerged as a friend and a powerful instrument against loneliness. When its print frequency was temporarily reduced in 1909 due to declining subscriptions, a reader wrote in frantically: "I feel as if I am losing a dear personal friend, whose intellectual society meant *so much* and to whose meeting I looked forward with such keen pleasure."[27]

This chapter tracks the responses of real and anticipated readers through a close examination of *The Indian Ladies' Magazine*, in dialogue with publication records, subscription information, and biographies. The magazine, like other examples of the form, archives its own reception. Its pages hold letters from exultant fans (and occasionally, from enraged ones). Subscribers hurried to send in answers to quizzes and participated in the publication's essay competitions. Those who wrote for the magazine should be counted among its readers, too. What they contributed, after all, was calibrated to how they perceived the publication and what they imagined other readers would be interested in. These are rich sources of readerly opinion, telling us what contemporary readers thought and felt about *The Indian Ladies' Magazine* and its place in colonial South Asia.

Alongside the voices of historical readers, I turn to the content of the magazine for evidence of reading practices. Reading for tone and rhetoric, I closely examine the magazine's literary essays and suggestions-for-reading columns, uncovering the ends to which contributors imagined their readers would approach an article. More broadly, this method also provides insight into the relationships that readers formed with literary texts beyond the pages of the magazine. For example, we will see how contributors anticipated that Coventry Patmore's *The Angel in the House* would prove difficult for South Asian readers, unlike a text like *The Merchant of Venice*, which readers would have repeatedly encountered in school. The chapter's exploration of *The Indian Ladies' Magazine* as a tool against provinciality concludes with a reading of Rabindranath Tagore's Bengali-language novella, *Nashtanirh* [The Broken Nest] (1901). As a story about loneliness, womanhood, and periodicals, *Nashtanirh* provides an important counterpoint to the chapter by making visible some of the evidentiary limitations to how we construct our histories of reading.

Kamala Satthianadhan's Magazine

After her husband's untimely death in 1906, Kamala Satthianadhan was struggling to support herself and her young children. By 1911, she was living in what her daughter described as a "mofussil town" that was "in reality no better than a poverty-stricken village."[28] It wasn't the life she'd expected to lead. Born into a family of Telegu Christians, she was the first woman to graduate with a college degree in South India, as well as the first to acquire a master's degree.[29] She'd collaborated with her husband, Samuel, a Tamil Christian educator, on several literary projects, including a volume of short stories, *Stories of Indian Christian Life* (1898), and a compilation of the writings of his first wife, the novelist Krupabai Satthianadhan.[30] The town she and her children now lived in was a book desert. A bright spot for the family was their subscription to the Literary Society in the city of Madras, from which they would receive boxes of books in the mail.³¹ More importantly, Satthianadhan was scrambling to keep *The Indian Ladies' Magazine* afloat.

Alongside the burden of her domestic duties and the imperative to educate her children, Satthianadhan needed an income. She took on the role of tutoring a local landowner's wife, which provided the family with some semblance of economic support. Between all her commitments, she worked on *The Indian Ladies' Magazine*. The task was onerous, as the magazine was, for the most part, a one-woman operation. Satthianadhan planned and edited each issue while also contributing articles herself. Despite the labor involved, the arrival of the printed issues at the family residence, ready for distribution, became something of a ritual. Her daughter, Padmini Sengupta, recounts the event as one of material wonder and pleasure:

> [t]he large packages of the journal would arrive each month, and we would avidly scan the pages. Our next task would be to sit and roll each journal separately for the post. How vividly I can see the neatly stacked piles rising before us, and my brother and I and the servants sitting on the ground busy with our task of rolling, gluing and stamping, while Kamala and "Nani" [maternal grandmother] would sit back and watch us.³²

Sengupta's biography of Satthianadhan, *A Portrait of an Indian Woman* (1956), describes her mother as a fiercely intelligent and well-read woman with no business acumen at all. She struggled to create an infrastructure for the magazine's production and source revenue from advertisements. As subscriptions fell, the production schedule of the magazine became increasingly erratic, finally ceasing publication in 1918. It was restarted in 1927, after the family returned from some years in England for the children's education and was finally discontinued in 1938.³³

The Indian Ladies' Magazine emerged in a crowded landscape of newspapers and periodicals. Spurred on by the availability of cheap print, magazines, both in English and South Asian languages, were mushrooming across colonial South Asia. Compared to the almanacs of chapter 3, the print runs of individual magazines were modest. *The Indian Ladies' Magazine*'s average monthly print run of eight hundred issues, amounting to a total of 9,600 copies a year, was but a fraction of the Gupta Press's yearly turnover of more than 100,000 almanacs.³⁴ But cumulatively, magazines as a genre represented a major presence in the print landscape of South Asia. For the first quarter of 1902, the Madras Presidency alone recorded thirty-six registered magazines in English with a total print run of 33,560. These were in addition to the fifty-seven other magazines being published in Tamil, Telegu, Sanskrit, or a combination of the three.[35] Households with literate members would have subscribed to multiple magazines, which were read alongside other printed materials, such as books and newspapers.

The nineteenth-century counterparts of *The Indian Ladies' Magazine* had circulated in a world of male publishers whose didactic impulses determined what were and weren't legitimate subjects for women's reading.[36] In the early twentieth century, by contrast, publications like Satthianadhan's periodical were written for and by women. As Francesca Orsini's history of Hindi magazines from North India tells us, early twentieth-century periodicals cautioned their readers that abstract conceptions of "Indian womanhood" shouldn't be left in the hands of Indian men. After all, women had as much a right to participate in defining this concept as men did.[37] A similar impulse shaped *The Indian Ladies' Magazine*, as it sought to encourage women to articulate opinions and intervene in social debates. As a cooperative, rather than a didactic, space, the magazine provided readers with the tools to think for—and write for—themselves, placing their voices on a national stage.

The table of contents of the magazine's very first issue demonstrated its commitment to being a collection of useful articles for its women readers (Figure 4.1). Articles geared toward the social reform project, in which Satthianadhan and her circle were invested, were threaded through the magazine. The first three articles—"Indian Women–Past and Present," "The Present Condition of Female Education," and "Female Infanticide in India"—were meant to be a rousing call for gender reform in South Asia. The magazine's interventions in debates about the state of the Indian woman were punctuated by articles of a more literary bent: original short fiction and poetry by the magazine's contributors. The "News and Notes" column portrayed stories of women in far-flung places who faced the same challenges and overcame the same hurdles as their South Asian counterparts. So did articles that described different parts of the country and world, whether "Rural Scenes in India" or "The Englishwoman in her Home." Then there were the pieces of domestic advice. A cooking column in July 1901 led to articles in later issues about needlework designs and knitting patterns, and others on sanitation and health in the home.

Throughout its life, the articles in *The Indian Ladies' Magazine* continued to span a wide range of topics. Essays recounting political meetings and events were interspersed with quotations from literary texts, just as essays on literature reminded women that the act of reading could be put toward the purpose

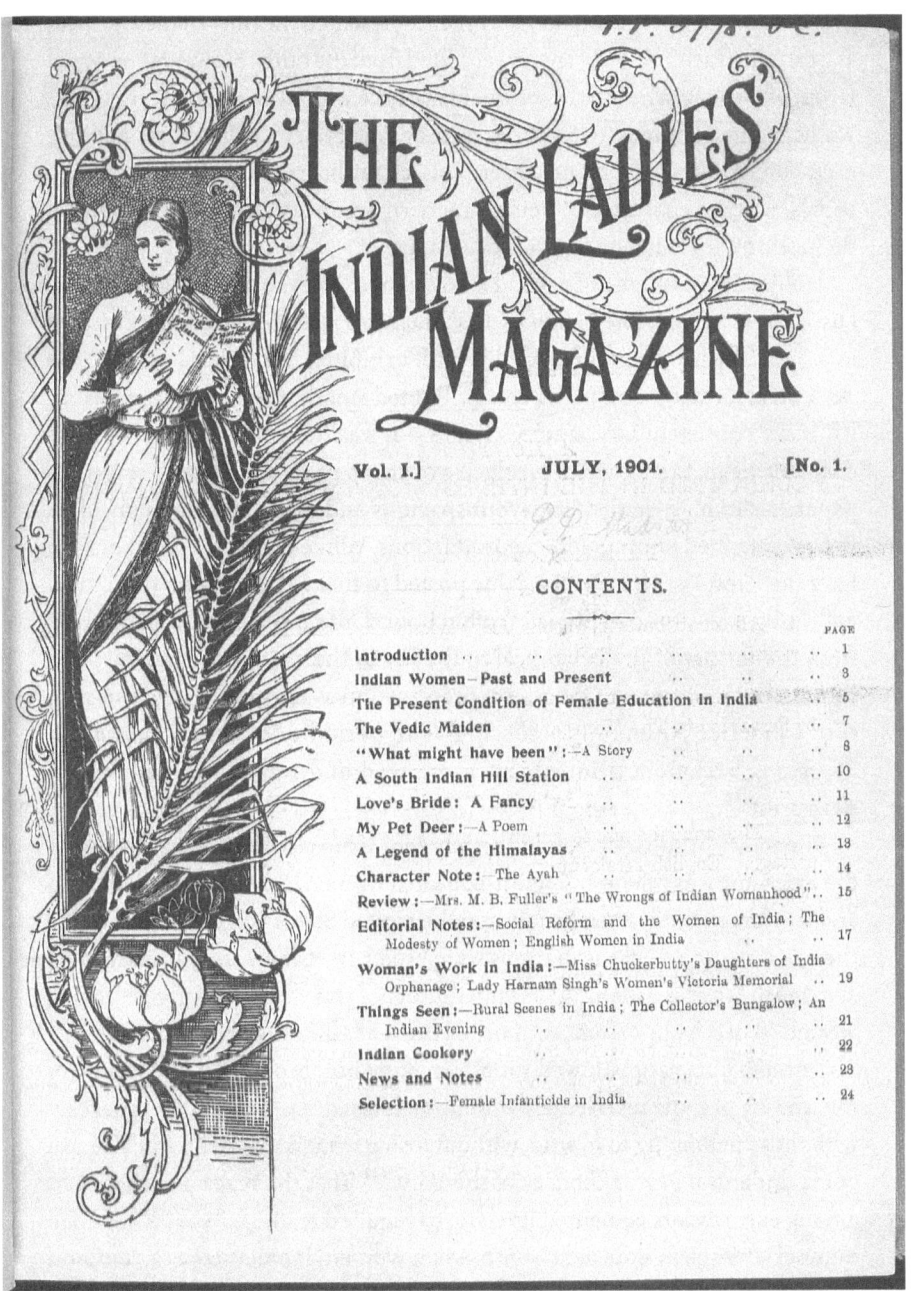

FIGURE 4.1. Cover of the first issue of *The Indian Ladies' Magazine* 1, no. 1 (July 1901), © British Library Board, P.P.3778.bc.

of self-improvement. The tables of contents presented the titles of these articles as a list, with each article discretely separated from the other. However, the actual layout of the magazine put the articles in dialogue with each other. In every issue, women's rights, recipes for South Asian food, and reviews of books jostled with each other for space on a single page. This, as Satthianadhan argued in her editorials, was the challenge of being a modern South Asian woman: balancing domestic duties with education and learning.

Unlike a newspaper of topical significance, or even the almanacs I discussed in chapter 3, *The Indian Ladies' Magazine* was presented to its readers as a desirable luxury object. While it still exhibited features standard to the periodical format—soft paper covers, limited length supporting its portability, and a consistent layout across issues—it was not curtailed by any of the cost-cutting tactics to which producers of cheap print often had to resort. Its paper was of high quality, its layout spacious and readable, and many of its issues contained photographic reproductions. While readers could choose to have the latest issue of the magazine posted to them each month, the annual collection was stored in libraries, often bound into a single volume. Moving from the format of the periodical to the book, the change in material form signified expectations of long-term preservation as opposed to the use-and-throw practice commonly associated with periodicals. *The Indian Ladies' Magazine* became a print object to be read and reread: *not* ephemeral newsprint.[38]

The terms of subscription in the July 1901 issue also made clear to whom the magazine was pitched: English-educated women located in India, Burma, and Ceylon, possibly even Britain and the United States (Figure 4.2).[39] While the magazine's political aspirations were broad, its readership was narrow. As an English-language monthly, its target audience was women who were "taking advantage of the opportunities afforded them of a liberal English education."[40] As Satthianadhan's opening editorial statement boldly declared, the "future of the women of India rests largely with this educated class; and more especially with those belonging to it, who, without losing what is distinctly Indian, have come under the best influences of the West."[41] That the magazine circulated among elite readers cemented its claim to required reading. Among the small number of English-educated South Asian women, it emerged as a common object that everyone read and consulted, fulfilling its role as a "bond of union" for the group.[42]

The magazine's imagined readership is materialized in subscriber lists that give us some sense of who was reading it. In the first of these lists, published

The Indian Ladies' Magazine.

A MONTHLY JOURNAL
CONDUCTED IN THE INTERESTS OF THE WOMEN OF INDIA.

Published on the 12th of each Month.

All contributions, books for review, &c., should be sent to Mrs. S. SATTHIANADHAN, "Myrtle Lodge," Royapettah, Madras.

All remittances and communications regarding advertisements, &c., should be forwarded to The Manager, *Indian Ladies' Magazine*, Royapettah, Madras.

Terms of Subscriptions.

The annual subscription in India, Ceylon and Burmah is Rs. 4 including postage. English rate of subscription including postage is 6 shillings. Subscriptions from America may be remitted for $1.50.

FIGURE 4.2. Terms of subscription, *The Indian Ladies' Magazine* 1, no. 1 (July 1901), © British Library Board, P.P.3778.bc.

THE INDIAN LADIES' MAGAZINE.

ACKNOWLEDGMENTS.

The following subscriptions received during the month of September for the "Indian Ladies' Magazine" are acknowledged with thanks :

		RS.			RS.
1.	Miss Lena R. Athim, Ferozepore	4	27.	Miss Moffat, New York, America	4½
2.	,, A. Bopanna, Bepunad, Coorg	4	28.	The Manager, Shantra Ashram, Muttra	4
3.	Mr. T. A. Comaraswamy, Mandalay	4	29.	Mrs. Maya Das, Ferozepore	4
4.	Mrs. Hemanta Kumari Chaudhuri, Sylhet.	4	30.	,, Sumatibai Nanuji, Bombay	4
5.	,, J. A. David, Palamcottah	4	31.	Miss Oxley, Madras	4
6.	,, Datta, Punjab	4	32.	Mrs. P. Ponsonby, Lahore	4
7.	,, Duthie, Nagercoil	4	33.	Mrs. M. Pereira, Trevandrum	4
8.	,, E. Dunlop, Mandalay	4	34.	,, S. A. Rahman, Purneah	4
9.	,, J. R. Dias, Travancore	4	35.	Dewan Bahadur Sreenivasa Ragava Iyengar, Madras	4
10.	,, Gates, Sholapur	4	36.	Mr. M. Venkataraghavulu Reddy, Zamindar, Sreeperambadur	4
11.	,, Gnanamuthu, Ellore	4	37.	Miss M. K. Scudder, Ranipettai	4
12.	Mr. A. K. Govindan, Madras	2	38.	,, Sell, Madras	4
13.	Mrs. A. George, Kottayam	4	39.	Rev. H. Schaffter, Tinnevelly	4
14.	,, Ibrahim Ahmadi, Bijapur	4	40.	Mr. M. Sudarsanam, Berhampore	2
15.	,, Veeramma Janakamma, Godavari	4	41.	Mrs. B. Shreenivassa, B.A., Madras	4
16.	Miss B. Kalliani Ammal, Trevandrum	4	42.	,, Stephenson, Gooty	4
17.	Miss M. S. Kukde, Ahmednagar	4	43.	Mr. K. V. Sreenivasa Iyer, Coimbatore	4
18.	,, Kugler, Guntur	4	44.	Mrs. Salmon, Almondsburry, England	4½
19.	Mrs. Kane, Amraoti	4	45.	Mr. P. Sundram, Madras	1
20.	,, F. M. Lake, Hassan	4	46.	Miss Tulsing, Tumkur	2
21.	,, D. Lazarus, Vizagapatam	4	47.	Mr. R. Venkataratnam Naidu, Hyderabad.	4
22.	Miss C. Middleton, Comilla, Bengal	8	48.	Mrs. J. R. Williams, Nellore	4
23.	Mrs. Malim, Trichinopoly	4	49.	Mrs. A. A. Williams, Madras	4
24.	,, Meiklejohn, Government House, Coorg	4	50.	,, C. J. Winckler, Cannanore	4
25.	Mr. Khitra Mohan Mitra, Krishnagar, Bengal	2	51.	,, Zephaniah, Bellary	4
26.	Miss Mee, Madras	4	52.	,, Zechariah, Calicut	4

☞ As the first and second issues of the *Indian Ladies' Magazine* are all exhausted, it is regretted that several applications for these numbers have not been complied with. New subscribers will have the Magazine supplied from September.

THE INDIAN SOCIAL REFORMER.

TERMS OF SUBSCRIPTION.

All Subscriptions are payable strictly in advance.

Per Annum				RS. A. P.
Town and Mofussil	....	....	....	4 0 0
For a single copy	....	....	....	0 2 0
Foreign countries	....		10 shillings per annum.	

Changes of address and all business communications, etc., must, as hitherto, be intimated to the MANAGER, and all literary communications must be addressed to the EDITOR, BOMBAY.

FIGURE 4.3. List of subscribers, *The Indian Ladies' Magazine* 1, no. 4 (October 1901), © British Library Board, P.P.3778.bc.
Note the inclusion of the terms of subscription for another magazine, *The Indian Social Reformer*, on the same page.

in the October 1901 issue, we see that the readership was predominantly married women interspersed with some men and unmarried women (Figure 4.3). While the bulk of the subscribers were from across the Madras Presidency, demand for the magazine also came from Lahore, Punjab, and Bengal, and further afield from Malaysia, the United States, and England. Aside from the information it contained, the list also dramatized the aims of the magazine: to encourage connections between South Asian women and their British and European counterparts. The alphabetical ordering of the list intermingles the names and addresses of South Asians, Americans, and Britons alike. It was something of a utopian document, reflecting the social and cultural intermingling that the magazine hoped to see in the world.

Subscription information provides a starting point for reconstructing who was reading *The Indian Ladies' Magazine*. But not everyone who encountered the periodical would appear on Satthianadhan's official list. For one, the periodical attempted to find ways of reaching non-anglophone speakers and, in doing so, to count them among its readers. Satthianadhan repeatedly encouraged English-educated South Asian men to subscribe to the magazine and translate its content for their wives. Further, hoping to "extend the benefits of *The Indian Ladies' Magazine* to a large circle of vernacular readers," several of its articles were translated and reprinted in South Asian-language journals that had a non-anglophone readership.[43] For example, a series of articles aimed at generating awareness about public health issues written by Isabel Brander were translated for publication in other periodicals: into Tamil for the *Dravidavarthamani* and the *Tamil Zenana Magazine*, into Telegu for the *Ravi*, into Malayalam for the *Manorama*, as well as into Kannada for the *Suvasari*.[44]

Even for elite anglophone readers, *The Indian Ladies' Magazine* was expensive, which necessarily limited the number of official subscribers. But its high-quality print also made it durable, enabling its circulation off the books, with copies being passed back and forth between friends. One such copy landed in the hands of Edwin Arnold, the author of the bestselling *The Light of Asia* (1879), a verse-biography of the Buddha.[45] Arnold claimed to have received his copy in London from a visitor in town from India to attend the coronation of Edward VII.[46] The visitor left Arnold with a copy of the magazine, and Arnold imagined them, in exchange, traveling back to India with "wonderful reports" of the ceremonies in London, to be discussed "in many a palace and hunting lodge."[47] Arnold's anecdote highlighted the formal and informal transnational networks through which information traveled across empire. It also positioned *The Indian Ladies' Magazine* at the heart of a larger infrastructure of cultural traffic.

Cut, Paste, Cite

Before I turn to how *The Indian Ladies' Magazine* framed English literature for its South Asian readers, I want to consider briefly how other forms of writing from the periodical also styled themselves as aids against the fear of provinciality. Take, for example, the periodical's relationship with other examples of the genre. The second issue of *The Indian Ladies' Magazine* ends with the "Opinions of the Press," a collated list of periodicals from across India that had noted (and praised) the event of its publication (Figure 4.4).[48] This simple tactic was intended as proof of the magazine's impact: even from its inception it was already being lauded as a contender by its peers. It was also a reminder that the magazine was but one node in a network of newspapers and periodicals that crisscrossed South Asia, even the world. Rather than obscure this interdependency, the magazine's editor embraced it. Every periodical in which *The Indian Ladies' Magazine* was referenced, mentioned, or discussed was like an individual reader, spreading word of its existence to friends and family.

The Indian Ladies' Magazine's relationships with other periodicals were more than a mutual admiration society. By making its relationships with other periodicals visible, it assuaged the magazine's readers of their anxieties of provinciality. If people from around the country were praising the magazine, they, too, as the magazine's readers, were visible on a national stage. Throughout its print life, the magazine adopted strategic practices, such as setting up collaborations with peer publications and reprinting content, to allow its readers to feel like they were both part of a global network and of contemporary cultural discourse.

Satthianadhan encouraged her readers to subscribe to peer publications with shared aims, such as the Bengali-language *Bharati* and *Antahpur* and the English-language *Indian Social Reformer*. She also kept her eye on British periodicals and newspapers, such as the *Daily Telegraph*, reporting back whenever it mentioned *The Indian Ladies' Magazine*. This was part of an overarching project to foster cross-cultural relationships between British and South Asian women, as she repeatedly stated in her editorial notes in the magazine. One of the magazine's extended relationships was with *Womanhood* (1898–1907), a London-based magazine that ran a column called "What Women are Doing in India." Authored by a Mrs. C. Besley—also an occasional contributor to *The Indian Ladies' Magazine*—the column became the impetus for a collaboration between the periodicals. Besley's articles that were published in the South Asian magazine, for example, were often reprinted in *Womanhood*.[49]

The Indian Ladies' Magazine.

A MONTHLY JOURNAL,

CONDUCTED IN THE INTERESTS OF THE WOMEN OF INDIA,

BY KAMALA SATTHIANADHAN, M.A.

Published on the 10th of each Month.

OPINIONS OF THE PRESS.

"We hope the Magazine will command great encouragement in India."—**Mysore Herald.**

"We hope that educated India will give the Magazine its ungrudging, generous and hearty support."—**Madras Standard.**

"The enterprise is indeed one of the noblest and, if favoured with a proper measure of success, is one that is calculated to produce immense benefit to the nation."—**The Hindu** (Madras).

"There are innumerable topics upon which women's views upon women's interests are sufficiently apparent to make the scope of such a Journal eminently useful and profitable."—**Daily Post** (Bangalore).

"As an attempt of unique journalistic enterprise by and in behalf of Indian women the *Indian Ladies' Magazine* is sure to meet with warm and sympathetic welcome and encouragement at the hands of every intelligent and patriotic citizen of this wide empire."—**Times of Malabar** (Calicut).

"The first number is edited with good judgment and most tastefully gotten up in every respect. We sincerely trust it may speedily win its way, as it deserves, to a large circulation and assured support."—**Indian Witness** (Calcutta).

"One of the interesting features of the Magazine is that the contributions, mostly from the educated ladies of India, are free from sectarian bias. . . . We wish that the educated college girls of Mysore will also join Mrs. Satthianadhan to make the Magazine a success."—**The Mysore Herald.**

"The *Indian Ladies' Magazine*, hailing from Madras, is an example of the capacity of our educated women to voice the feelings, grievances and aspirations of their sex. . . . The get-up of the Magazine is creditable to the feminine sense of beauty."—**Subodha Patrika** (Bombay).

"The first number is excellent in every respect. . . . We trust that the Magazine will have a long and useful life and be of great assistance in realising the object for which it has been started. . . The venture has much to commend it, and we hope that it will achieve the success it so well deserves."—**The Madras Mail.**

"The first number of the *Indian Ladies' Magazine* answers expectations. It is charmingly got up. The articles are short and sweet, and treat of the past, present and the future in a tone of healthy, but not morbid, optimism. . . We should very much like to see the Magazine widely read by Indian ladies."—K. Natarajan Esq., B.A., in the **Indian Social Reformer** (Bombay).

"We would appeal to all educated Indians to support the present deserving venture of Mrs. Satthianadhan's, which—if it can keep up to its present high standard as we have no doubt that it will—would soon be a power in the land in all matters pertaining to the cause of Indian women."—S. Sinha Esq., Bar-at-Law, in the **Kayastha Samachar** (Allahabad).

"The new Magazine promises, from its first number, to be an interesting and useful journal. . . . The aim of the Magazine is certainly a noble one and it is needless to say that there is ample scope and opportunity for any one who aspires to help the noble and urgent work of the advance of the cause of the women of India."—**Indian Messenger** (Calcutta).

"Madras, the Benighted Presidency, which so often comes in suddenly ahead of clever Bengal, able Bombay, and solid Hindoostan has just produced the *Indian Ladies' Magazine*, edited, and, in a great part, written by Native Ladies. It has, we think, the

FIGURE 4.4. First page of "Opinions of the Press," *The Indian Ladies' Magazine* 1, no. 2 (August 1901), © British Library Board, P.P.3778.bc.

Peer publications like *Womanhood* were also sources of content for Satthianadhan. *The Indian Ladies' Magazine*'s original pieces of writing (literary essays, short stories, and editorial notes) existed in a collection of articles repurposed from other sources. Each article traveled a significant geographical and temporal distance, often undergoing transformations in genre and length before it was printed in the magazine. Take, for example, an article titled "Women in China." The article's original source was a report written by a Mrs. J. L. Whiting for the International Suffrage Conference in Washington, D.C. An excerpt from the report was published in the Boston-based *The Woman's Journal* in May 1902 and then reprinted in the July 1902 issue of *The Indian Ladies' Magazine*.[50] This act brought together three different countries (China, the United States, and India) and shifts between two different genres (report, extract). Behind the transformations that characterize the final article was a reader and an editor whose fingerprints were all over the decision of how to synopsize, how to excise, and how to extract the original source.

A part of the magazine that relied exclusively on reprinting was the "News and Notes" column. Loosely aggregated around the theme of women's issues, this column provided readers with discontinuous snippets of information from places as far apart as Bosnia and the rural United States.[51] The September 1904 issue carried news of the botanist Marie Stopes's appointment at the University of Manchester.[52] Many of the entries had a distinctly anecdotal flavor. For example, the news of Stopes's success is instantly followed by: "The Czarina frequently reads, before bed-time (which comes about 11 o'clock) an English novel or the *Times* aloud to her husband."[53] Similarly, the April 1907 issue recounts the story of one Agatha Troy, a sixteen-year-old Sicilian girl and current resident of Utica, New York. The note describes her as "a skilful assistant to her father in his work as a marble and granite cutter." A "slip of a girl, less than five feet high," she wields her five-pound hammer, we are told, with more grace than a man.[54]

In its search for reprintable content, *The Indian Ladies' Magazine* was well served by what Isabel Hofmeyr and Antoinette Burton call an "imperial commons": an expansive space in which books, documents, and newspapers circulated outside of copyright regulations.[55] The mutual agreement to borrow from each other was known as "The Exchange."[56] Periodicals across the Indian Ocean, West Africa, the Caribbean, and Australasia were commonly formed through the textual intermeshing of bite-size news items originally published elsewhere. The reasons for this were as much economic as ideological: these snippets filled up dead space, cost nothing to reproduce, and, in the provincial outposts, were often the sole source of international news. On each page, the world was fragmented and reconstituted at the mercy of an editor's scissors.[57] The result was a periodical that was something like a public-facing scrapbook, a collation and compilation of articles that were worthy of preservation.

But why would a South Asian reader care about the Czarina's bedtime reading habits or Marie Stopes's academic appointment? Remember that one of the aims of *The Indian Ladies' Magazine* was to generate meaningful connections between South Asian women and their British and European counterparts. As Kwame Antony Appiah writes, the novel has always been held preeminent for its power to represent otherness, to inculcate sympathy, and to remind us, despite our differences, of our shared sense of humanity.[58] To read, then, is to "travel in books to learn 'mutual toleration.'"[59] The "News and Notes" column reproduces this model of novelistic reading by attaching it to a non-novelistic object.

The "News and Notes" column took the twin mandates of sympathy and solidarity and placed them in a global context. Its format reinforced this. Composed in a double-columned structure and running into multiple pages, a new entry was marked by a dash. The aim of the editor was to include as many news items as possible. Countries like Britain, Russia, Japan, and France intermingled in the colonial outposts of this local South Asian magazine, in defiance of geographical limits. The fragmentary form of the column—remember that no item was more than a few lines long—meant that news items followed rapidly on the heels of another, barely separable from each other. One reason for this was accessibility: readers could rapidly skim the pages for stories that appealed to them. But as a result, the "News and Notes" column gave the world a provincial form, downsized into approachable and interchangeable nuggets. With just a quick glance, the world was within the reader's grasp.

The impulse to make the world provincial was also reflected in the kinds of snippets the magazine chose to reproduce. Recall the story of Agatha Troy's marble-cutting success in New York. At first glance, Troy's story seems completely random, an incidental footnote. But reprinting Troy's exploits in a South Asia-based periodical transforms an anecdote into a story with universal potential, easily read and understood in a local context. It's representative of the kind of content that "News and Notes" regularly showcased: stories about women's achievements or instances in which they outcompeted men. Troy's story, then, is relevant not because it's exceptional, but because it exemplifies a pattern. It repeats the themes and mottos of the stories that surround it in the column, toggling between the familiar and the aspirational. It also inspires acts of repetition in its readers. Each item in "News and Notes" was an occasion for South Asian women to remind themselves, again and again, that the struggle for autonomy was a global project, uniting aristocrats and working-class people, South Asians and Europeans alike.

In the next two sections of the chapter, I show how the struggle against provinciality and the desire to feel like a part of a community were shaped by other parts of *The Indian Ladies' Magazine*, ranging from reading suggestion columns to puzzles to long literary critical essays. While the magazine is a fascinating source of information about what women were reading, I turn instead to the textual apparatus that guided their reading choices and practices.

A Reader's Guide to English Literature

Between March 1903 and January 1904, *The Indian Ladies' Magazine* ran a column titled "Suggestions for English Reading." The column was authored by an "Englishwoman in India," a frequent pseudonymous contributor. Its goal was to "encourage the reading of English literature among Indian ladies," with the aim of providing "brief summaries of works of well-known English writers, specially useful to Indian readers."[60] These works ranged widely, including John Ruskin's *Sesame and Lilies*, Augustine Birrell's *Obiter Dicta*, and R. L. Stevenson's *Virginius Puerisque*, among others. The column was unambiguously prescriptive. Focusing on "difficult" but essential works, it was meant to be a guide to an English literary landscape, putting up signs and road maps for South Asian readers to follow. The column, in short, was a link between the reader and her relationship with a literary text outside the pages of the magazine.

How was a reader supposed to go about planning and organizing their reading? As articles in *The Indian Ladies' Magazine* repeatedly reminded its subscribers, there was an impossible number of books in the world to read. One Mrs. A. Zechariah pointed out, for example, that it would take "hundreds of years to read the titles alone of all the books in the World's Libraries."[61] There was also the question of considering what kinds of books would even be appropriate for South Asian readers. A subscriber to the magazine wrote in to complain about how most of the English books South Asian women were encouraged to read were embarrassingly juvenile, "enchanting fairy stories for childhood."[62] But most English novels outside of pedagogical texts and primers were written for English readers, assuming knowledge of local customs and dialects. Priya Joshi notes that many South Asian readers, even English-educated ones, felt alienated by references to unfamiliar landscapes and unattainable objects in the books they encountered.⁶³ Even earnest intentions to read ran into inevitable obstacles.

Through the "Suggestions for English Reading," *The Indian Ladies' Magazine* sought to provide its readers with some direction: a helping hand, a reading list to get them started. By presenting the column as an indispensable guide to English literature, the magazine sought to consolidate its status as required reading. Contributors to *The Indian Ladies' Magazine* had strong feelings about what the South Asian woman's bookshelf should look like. Shakespeare was a universal favorite. Zechariah's article ends in a pseudo-syllabus that lists all the usual suspects: Eliot, Dickens, Carlyle. It doesn't include a single book written by a South Asian, whether in English or any South Asian language, even though Satthianadhan routinely exhorted her readers not to neglect their vernacular reading. "Indian History" makes the cut as an important subject of study, but only through the inclusion of historical novels and accounts written by British administrators such as George Trevelyan.⁶⁴ Another contributor suggested that some readers would find Rosa M. Carey, Charlotte Yonge, and Rhoda Broughton "delightful," while others would enjoy the "quaker-like purity and primness" of Jane Austen and Charlotte Bronte.⁶⁵ There's often no clear sense why some books are presented as recommended reading and others aren't.

What suggestions for reading universally did was provide the assurance that with some help, readers could build their own reading lists outside the pedagogical space of the classroom. Take, for example, the opening paragraph of the January 1904 column, in which "The Englishwoman in India" urges her readers to pick up Edwin Arnold's blockbuster epic, *The Light of Asia* (1879). But before she turns to the merits of the book, she conjures up a scene in which the readers of the article are standing in her library:

> Look up at my book-shelves. What shall I lend you this month?—that is how I always feel about our talks about books. All the books I have advised you to read stand on my book-shelves, dainty in their bright covers. I like my books to please me with their appearance, just as I like my children nicely dressed, but I do not like my children in new dresses nor my books in new covers. I like my children in the dresses they have worn so long that they seem part of their dear little selves; and the books,—let their color be a little mellowed with much handling, yes, even with much lending.⁶⁶

The passage transforms the immaterial form of the book recommendation into the material form of the book: standing in a row on a bookshelf, wrapped in bright covers. But take a closer look at the extended analogy that undergirds the passage's material metaphors: children: dresses :: books: covers. The comparison of children to books enacts the central tension between education and motherhood that animated *The Indian Ladies' Magazine* from its very inception. From its earliest issues, the magazine featured discordant voices that violently disagreed with each other on the subject. In an article titled "The Higher Education of Women," a barrister called Alfred Nundy decried educational opportunities for women as a farce, arguing that men were looking for wives capable of making "a good omelette or delicious *hulwa*, and be otherwise an expert housekeeper" rather than one who would "quote Shakespeare and Milton when a badly cooked dinner is served before him."[67] By suggesting that children and books are analogous to each other, the "Englishwoman in India" purposefully seeks to undermine Nundy's argument. Refusing a division between the public and the private, she boldly places books at the very center of domestic life, as objects and texts with which women could and should engage.

A voracious reader not afraid to articulate strong opinions, the "Englishwoman in India" models mastery over her library and its titles for her readers. To a shy South Asian reader, looking for new things to read and forever afraid of lagging behind, the child/book analogy softens the intimidating space of the imaginary library. Books with frayed covers, like children in old clothes, are symbols of familiarity and bear the imprint of the intimacy created by acts of reading and rereading. Books elicit—and deserve—the same level of love as children themselves. Borrowing the language of familial relationships for the act of reading, the passage serves as a reminder that mastery over books is within every woman reader's grasp. The absence of a subject in the final line of the passage—"let their color be a little mellowed with much handling, yes, even with much lending"—is aspirational: the reader is meant to insert herself into the sentence, as one with the knowledge and authority to handle and lend books to others. With enough time and enough study, even the most daunting of things can become objects of affection.

Contributors to the magazine often emphasized the aesthetic value of literature, remarking on the beauty of specific lines or the feeling of reading a poem. The articles in the "Suggestions" series did, too. But they were also very much interested in the everyday ends to which one's reading could be deployed. They provided a clear rationale for what readers would get out of their reading exercises. The uses to which English literature was put were eminently practical, a set of how-tos: how to acquire knowledge, how to learn about the histories and geographies of different countries. For example, readers were encouraged to peruse Twain's *The Prince and the Pauper* for an introduction to Tudor history.[68]

But for the most part, English literature was seen as a vehicle for moral self-improvement: how to be a better mother, how to be a better wife.[69] The very first column on John Ruskin's *Sesame and Lilies*, for example, clearly orients the reader toward the woman's role in the family. The book "helps each of us to find out for ourselves, just what we are, just what we ought not to be, how 'to right the wrong,' and to try to make ourselves a little better than we were." The goal of reading the book, as the "Englishwoman in India" notes, is to "become more like Ruskin's ideal woman each day."[70]

A similar thread emerges in an article published in the May 1903 issue encouraging readers to turn to Coventry Patmore's *The Angel in the House* (1854–1862). This narrative Victorian poem is remembered today mostly for its unhealthy idealization of the figure of the wife. In the article, the poem is presented to South Asian women as a primer of sorts for how to be the ideal wife.[71] The "Englishwoman in India" outlines a contrast between British ideas of marriage and her own perception of South Asian ones. Calling attention to the centrality of love in Patmore's poem, she remarks to her readers, that "[a]ll this [descriptions of a husband's love for his wife] must be so new, even the idea of it is all strange to you Indian ladies, you, who dare not even mention your husband's name."[72] While the contributor places these two cultures of marriage in direct opposition to each other, in reality, discussions about the model of a companionate marriage had dominated nineteenth- and early twentieth-century debates about gender reform in South Asia. Patmore's poem and its portrayal of a loving marriage is presented to its South Asian readers as self-help in the mode of conduct manuals, domestic treatises, and pamphlets circulating across the colony. By imagining acts of reading leading to acts of emulation, the "Englishwoman in India" suggests that the poem provides the building blocks for the ideal companionate marriage, one in which the wife comes to the realization that "God never meant woman to be a mere appendage of man."[73] By presenting readers with an alternative conception of marriage, the poem has a clear function in the hands of a South Asian reader: to allow women to reimagine themselves outside of the cultural roles cut out for them. The point of reading Patmore, in short, is to gather the tools to conceptualize a different life path for oneself, one that lay outside the bounds of South Asian provinciality or, at least, in some sort of critical relationship to it.

The column drew on formal and narrative features to reinforce its functional role as a guide to reading English literature. The article on Coventry

Patmore, for example, details the arc of the poem chronologically, while pausing to dwell on specific important lines and stanzas. This excerpt is representative of the article's style as a whole:

> The poem begins with the poet's answer to his wife's question, as to what theme he is going to choose as the one to make his fame in the world of letters,—he says to all her suggestions,
>
>> "Your gentle self, my wife,
>> And love, that grows from one to all."
>
> and then he explains how he is going to do it. On the following anniversary of their wedding day he reads the first part to her.
>
>> "If I to men have here made known
>> New truths, they, like new stars, where there
>> Before, though not yet written down."[74]

Moving between explanatory commentary and lines from the poem, the "Englishwoman in India" conjures up multiple scenes of reading together. There's the scene of the family reading together in the drawing room, a scene invoked multiple times in the magazine itself: husbands reading to their wives; literate members of the family reading to the illiterate. Most enduringly, there's the scene of pedagogical instruction, set in the colonial classroom. One of the common roles in which British women found themselves in the colonies was as teachers in missionary schools.[75] This is the most likely context in which the South Asian women readers of the magazine would have encountered their British counterparts, as their native students and tutees. Across late nineteenth- and early twentieth-century South Asia, the white missionary teacher is valorized as a confidant and guide, a central actor in the struggle for gendered reform.

The "Englishwoman in India" borrows from the well-known tropes of being a teacher in a classroom. After convincing her readers of the value of *The Angel in the House*, she writes: "I feel that this poem may be difficult for you to follow, because the ideas in it are all so new to you, so we will go through it together."[76] This immediately positions her as a keeper of the keys, a guide to helping the provincial South Asian reader walk through and understand a long and complicated poem. But it's hard to ignore the flipside of the teacher in the colonial imagination: as a cruel and exacting presence. Teachers guide and assist, but at the end of the nineteenth century, they also judged, scolded, and inspired fear in their students. Trapped in an imaginary classroom, the South Asian woman was constantly reading with the Englishwoman looking over her shoulder, continuously scrutinizing and correcting. To experience more inclusive reading communities, she would have to look elsewhere in the magazine.

A Rereading Public

In 1886, the Bengali novelist Bankim Chandra Chattopadhyay published an essay called "Shakuntala, Miranda O Desdemona" [Shakuntala, Miranda, and Desdemona].[77] He compares Shakespeare's heroines, Miranda and Desdemona, to Shakuntala, the titular character of a Sanskrit play by Kalidasa. Tucked in between arguments about how the European characters are more loyal wives than Shakuntala is a claim about the dissemination of English literature in South Asia. Bankim confessed to his readers that he "wanted to quote the entire first dialogue of love [between Ferdinand and Miranda from Shakespeare's the *Tempest*]" but that ultimately, he felt such a gesture would be unnecessary.[78] His reasons were practical: "Everyone has the texts of Shakespeare, and they can all read the original versions. They will find that this is no less powerful than the dialogue of Romeo and Juliet in the garden, famous all over the world and memorized by all college students."[79]

Bankim's evocation of a hardbacked version of the "collected works" residing on the bookshelves of elite households, schoolrooms, and university libraries made an assumption: that most elite South Asians were familiar with the playwright's work. He wasn't wrong about his audience's intimate knowledge of Shakespeare. By the late nineteenth century, Shakespeare had a widespread presence across South Asia. His plays were performed on stages across the country. Translations into local languages circulated widely in pamphlet form. His works were included on school literature syllabi; extracts and speeches were reproduced in textbooks.[80] Adapted versions and retellings of the plays—most famously, Charles and Mary Lamb's *Tales from Shakespeare* (1807)—gained a popular readership. Bankim didn't need to support his arguments by reproducing sections from the *Tempest* or *Othello*, because his audience had already read them.

Like Bankim, *The Indian Ladies' Magazine* repeatedly evoked literary texts it assumed most of its audience had read. The magazine published a plethora of articles on Shakespeare that took different forms, ranging from forums simulating panel discussions focused on an exemplary character from a play to articles exhorting South Asian women to be more like their early modern, if fictional, counterparts. And it wasn't just Shakespeare. The editor and contributors performed the same task of opining on well-established literary objects ranging from early modern works like Edmund Spenser's *The Faerie Queene* to long narrative Victorian poems like Alfred Tennyson's *In Memoriam* to sentimental novels by Oliver Goldsmith and Marie Corelli.[81] These examples formed part of a colonial canon of literature: a set of texts that, if read, reread, and understood, signaled a reader's inclusion in the literary and cultural discourse of anglophone South Asia. They provided the modern South Asian woman with a tool kit designed to make her both a useful companion to the modern South Asian man and a worthy counterpart to the English woman. In doing so, *The Indian Ladies' Magazine* created what I call a *rereading public*: a community of readers brought together by a sustained and repeated engagement with specific texts. This community coexisted and overlapped with the community created by the "Suggestions for English Reading" column.

The Indian Ladies' Magazine staged the repeated intimacy between English literature and elite South Asian readers in several different forms, each harnessing the relationship between reading, rereading, and memory. Let's turn to an example: the puzzle. In 1908, the magazine organized a series of competitions, all of which centered on literary themes of increasing complexity. In April, readers were asked to solve a word jumble by finding names of characters from Shakespeare's plays (Figure 4.5).[82] By May, the same readers were given the task of identifying passages from "well-known" poems that had been incorrectly quoted, submitting the poem's name and the correct quotation as their answer (Figure 4.6).[83] In July, the competition reached new levels of difficulty (Figure 4.7). Readers were presented with a poem with blanks. Each blank was matched with a corresponding author's name and was to be replaced by the title of one of their literary works. The result, if the puzzle solver was successful, was to be a "set of nonsense verses in the same metre as that in which Wordsworth's 'We are Seven' is written."[84]

Designed to test a reader's repertoire, these puzzles are an index of what South Asian women were reading, giving us a clear sense of the texts with which the early twentieth-century reading public was expected to be familiar. Taken collectively, the puzzles are a test of memory. Could the reader remember the names of all the books they'd read? The names of the characters in those books? Did the reader read attentively—attentively enough to identify misquotations so minor that they would escape even the closest of readers? The demands of this puzzle may seem absurd to a contemporary reader, even redundant in the age of Google. But *The Indian Ladies' Magazine* reported that

A Puzzle Competition
THE SHAKESPEARE-NAMES PUZZLE.

(Taken from the Girls' Own Paper.)

DIRECTIONS.

The 144 letters make up the names of characters in Shakespeare's Plays. To find a name begin at *any* letter for the initial, but each succeeding letter must be in a square touching the one just used. No square may be used twice in the same name.

Lists should be sent in thus—
A D A M   14, 13, 26, 27.
D I A N   13, 1, 14, 2, 3, etc.

Lists must be addressed to The Editor, The *Indian Ladies' Magazine*, Royapet, Madras. "Shakespeare-Names Puzzle" to be written in the top left-hand corner of the envelope. Each list must be headed with the name and address of the sender.

No lists will, in any case, be returned.

A prize of Rs. 5 will be given for the longest list of names sent in; and, if they so desire, the names of the competitors will be mentioned. The last day for receiving the lists is the 31st May, 1908.

1	2	3	4	5	6	7	8	9	10	11	12
I	N	A	I	A	I	L	C	A	L	N	E
13	14	15	16	17	18	19	20	21	22	23	24
D	A	L	S	C	J	O	E	I	A	G	R
25	26	27	28	29	30	31	32	33	34	35	36
R	A	M	E	A	B	Y	T	U	B	P	E
37	38	39	40	41	42	43	44	45	46	47	48
I	A	N	X	S	S	R	T	M	S	G	U
49	50	51	52	53	54	55	56	57	58	59	60
R	G	D	A	N	E	U	A	O	V	C	S
61	62	63	64	65	66	67	68	69	70	71	72
I	E	U	S	T	I	C	S	N	I	D	E
73	74	75	76	77	78	79	80	81	82	83	84
L	H	O	I	O	U	I	N	S	S	C	A
85	86	87	88	89	90	91	92	93	94	95	96
O	C	Y	N	Q	G	R	E	L	U	E	Y
97	98	99	100	101	102	103	104	105	106	107	108
H	E	Y	U	A	T	O	C	W	L	L	F
109	110	111	112	113	114	115	116	117	118	119	120
L	R	M	R	B	E	D	M	E	D	S	O
121	122	123	124	125	126	127	128	129	130	131	132
E	O	D	E	N	A	R	O	N	D	E	R
133	134	135	136	137	138	139	140	141	142	143	144
L	P	H	I	C	K	D	I	O	A	L	D

N.B.—In the January number of the *Indian Ladies' Magazine*, a prize competition was given, more as a trial than as competition. To this many answers were sent in; and the Editor encouraged by the ready answers to the puzzel is giving this new competition, in the hope that it will meet with the same success as the former one. This time, a prize will be given.

FIGURE 4.5. "A Puzzle Competition: The Shakespeare-Names Puzzle," *The Indian Ladies' Magazine* 7, no. 10 (April 1908): 333, © British Library Board, P.P.3778.bc.

THE INDIAN LADIES' MAGAZINE   363

New Prize Competition.

THE "CORRECT-PASSAGES" QUOTATION.

THE following passages are *incorrectly* quoted from well-known poems, written by poets now deceased. Mention the poem, its author, and give the correct quotation of each.

(1) "What thou art we know not.
     What is most like to thee?
     From rainy clouds there flow not
     Drops so bright to see,
     As from thy presence showers a flood of melody."

(2) "Till then, ye ancient warriors,
     Our song and feast shall flow
     To the fame of your name
     When the stormy tempests blow."

(3) "Come unto these yellow sands,
     And then take hands . . . .
     Foot it neatly here and there
     And sweet sprites the burden bear."

(4) "Earth has not anything to show more fair;
     Dull would he be of soul who would pass by
     A sight so touching in its majesy."

(5) "His house was known to all the vagrant train;
     He chid their wandering, but relieved their pain.
     The long-remembered beggar was a guest . . . . .

Pleased with his guests, the good man seemed
     to glow,
And quite forgot their vices in their woe."

(6) "There in thy scanty mantle clad
     Thy snowy boson sunward prest,
     Thou lifts thy unassuming head
     In humble guise;
     But now the share upturns thy nest,
     And low thou lies!"

(7) "If I am right, thy power impart,
     Still in the right to say;
     If I am wrong, then teach my heart
     To find that better way."

(8) "When can their glory fade?
     Oh, the grand charge they made
     While everyone wondered."

(9) "Smack went the whip, round rolled the wheels,
     Where never folk so glad,
     The stones did rattle underneath
     As if Cheapside were mad."

A prize of five rupees will be awarded to the most successful competitor.

Answers to be written on one side of paper only. Name and address to be written on top of each page. If more than one sheet is used, they must be fastened together. When possible lists should be numbered and in alphabetical order.

*** No questions concerning the working of the competitions will be answered in the magazine, or by post, even if stamps be sent for that purpose. Should a greater number of competitors present equally correct answers, that shall be deemed most deserving whose MSS is most clear, clean, plentiful and pleasing.

The last day for receiving the answers is June 20th 1908.

FIGURE 4.6. "New Prize Competition: The 'Correct-Passages' Quotation," *The Indian Ladies' Magazine* 7, no. 11 (May 1908): 363, © British Library Board, P.P.3778.bc.

each puzzle had multiple winners, often too many for a prize to be meaningfully awarded.[85] This is evidence that the puzzles were an accurate reflection of the reading habits and skills of the magazine's readers and that they, too, believed in this intellectual performance. It wasn't enough to have simply read a literary text. Readers had to have memorable lines, the names of characters, and discussion points at the tips of their fingers, all as visible markers of the act of reading.

Another form that literary opining took in the magazine was the long essay, a prolonged rumination on the value of a single literary text. At first glance, these essays look somewhat like the essays that made up the "Suggestions for English Reading" column. There was, however, a crucial difference. *Those* essays were designed to entice readers to pick up a book they hadn't the cottagers, but give themselves free access to the lake. How was the wall to be built?

(The correct answers to the last two little puzzles will appear in our next number.)

Our Prize Competitions.

here were many answers to our "correct verses" competition, and most of them were correct and neatly written. Consequently, it is difficult to award the prize. I have, therefore, decided to transfer the prize to the following new competition, which will have a prize of Rs. 10.

New Prize Competition.

PUZZLE VERSES.

In the following verses take away each author's name and replace it by the title of one of his books. The result will be a set of nonsense verses in the same metre as that in which Wordsworth's "We are Seven" is written.

To (CHARLOTTE BRONTE).

Farewell! my (W. W. Jacobs)
  We met (C. Kingsley)
And now I've lost (C. M. Yonge)
  I'm sailing (C. Kingsley)
Over the sea shores (N. Gale)
  While with (C. Dickens)
I read strange (E. A. Poe)
  I wish they'd never end!

We pass near (Sir W. Scott), and then
  With (Sir W. Scott) for our mate,
We travel all (Mrs. Henry Wood)
  At most terrific rate,
(Jules Verne),
  We near (H. Cockton)
Our craft is bound for (D. Sladen)
  At last it runs aground!

"(S. Smiles) and (S. Smiles) are all we need,"
  Exclaims (Sir W. Scott)
"(H. Sienkiewicz)?" questions (F. H. Burnett)
  We answer, "On (J. F. Cooper)."
(J. F. Cooper) are with us now
  And (L. Carroll)
So through (R. N. Carey)
  We (T. Carlyle) bravely go.

We meet with (A. Dumas)
  And shoot at them with (Mrs. Molesworth)
The noise when (W. M. Thackeray) fires
  Is like the screech of parrots.
We run into (Mrs. Molesworth)
  The (G. A. Henty)
And tumble (L. Carroll)
  (S. R. Crockett) to save.

Our (Rev. W. H. Fitchett) vast
  Would startle (R. D. Blackmore)
(W. Irving) bold are they!
  I'll tell them to you soon.
For shortly, (Edna Lyall)
  With (F. Anstey) to carry
My (C. Bronte), I'll come home to you,
  At (W. H. Ainsworth) we'll marry.

A prize of Rs. 10 will be awarded to the most successful competitor. The papers to be sent in not later than July 31st.

Our Needle Work Column.

APPLIQUE EMBROIDERY.

A VERY effective style of work, especially suitable for large pieces which will be seen at a distance when finished, or for curtains or hangings, is applique. There is no single word in English which expresses it, probably because it did not originate with us. The nearest is "applied work," and it is really the art of laying one material on to another to form a pattern. This pattern may be designed to require more than one colour in the treatment, but these colours will be distinct in themselves, without shade.

The rule in applique is to put the richer material you are using on to the inferior one. For instance, silk, satin, or velvet may be applied on to serge or linen, or on to materials of their own quality; linen may be applied on to linen, but never apply serge or linen on to silk or satin. The material you are applying must first be backed, to make it thoroughly strong, and to prevent it ravelling or turning up at the edges when it is cut out.

First make an embroidery paste in the following way:—Mix well together three tablespoonfuls of flour, and half-a-teaspoonful of powdered resin, in a one pound jar nearly full of cold water. Place the jar in a saucepanful of water and stir continually until the paste boils. Let it boil slowly for two or three hours, with an occasional stir, and allow it to grow cold before using. This paste will keep for several days. Then either frame, or stretch tightly on a board with drawing pins, a piece of nainsook or fine linen, and with your hand, from which you will have removed any ring or rings you may be wearing, paste this all over very smoothly and evenly with the paste you have ready, taking especial care to remove any lumps that may be in the paste, from the baking, or these will show through your material. Wash your hands quickly, and place the material you are applying wrong side down on to the pasted backing. Press this down very firmly and smoothly and leave it to dry thoroughly, if possible, for twelve hours.

read before, signaled by how they framed the text under discussion as uncharted territory. Instead, *these* articles leaned on haphazard forms of plot summary sprinkled with occasional commentary to present their literary objects as excessively familiar landscapes. As a mode of reengagement with a text, they pose an important question: Why write an essay about books that everyone's read?

The impulses of *The Indian Ladies' Magazine*'s literary output find an anachronistic counterpoint in a contemporary form of writing: the television show recap. Linked to the rise of internet forum cultures in the early 2000s, the recap emerged as the distinctive genre for writing about television. Taking a single episode as its unit for analysis, the recap was an elaborate act of re-narration. Walking the reader through the episode's narrative arc, a typical example of the genre recounted the major plot points interspersed with reflections, reactions, and analysis. Unlike a review, it wasn't oriented toward a future relationship, designed to recruit potential viewers to watch a show (or ward them off). Unlike a summary, it wasn't just a simple aid to memory or a substitute for the act of watching the episode. Rather, the form of the recap was directed at a very specific slice of the television-watching public. It was aimed at the subset of people who had already watched the episode under discussion.[86]

For this reason, many recaps came with a warning label: "Don't read this article if you haven't watched Episode X of Show Y." Recaps were, after all, not designed to spoil the fun of watching an episode for the first time. As miniature, condensed versions of the original, they provided an opportunity to relive the experience of watching through the mode of reading and the medium of print. It's worth remembering that the form of the recap was fueled by the so-called Golden Age of Television, when prestige shows occupied an outsized and unified position in cultural discourse and conversation. Beyond considerations of plot, the recap provided a space for viewers to mull collectively over the latest episode of *The Sopranos*, *Mad Men*, or *Game of Thrones*, rationalizing events, siding with characters, and expressing feelings of excitement or disappointment about how the series' stories were unfolding.[87]

There were logistical reasons for why the literary recap was a key mode of textual engagement. Again, there was the question of memory. Mrs. A. Zechariah, the author of "Books and Reading," published in the magazine's December 1908 issue, outlined the importance of reading to the intellectual development of young women. Zechariah's culminating advice to readers was: don't forget what you read. "Young people are apt to think they can remember all they can read, but experience will teach you to think differently," she scolded.[88] The lecture culminated in a series of techniques to compensate for a reader's memory. Among these were making notes, underlining salient portions of texts, memorizing speeches and stanzas, and writing summaries of books and sketches of their characters. More than just an aid to remembering, these practices were intended to ensure that "what you read may become part of you."[89] These were crucial modes of recapitulating the highlights of a literary text. Put another way, Zechariah's advice for young readers was to develop private, individual forms of recapping, whether through marginalia in a book or carefully written and preserved in a diary, to both sustain and recall the original act of reading.

Read alongside Zechariah's mandate, the literary recaps in *The Indian Ladies' Magazine* emerge as a practical tool. Drawing on all the techniques Zechariah recommends—summaries, character sketches, selecting memorable passages—they served as sites for rereading. Through an interplay of plot reconstruction and critical commentary, readers reexperienced the act of reading *through* the form of the literary essay. Recreating pivotal moments from the plot of a novel or reproducing memorable stanzas from a poem, the literary essay allowed readers to relive the gist of their experiences reading the original text. With the literary recap operating on the assumption of an act of original reading—that is, that the text under discussion had already been read by the magazine's audience—it eliminated the need to revisit that text, insisting that the recap could substitute for an act of reading again. That is, *The Indian Ladies' Magazine* recapped *In Memoriam* or *The Merchant of Venice*, not despite the fact that its audience had already read these texts, but because of it. The recap enabled what the act of reading a book in isolation didn't quite achieve successfully: it allowed women to form invisible communities with fellow readers from across the subcontinent or even, potentially, from across the world, who shared the same reading list.

Michael Warner has shown us that reading any literary text—or indeed, any text at all—allows a reader to imagine themselves in an abstract public constituted of far-flung strangers.[90] Patricia Spacks puts this pithily: "No one ever reads alone."[91] As Gillian Silverman has argued for the nineteenth-century United States, reading provided an "alternative route to intimacy," allowing people to connect across race and class divides. Reading could "enable unfamiliar or illicit forms of social intercourse, avenues for imagined contact with individuals who were otherwise unreachable. In so doing, reading offered a different mode of *being* in the world, one less constrained by norms of privacy, propriety, and individuation."[92] Against historical conditions of segregation and racialized forms of power, the reading public could emerge as an imagined, and therefore egalitarian, space.

My contention is that the recap essay and the modes of rereading it inculcated created forms of sociality that exceeded the ambit of the original literary text. It was this ability that made the magazine required reading. As I argued in the introduction to this chapter, stories of elite South Asian women reading English books were commonly stories of isolation and loneliness. Publics reproduce the racial hierarchies of the worlds from which they draw members. The form of the recap, published in the pages of *The Indian Ladies' Magazine*, made an important amendment to these anxieties of belonging. By identifying *South Asian* readers as part of the audience of the recap, it also acknowledged them as readers of the English books under discussion. Crucially, by bringing together South Asian and English readers and contributors in proximity to each other, the magazine's form dramatizes a reading public in which strangers became friends. Drawing on tropes of reading together, talking together, and watching together, it recast its readers not as silent participants, reading alone in their homes, but as active interlocutors discussing and arguing the merits of a literary work. In doing so, the reading public of the magazine—a self-proclaimed conduit between South Asian and British women—did something the English literary text could not. It allowed South Asian women readers to feel in communion with their British, often distant, counterparts, brought together by their shared reading material. The recap, in short, was a textual infrastructure, laying out the pathways and building the bridges that allowed South Asian women to seek out the company of like-minded readers, if only in the thin pages of *The Indian Ladies' Magazine*.

Let's consider two extended examples from the magazine. The first is an essay titled "My Impressions of 'East Lynn'[*sic*]."[93] Published in the November 1901 issue of the magazine, the essay recounts the plot of Ellen Wood's popular sensational novel, *East Lynne* (1861). The novel follows the marriage of Isabel Vane and Archibald Carlyle and has all the stereotypical markers of a Victorian melodrama: disinherited property, suspected infidelity, actual infidelity, illegitimate children, sudden and tragic accidents, death by tuberculosis, and a concluding scene of deathbed forgiveness. The essay's author, Stephen Balm, starts by announcing the immense popularity of the novel: "Thousands have admired Carlyle for his untainted character and nobility of mind and ten thousands have wept over the sad fate of Isabel, the heroine of the tale."[94] The loose quantification of the novel's readership—thousands and ten thousands—confirms that it was a bestselling hit in its own time, even as it has been mostly forgotten by contemporary readers. Beyond the availability of *East Lynne* in its original form, translations and adaptations into local languages circulated across South Asia from the novel's publication into the early twentieth century.[95] Charles Wood, the author's son, wrote in his biography about the novel's particular resonance with South Asian readers: "Indian readers will gather a large circle of Hindoos around them, and read the book to them in their own tongue; seated upon the ground, the listeners rock themselves to and fro and laugh and weep by turns."[96]

It's highly likely that the readers of *The Indian Ladies' Magazine* would have already read or encountered *East Lynne* in one form or another, whether through the original or an adaptation. This expectation is further reflected in the structure of the recap. Here is a passage that summarizes the events of chapter 12 of the novel:

> Every reader knows how business takes Carlyle to Castle Marling; how, he pays a flying visit to Isabel; how he meets her with tears in her eyes; how, on seeing him, she tries to suppress her tears and will not tell him why she is crying; how her little cousin comes out innocently with the truth: "Oh! mamma, beat Isabel;" how Carlyle, moved by the sight of her weeping and eager to emancipate her from the thraldom of her jealous and cruel aunt, asks if she loves him and will consent to be his wife, and how she replies "I don't love you, but I like you as a friend," and how, with a magnanimity of mind, he asks her "to learn to love him."[97]

The synopsis focuses less on the literary style or the development of characters in the novel than on the meaty, dramatic parts of its plot. The recap's reliance on plot summary wasn't intended as a teaser of the novel-to-come. Indeed, if the readers of the article *hadn't* read the novel already, the techniques of recapping would spoil the suspense of encountering the novel for the first time. Instead, the recap became a space for staging rereadings of *East Lynne*. Reconfiguring the relationship between the part (the article) and the whole (*East Lynne*), the form operated under the assumption that rereading the plot of the novel would recreate the feeling of reading it for the first, second, or third time.

The passage, a condensed version of events in chapter 12 of the novel, is set up as a moment of remembering. As the reader of the essay reads the plot point being described, she remembers the moment in which that point occurs in the novel. Toggling between a past experience of reading and a present one, between the absent book and its impression in one's memory, the recap is the bridge through which to rekindle the first instance of reading. The cascading effect of the run-on sentences relays the visceral experience of reading the novel, heightened by an entire chapter's events summarized in just over a hundred words. Some paragraphs down, the essay's author asks the readers: "Need I relate what occurred after she had witnessed this heartrendering [sic] scene?"[98] He then immediately proceeds to do so, not because the readers don't remember, but because telling them what occurred is integral to their individual acts of rereading. We might say that to read the recap was to read the novel again.

By drawing readers back into a novel they'd already read, the recap of *East Lynne* purposefully curates a sense of community. Take, for one, the references to "every reader" in the passage above. In this rhetorical gesture, Balm's recap poses a question for the audience of *East Lynne*: Did *you* feel the sentiment the recap describes when you read the novel? If the answer is yes, the reader's response not only resonates with Balm's. To establish a commonality between their response and the critic's is to remind them that their experiences of reading the novel are universal. Their reading is representative of the reading of others. This realization is key to the intent of the recap, reminding us that we always read in the company of others. While the novel's public was invisible, *The Indian Ladies' Magazine*'s wasn't. Satthianadhan published records of new subscribers in early issues, allowing readers to see exactly who else was reading the magazine. These lists put a name to some of the imaginary readers evoked by Balm and other contributors. The recap recasts the public as more than a relationship between strangers. Perhaps a relationship between almost-friends?

This sense of reading community is staged differently elsewhere in the essay. Most commonly, it is presented as a debate between the author of the essay and the novel's readers. Two pages into his three-page article, Balm abruptly stops his act of re-narration: "We must stop here, for it is unnecessary to go further into the narrative for our present purpose."[99] Instead, he presents his audience with a question for discussion: "[W]ho was to blame—Carlyle or Isabel?" Balm's own response is even-keeled. Carlyle is a "man of irreproachable character." Since "everything looks yellow to the jaundiced eye," Isabel's irrational jealousy should be excused, too.[100] Balm was clearly wading into a hot topic of discussion among *East Lynne*'s readers, following up his opinion with an exhortation: "Blame not, therefore, ye readers of East Lynn, the conduct of Isabel!"[101] Key here is Balm's tone, which is dramatic, attesting to the passionate heights to which the debate might be taken. But presented as an imperative and addressed to a collective of readers, it's also didactic, attesting to his position of authority as a critic. Addressing "ye readers of East Lynn" as a group, Balm's words set up conditions for further (imagined?) debate among eager readers and fans: Did they support Carlyle and blame Isabel? To participate in the novel's recapping was to place one's opinion in conversation with that of other, unseen, interlocutors.

My second example takes up the subject of the reading community even more forcefully. The May 1911 issue of *The Indian Ladies' Magazine* contained an article on Shakespeare's *The Merchant of Venice*, a magazine favorite.[102] While the *East Lynne* recap walked its readers through the major plot points of the novel, this essay starts at the final moments of the play:

> [T]he curtain falls and "The Merchant of Venice" comes to a close. Ah! what a feeling of regret overtakes us when our dear old play is no more before us! Our revered Antonio was familiar to us in the calm and sad gravity from which he was not often separable. Our friends, the gallant Bassanio, the revengeful and avaricious Shylock, the clever and noble Portia triumphing over all, the pedantic Lorenzo, and his pretty Jessica, have all disappeared from our vision.
>
> When we were engaged in "the two hours' traffic" of the stage, there was a source of new delight. The good old tale of Venice brought us friends in the fascinating and romantic characters of the signiors and ladies of medieval Venice. The performance which we gave diverted our attention and exercised our fancy. We were transported to a new world and altogether an attractive one. We lived in the unreal void of material concerns. We met our friends, talked to our ladies and ordered our servants about, with perfect ease.
>
> When we bid farewell to a friend, we fondly recollect the hours we have spent with him in the past; and so let us take ourselves back through the changing scenes of "The Merchant of Venice." The curtain rises . . .[103]

The passage describes *The Merchant of Venice* not as a text—printed, bound, and circulated—but as its ephemeral version, the stage play. Switching out metaphors for reading a book for metaphors for watching a play undergirds *The Indian Ladies' Magazine*'s project of community building among and across its women readers. No play has an audience of one. The structure of the theater reminds us that watching a performance of a play is, by necessity, a social activity, predominately conducted with friends and other companions, with whom the performance can be discussed retrospectively. Even the individual theatergoer can't avoid encountering others in the space of the playhouse, as they brush shoulders with other audience members, whether in a line outside the theater or in their seating row. In contrast to the public act of watching a play, by the early twentieth century, most scenes of reading were individual and private. Through its extended analogy to the theater, the recap of *The Merchant of Venice* attempts to recapture the sociable aspect of theatergoing for women's acts of solitary reading, simulating moments of intellectual companionship that the readers would have experienced together in the space of the school or university classroom, and in the family drawing room.

Elsewhere in the magazine, contributors emphasized the value of reading as a tool for gender reform, intellectual growth, and moral development. The recap of *The Merchant of Venice* provides no pedantic thoughts on Portia as a role model for South Asian women or any elaborate description of the play's literary value. Rather, rereading (or rewatching, as it were) is described in terms of friendship. Just as one misses the company of friends and loved ones, one can miss the company of a book. The goal of rereading, then, is not to know more or better, but rather to reproduce conditions in which one wasn't alone. But it's not just that the experience of watching or reading *The Merchant of Venice* is analogous to friendship. Characters in the play also court familiarity as friends. This conceit—of referring to characters in books as friends—appears across *The Indian Ladies' Magazine*. In March 1902, Satthianadhan commended Shakespeare on the vividness of his writing, comparing Portia to a "portrait [that] ever afterwards lives in our mind like that of an old and dear friend."[104] In December 1906, an "Indian Lady" remarked in "An Estimate of Shakespeare's Desdemona": "In my hours of reflection, my fancy revels in confounding my personal friends with those I have among Shakespeare's characters."[105] To cast fictional characters into human relationships is to imagine oneself not just in the public of the play and in the company of others, but as a silent participant in the play itself.

Coda: *Nashtanirh* and the Failures of Reading Together

The Indian Ladies' Magazine presents itself as a practical tool, one that allowed women to reimagine radically what it meant to be part of an intellectual and affective community. Where its readers might have been isolated in colonial outposts, the magazine filled a void, creating the possibility of dialogue—if only imaginary—with other readers from across South Asia, even the world.

By deploying specific genre conventions, ranging from reprinting to reading lists to recap articles, *The Indian Ladies' Magazine* operated as a technology of recognition, allowing South Asian women to be seen and acknowledged as readers, often in contradiction to prevailing gendered and racial dynamics.

This coda presents a cautionary footnote to the aspirational story of *The Indian Ladies' Magazine* by turning to Rabindranath Tagore's Bengali-language novella, *Nashtanirh* [The Broken Nest] (1901).[106] Published in the same year as the first issue of *The Indian Ladies' Magazine*, its protagonist, Charulata (or Charu, as her family calls her), bears many similarities to the readers of the magazine. She's from an elite Bengali Brahmin family. She's literate (in Bengali) and her desire for education is supported by her liberal husband, Bhupati. Like many of the readers of *The Indian Ladies' Magazine*, Charu is also desperately bored. She has no children and few domestic duties. Over the course of the novella, she doesn't leave the house even once. Satyajit Ray's sensuous filmic rendition of the novella is called *Charulata* (1964), taking its name from the protagonist.[107] Tellingly, the English title of the film is "The Lonely Wife." That's what Charu is throughout the novella and film: lonely.

Like many late nineteenth- and early twentieth-century colonial novels, *Nashtanirh* is filled with references to material texts. Volumes of Tennyson's poetry and Bankim's novels, letters, telegrams, blank and filled notebooks, and unpaid bills accumulate in the novella's plot. But the drama of the novella is propelled by the characters' interactions with two printed genres: the periodical and the newspaper. While these genres are defined by their communitarian aspects, their capacity to open up worlds and build relationships, *Nashtanirh* is marred by the failure of these characteristic functions. The novella's characters use the periodical and the newspaper to hone private fantasies that prevent them from participating in the kinds of intellectual communities we associate with a publication like *The Indian Ladies' Magazine*. Reading, in short, is no cure for loneliness. By the end of the novella, newspapers and periodicals have only served to drive people apart, creating unfulfilled desires, ruining friendships, and destroying marriages.

The Indian Ladies' Magazine, like other examples of the form, was filled with readers' thoughts and comments on the publication's content. Ranging from letters to the editor, responses to literary quizzes, and articles submitted to the "Our Special Indian Lady Contributors' Column," these forums provided readers with opportunities to shape the magazine's future issues through their critiques and praise. These are crucial sources for writing the reception history of the magazine, but it's worth considering their limitations. First, there's the problem of selection bias. The magazine was an intensely curated space, with Satthianadhan single-handedly deciding what was included in each issue. There's no way of determining, for example, which submissions and letters *weren't* published and what opinions they contained. Second, there's the problem of self-curation. Unlike the scribbles on the pages of the almanacs of chapter 3, articles and letters to the editor were intended for an audience greater than one. They were carefully crafted performances in erudition. In short, they replicate the anxieties of self-presentation that the magazine seeks to assuage in its readers.

Nashtanirh provides us with an opportunity to read *The Indian Ladies' Magazine* against the grain. As a novella focused on the interiority of its characters, it is a representation of the deepest, most private acts of periodical reading outside the glare of public judgment and prying eyes. Rather, at its highest level, *Nashtanirh* presents a portrait of how readers responded to the *genre* of the periodical, a genre of which *The Indian Ladies' Magazine* is exemplary. In what follows, I provide an instance of a recursive reception history that places functional and literary archives in dialogue with each other. If the earlier sections of the chapter showed how the magazine can be used as a source for the reception of literary works, this coda shows how a literary work can provide insight into the reception of the genre of the magazine. Together, reader responses documented in magazines *and* literary representations of their circulation, allow us to construct the uses and misuses to which periodicals were put at the beginning of the twentieth century in colonial South Asia.

As we've seen in the earlier sections of this chapter, reading together is imprinted in every issue of *The Indian Ladies' Magazine*, whether through the formal adoption of the tropes of pedagogical instruction or the invisible communities that the "News and Notes" column and the recap articles constructed. Similarly, in *Nashtanirh*, whom characters choose to read with signals shifts in plot and sentiment. At various points in the novella, Bhupati presents different projects of reading together to save his marriage to Charu. He reads Tennyson to her, translating the English lines into Bengali as he goes along. When the English-language daily that preoccupies him is shut down, he proposes a new joint endeavor: a bilingual newspaper with him overseeing the political English-language content and Charu the Bengali-language literary content.

Unlike many of *The Indian Ladies' Magazine*'s readers, Charu reads not for self-improvement or the development of some inchoate interiority. Instead, literature serves a literal and material prop in her relationship with Amal, her brother-in-law and love interest. Reading is the primary way in which the two can legitimately spend time together, with Amal playing the role of tutor and Charu of tutee. In these moments, the two share their time reading literary periodicals, discussing contemporary fiction, and poring over Amal's florid, pretentious literary experiments. But Charu and Amal's exercises of reading together are short-lived. When Amal's composition, "Notebook," is published in *Sharoruha*, a local literary periodical, Charu realizes that she is no longer Amal's sole reader. He begins to receive public attention, followed by flirtatious fan letters from his women readers, populating their literary space with hundreds of readers and commentators: "Now everyone would read that composition, and many would praise it."[108] The emphasis falls on the word *everyone*. *Everyone* is the imagined community of readers aggregating around Amal's literary composition and intruding forcefully upon Charu's consciousness. In Charu's worst moments, she worries that "all at once the closed doors to their committee sessions stood open, and a Bengali readers' circle stood between them."[109]

Recall that the aim of *The Indian Ladies' Magazine* was to create a space for debate, allowing readers to participate in cultural and literary discussions from which they were often far removed. The hypothetical "Bengali readers' circle" does just that, making Amal's writing a subject of multiple conversations among a wide range of interlocutors. The periodical in which he publishes his composition has the effect of breaking down barriers and forging intellectual communities. Amal soon realizes that replacing real-world relationships with imaginary ones has its upsides. Imaginary communities never disappoint because they're imaginary. Charu, by contrast, continuously disappoints, failing to be the co-reader Amal wants her to be. Her jealousy mars Amal's success, and she starts to write compositions of her own that gain local fame and popularity, to the detriment of his own literary reputation.

For Charu, the scenario presents differently. Breaking down the doors to Charu's committee meetings of two, these readers violently burst in, intrusively inserting themselves into a private space and a private conversation. Rather than imbuing the "Bengali readers' circle" with the liberatory potential of an imagined community, the periodical evolves in her mind instead into a fearsome document, threatening to rip the covers off existing relationships. Charu panics. Her response to Amal's success is to suggest that they start a periodical of their own. Copied by hand, the periodical, she tells him, will be "just yours and mine," "[n]o one else will read it. We'll put out only two copies, one for you, one for me."[110] Contrast this with *The Indian Ladies' Magazine*'s promotion of reading as a sociable, if often solitary, activity. Instead, Charu's proposed project fundamentally misunderstands the role of a periodical, reappropriating the form to private ends. Radically putting the periodical out of circulation, she transforms it into a document for the smallest of coterie audiences. The periodical remains the cornerstone of the act of reading together, but only when Charu can dictate who is permitted to participate. The failure of Charu, Tagore suggests, is ultimately a failure to see the alternative networks of community that a literary career could cultivate for her. Put another way, it's a failure to imagine the power of reading with others.

While *The Indian Ladies' Magazine* is constantly described by its readers as a friend, ultimately there's no comfort to be found in the pages of a periodical for the characters of *Nashtanirh*. This is true not only for Charu and Amal, but also for Charu's husband, Bhupati. Bhupati has little to say about the couple's literary endeavors, absorbed as he is in his role as the editor and publisher of an English-language daily. This newspaper, like the literary periodical, is the novella's specter of failed or misplaced intimacy. Whereas Charu finds herself in an open room with unwanted readers of Amal's work, when it comes to Bhupati, she finds herself on the other side of the door: she is unable to "break down the newspaper barrier and get possession of her husband."[111] Bhupati is described as being "hypnotized" by the newspaper.[112] Replacing the language of friendship from *The Indian Ladies' Magazine* with the language of seduction, the newspaper is cast as a malevolent force, competing with Charu and destroying the possibility of a relationship with Bhupati.

The novella ends with the household falling apart. Amal gets married and leaves in a huff for England to study law; Bhupati's newspaper is shut down and Charu is desolate. In these final moments, Tagore returns to material metaphors to describe Charu's devastation: "All the color drained from her face and left it white and dry, like a piece of paper."[113] The image of the blank piece of paper reminds readers of Amal's essay, "Notebook," the exaggerated paean to white paper that starts the downward spiral of his relationship with Charu:

> "Oh my pure-white notebook, my imagination has not touched you yet. You are unstained. You are as mysterious as the forehead of a child still unmarked by the god of destiny. How distant is the day when I shall finish writing the last line of the conclusion on your last page! Today, not even in dreams do your shining infant pages imagine the concluding words recorded in ink for all eternity . . ."[114]

Written at the beginning of his relationship with Charu, the image of the blank "unstained" page connotes the potential of the unwritten: nothing has been written yet and so anything could be written. Yet when we come to the last page of the novella, that potential has been completely devastated for the characters of *Nashtanirh*, leaving nothing but fragmentary connections in its wake. The notebook fails to fulfill its promise; instead, its last page is the image of Charu's face. If Amal's poem—and *Nashtanirh*—was meant to excite us with the potential of what was not yet written, the last page of the novella and the notebook converge on Charu's paper-white face, a document of being unwritten; not blank, but erased.

Epilogue

FOR CONTEMPORARY SOUTH ASIANS, Dayanita Singh's *File Room* (2013) is a familiar scene of required reading. The collection's photographic subject is paperwork, the routine files and folders that accompany any action in the postcolonial state. Through a series of stunning black-and-white images, Singh follows these objects into the heart of "Indian courts, municipal offices, state archives" to give us a visual depiction of the postcolonial state's entanglement with writing.[1] Some of the photographs depict clerks, peons, and archivists, surrounded by the tools of their trade. These are the people who spend their time curating, transporting, and containing this flood of administrative writing. Other photographs take us deep into the bowels of the archive, peering into storage rooms and cupboards.

The photograph in Figure E.1 is part of Singh's collection. I am immediately struck by its evocative play of presence and absence. To me, the photograph is a throwback to a typical bureaucratic office, familiar to South Asians in the 1960s and 1970s. The files we see, well-worn with frayed edges, suggest active handling and reading. Yet the photograph shows us no readers. We see none of the frenetic activity or the long lines that characterize government offices open for business. Noticeably absent are the streams of visitors we would expect in an office like this, people whose lives are wrapped up in the constant back and forth of the bureaucratic process and, as a result, in the endless cycle of writing and filing. The empty chair is a stand-in for a delinquent bureaucrat, perhaps off on an extra-long lunch break. In this universe, readers can only be invoked through the objects they read, the files that embody their aspirations, struggles, and labor.

None of the folders in this photograph are open, so we're unable to take a peek at the writing they contain. Instead, the image emphasizes Singh's interest in the material life of writing, forcing us to register the moments in which the

FIGURE E.1. Dayanita Singh, Untitled Image, *File Room* (Göttingen, Germany: Steidl, 2013). Reproduced with permission of Dayanita Singh.

file-as-object overwhelms the file-as-text. Tied together by threadbare strings, each file appears to contain more paper than it can reasonably hold. Bursting at the seams, folders accumulate and cluster just about everywhere in the office. They fill up metal cupboards, threaten to fall off metal shelves, spill over tabletops and onto the floor. They overwhelm us with their sheer numbers, at once disorganized and artfully orchestrated. The image, like the room it depicts, is cluttered, unable to frame its subject. *File Room* is an "elegy to paper in the age of the digitization of information and knowledge," a mournful acknowledgment of the mattering of paper against the disembodiment of the digital.[2] The scene of the office, a space where files are living, breathing, reading material, is slowly transformed into the space of the archive, where they are stored, filed away, and rarely consulted.

But Singh's photographs, capturing feelings of nostalgia and memory making, are also a reckoning with the crushing weight of the system, a "confrontation with chaos, mortality, and disorder" that characterizes the administration of a country as populous as India.[3] *File Room* is a meditation on the entanglement of paperwork and the postcolonial state, an entanglement that, as this book has shown, has its roots in the history of British colonialism in South Asia. When I first saw Singh's photographs, I was surprised by how closely they resembled my imagination of what a colonial-era office might have looked like, pieced together from descriptions in literary and historical sources. *Required Reading* has told the history of the British empire in South Asia as the story of an obsession with paper. Developed as a system of governance at-a-distance, British rule was so tightly bound to the acts of writing, recording, and documenting, that its subjects colloquially referred to it as *kaghazi raj* (the "rule of paper"). What started as a penchant for paperwork quickly spiraled into large-scale projects of data collection targeting any and all aspects of life in South Asia. Equally important are the ways in which colonial rule shaped the endeavors of South Asians, who, by the second half of the nineteenth century, had made significant forays into the industry of publishing. Whether produced by the British or by South Asians, petitions, almanacs, magazines, and handbooks came to be the very texts through which empire's subjects and agents confronted, tolerated, and resisted the possibilities and limits of a life under British rule. These texts formed material networks that I have called the functional archive, remnants of which fill our institutional and noninstitutional repositories today. The concept of the functional archive has held the chapters of this book together, allowing us to uncover the ways in which individuals read and felt under the aegis of empire.

Empire's subjects and agents produced a glut of paper of all shapes and sizes with which readers did all kinds of things. This book has made a case for the functional archive as a historical formation, emphasizing that readers encountered ordinary forms of writing as constellations rather than singular objects. Here, I also want to point out the concept's methodological implications and uses. The number of files, records, and books that we still have from the nineteenth century is but a tiny fraction of historical circulation. In the shadow of these objects are the missing, destroyed, and decomposed records that leave indelible gaps in our ability to reconstruct historical narratives. Deployed methodologically, the functional archive can help address historical gaps in the archive. Focusing not just on individual archival items but on the ways in which they make things happen in relation to each other can help us identify lost nodes, even in the absence of documentation. In this way, the functional archive isn't tied to colonial South Asia, even as it takes a particular shape under the historical circumstances of my book. It is my hope that the concept will prove useful to scholars across a number of colonial and postcolonial contexts, where our ability to grasp fully the relationship between people and paper is hindered by the limits of our archival records.

What pulls a military handbook, bureaucratic documents, almanacs, and a magazine into the same story is their shared status as objects that are read. This book's literary and archival explorations reveal the range of reading practices that individuals brought to bear on these constituents of the functional archive. As people rubbed shoulders with these texts, they refused to read, read defiantly, deliberately misread, listened to others read, couldn't read, couldn't understand what they read, weren't acknowledged for the reading that they did. The point of this long list is not to claim exhaustiveness but rather to emphasize that these are merely some ways in which people did (and still do) make sense of the forms of writing that cluttered their daily lives. Throughout this book, I have claimed a capaciousness for what we call reading, pushing the boundaries of what kinds of interpretive, noninterpretive, even anti-interpretive practices can be included under the wide umbrella of this slippery term. Refusing to label some responses as more valuable or intellectually hefty than others, each chapter works against a hierarchization of readerly engagement.

The different reading practices I identify have led me to assemble an entire cast of unlikely readers: annoyed soldiers, overwhelmed bureaucrats, confused peasants, conniving headmen, hurried clerks, and anxious women. In the spirit of acknowledging their common reading material—the functional archive—the history I have constructed in this book juxtaposes readers from across literary, class, and racial divides. The result looks quite different from the demographic models of traditional histories of reading. Chapter 2, for example, drew on evidence from Leonard Woolf, an over-literate, Cambridge-educated intellectual and administrator, but also from illiterate and semiliterate Sinhala readers who left their readerly imprints in the colonial archive. By acknowledging that readers come to texts for different reasons and outcomes, we can write a more inclusive history, one that doesn't just focus on elite, lettered readers who leave thick traces of their textual engagement in the archive for future scholars to find.

The reason that the functional archive, the reading practices that surround it, and the readers who cathect to it have elided sustained scholarly attention is because they don't quite fall into the realm of what, for the lack of a better word, we might call the literary. Our theories of reading come out of the experience of reading literature, or, more specifically, from the model of immersion and transformation that is associated with the form of the novel. Yet these modes of reading hew more closely to each other than is apparent at first glance. Novels can be read in all the ways that my readers approach the functional archive, eliciting forms of not reading, material attachment, and casual perusal, even as these modes of reading remain marginal to our understanding of the novelistic experience. Similarly, an almanac or a handbook can spark effects in its readers that look a lot like those we associate with the realm of the literary text. What this does is open up the possibility of claiming the literary not as an inherent property or quality of a text but rather, as an effect that is generated in the productive interface between a text and a reader.

Required Reading takes as its focus the experiences of historical readers, following their textual encounters and dissecting their responses. But I want to end with a note about a contemporary reader: the literary scholar. Across this book, as I have claimed an aesthetic life for the functional archive, I find myself returning to the methodological affordances of literary studies. This book makes a case for close reading as a tool that has resonance beyond our narrowly defined disciplinary objects. Just as we can close-read a passage from a novel or a couplet from a poem, so we can close-read less charismatic, more mundane texts.

One of the enduring lessons of this book is that literary form and feeling can lurk in the most ordinary of places, in the pleading narratives of melodramatic petitions and in the bored doodles in the margins of almanacs. By reclaiming the files and folders of the functional archive for our shared discipline, this book's ambition has been to use literary methods to reanimate a whole range of everyday forms of writing. Like the historical readers that populate the pages of this book, we might uncover aesthetic power where we least expect it.

NOTES

Introduction

1. Rudyard Kipling, *Departmental Ditties and Other Verses* (Lahore: Civil and Military Gazette Press, 1886).

2. Kipling was born in India in 1865, living in the region till he was five years old. He spent the rest of his childhood in England, returning to Lahore in 1882.

3. Rudyard Kipling, "My First Book," in *The Idler Magazine: An Illustrated Monthly*, Vol. 2, August 1892 to January 1893, eds. Jerome K. Jerome and Robert Barr (London: Chatto and Windus, 1893), 481. Kipling's essay appeared in the December issue.

David Alan Richards's bibliography of Kipling's works estimates a print run of five hundred copies for *Departmental Ditties*. See David Alan Richards, *Rudyard Kipling: A Bibliography* (London: Oak Knoll Press/British Library, 2010), 12. James McG. Stewart puts the number at around 350 copies. See James McG. Stewart, *Rudyard Kipling: A Bibliographical Catalogue*, ed. A.W. Yeats (Toronto: Dalhousie University Press and Toronto University Press, 1959), 21.

4. Kipling, "My First Book," 481.

5. Kipling, "My First Book," 481. For the legal and copyright implications of the form of *Departmental Ditties*, see Shafquat Towheed, "Two Paradigms of Literary Production: The Production, Circulation and Legal Status of Rudyard Kipling's *Departmental Ditties* and Indian Railway Library Texts," in *Books Without Borders, Volume 2: Perspectives from South Asia*, eds. Robert Fraser and Mary Hammond (Basingstoke, UK: Palgrave, 2008), 127–34.

6. Kipling, "My First Book," 481.

7. I take the term "contact zone" from Mary Louise Pratt. Pratt defines "contact zones" as "social spaces where cultures meet, clash, and grapple with each other, often in contexts of highly asymmetrical relations of power, such as colonialism, slavery, or their aftermaths as they are lived out in many parts of the world today." See Pratt, "Arts of the Contact Zone," *Profession* (1991): 34. See also Pratt, *Imperial Eyes: Travel Writing and Transculturation* (London: Routledge, 1992).

8. My use of the word "duress" follows from Ann Laura Stoler's discussion of duress as a concept that can help illuminate the violence of colonial legacies. See Stoler, *Duress: Imperial Durabilities in Our Times* (Durham, NC: Duke University Press, 2016), especially 3–36; 336–80.

9. John Stuart Mill, "The East India Company's Charter," in *Writings on India* [1852], eds. John M. Robson, Martin Moir, and Zawahir Moir (Toronto: University of Toronto Press, 1990), 33.

10. Thomas Richards, *The Imperial Archive: Knowledge and the Fantasy of Empire* (London: Verso, 1993), 1.

11. A full account of the precolonial histories of writing and bureaucracy is outside the scope of this book. It's worth noting that in its early years, the East India Company built on the extant infrastructure of the Mughal empire, in an effort, as Robert Travers puts it, "to colonize the personnel, protocols, and idioms of late Mughal governance." See Travers, *Empires of Complaints: Mughal Law and the Making of British India, 1765–1793* (Cambridge: Cambridge University Press, 2022), 3. For more on the relationship between Mughal and British forms of governance, see Travers, *Empires of Complaints*; Nandini Chatterjee, *Negotiating Mughal Law: A Family of Landlords Across Three Mughal Empires* (Cambridge: Cambridge University Press, 2020).

In the period leading up to 1852—the year we hear from Mill—the East India Company's system of written accountability had reached an unprecedented scale, drawing on a range of written genres, the quantitative powers of statistics, and a complex system of cross-referencing to track written documents. For the relationship between colonial rule and bureaucratic writing in South Asia, see, among others: C.A. Bayly, *Empire and Information: Intelligence Gathering and Social Communication in India, 1780–1870* (Cambridge: Cambridge University Press, 1996); Miles Ogborn, *Indian Ink: Script and Print in the Making of the English East India Company* (Chicago: University of Chicago Press, 2007); Bhavani Raman, *Document Raj: Writing and Scribes in Early Colonial South India* (Chicago: Chicago University Press, 2012).

12. These anecdotes, taken from another report written by Tennent, are republished in James Emerson Tennent, *Ceylon: An Account of the Island, Physical, Historical, and Topographical with Notices of Its Natural History, Antiquities and Productions*, Vol. 2 (London: Longman, 1859), 173.

13. Quoted in Ranajit Guha, "Not at Home in Empire," *Critical Inquiry* 23, no. 2 (1997): 483.

14. Bernard S. Cohn, *Colonialism and Its Forms of Knowledge: The British in India* (Princeton, NJ: Princeton University Press, 1996).

15. George Abraham Grierson, ed., *Linguistic Survey of India* (Calcutta: Office of the Superintendent of Government Printing, 1903–28), 11 vols. For more on Grierson's project, see Javed Majeed, *Nation and Region in Grierson's Linguistic Survey of India* (Delhi: Routledge, 2019).

16. *The Imperial Gazetteer of India* (London: Trubner, 1881), 9 vols. A second edition of fourteen volumes was produced in 1886. The 1900 edition of twenty-six volumes was published posthumously.

17. Antoinette Burton and Isabel Hofmeyr, "Introduction: The Spine of Empire? Books and the Making of an Imperial Commons," in *Ten Books That Shaped the British Empire: Creating an Imperial Commons*, eds. Antoinette Burton and Isabel Hofmeyr (Durham, NC: Duke University Press, 2014), 1–2.

18. If of interest to my readers: Major C., *Indian Horse Notes: An Epitome on Useful Information, Arranged for Ready Reference on Emergencies Specially Adapted for Officers and Country Residents* (Calcutta: Thacker, Spink, and Co., 1885).

19. While I focus on the functional archive in colonial South Asia, similar versions of the formation appear across diverse historical and geographical contexts. For example, Oz Frankel explores how the US and British governments embarked on projects of collection and publication targeted at their domestic populations who, in turn, also responded to these programs through the medium of print. See Oz Frankel, *States of Inquiry: Social Investigations and Print*

Culture in Nineteenth-Century Britain and the United States (Baltimore, MD: Johns Hopkins University Press, 2006).

20. For the idea of colonialism as a literary transaction, see Harish Trivedi, *Colonial Transactions: English Literature and India* (Manchester: Manchester University Press, 1995). For the idea of colonialism as an anthropological and ritual transaction, see Florence Bernault, *Colonial Transactions: Imaginaries, Bodies, and Histories in Gabon* (Durham, NC: Duke University Press, 2019).

21. Charles Hardless, *The Clerk's Manual: A Complete Guide to General Office Routine* (Calcutta: Thacker, Spink, and Co., 1903), 126.

22. Ulrike Stark, *An Empire of Books: The Naval Kishore Press and the Diffusion of the Printed Word in Colonial India* (Ranikhet, India: Permanent Black, 2008), 1.

23. Leah Price, *How to Do Things with Books in Victorian Britain* (Princeton, NJ: Princeton University Press, 2012); Adam Smyth, "Almanacs, Annotators, and Life-Writing in Early Modern England," *English Literary Renaissance* 38, no. 2 (2008): 203.

24. Natasha Glaisyer and Sara Pennell, quoted in Francis E. Dolan, *True Relations: Reading, Literature, and Evidence in Seventeenth-Century England* (Philadelphia: University of Pennsylvania Press, 2013), 158–59.

25. Laurel Brake and James Mussell, "Digital Nineteenth-Century Serials for the Twenty-First Century: A Conversation," *19: Interdisciplinary Studies in the Long Nineteenth Century*, 21 (2015). Priti Joshi is right to be cautious about celebrating digitization efforts, pointing out that for-pay digital databases reinscribe questions of ephemerality as questions of institutional access. See Joshi, "Scissors-and-Paste: Ephemerality and Memorialization in the Archive of Indian Newspapers," *Amodern* 7: Ephemera and Ephemerality (December 2017), https://amodern.net/article/scissors-and-paste/.

26. Mike Esbester makes a similar point, but from the perspective of reading and design history. See Mike Esbester, "Nineteenth-Century Timetables and the History of Reading," *Book History* 12 (2009): 156–57.

27. Thomas B. Macaulay, "Minute on Indian Education" [1835], in *Archives of Empire: From the East India Company to the Suez Canal*, Vol. 1, eds. Barbara Harlow and Mia Carter (Durham, NC: Duke University Press, 2003), 230.

28. Macaulay, "Minute on Indian Education," 237.

29. Gauri Viswanathan, *Masks of Conquest: Literary Study and British Rule in India* (New York: Columbia University Press, 1989).

30. Edward Said, *Culture and Imperialism* (New York: Knopf, 1993).

31. Priya Joshi, *In Another Country: Colonialism, Culture, and the English Novel in India* (New York: Columbia University Press, 2002), 1–138.

32. Stephanie Newell, *Literary Culture in Colonial Ghana: "How to Play the Game of Life"* (Manchester: Manchester University Press, 2002), 98–119.

33. Anindita Ghosh, *Power in Print: Popular Publishing and the Politics of Language and Culture in a Colonial Society, 1778–1905* (Delhi: Oxford University Press, 2006).

34. Francesca Orsini, *Print and Pleasure: Popular Literature and Entertaining Fictions in Colonial North India* (Ranikhet, India: Permanent Black, 2009).

35. Of course, the lack of evidence doesn't imply that a text hasn't been read, even as it is impossible to say so authoritatively.

36. Santanu Das, *India, Empire, and First World War Culture: Writings, Images, and Songs* (Cambridge: Cambridge University Press, 2018), 335.

37. Elizabeth McHenry, *Forgotten Readers: Recovering the Lost History of African American Literary Societies* (Durham, NC: Duke University Press, 2002), 13.

38. See, for example, Ghosh, *Power and Print*, 182–84.

39. For an example beyond South Asia, see Archie Dick, *The Hidden History of South Africa's Book and Reading Cultures* (Toronto: University of Toronto Press, 2012), 3.

40. In the African American context, Elizabeth McHenry writes that "[m]any early nineteenth-century literary societies endorsed a broader notion of oral literacy that did not valorize the power of formal or individualized literacy over communal knowledge." See McHenry, *Forgotten Readers*, 13.

41. Isabel Hofmeyr, Sarah Nuttall, and Cheryl Ann Michael, "The Book in Africa," *Current Writing* 13, no. 2 (2001): 1–8.

42. Price, *How to Do Things with Books*.

43. Mark Amsler, "Affective Literacy: Gestures of Reading in the Later Middle Ages," *Essays in Medieval Studies* 18, no. 1 (2001): 83–110.

44. Isabel Hofmeyr, *Dockside Reading: Hydrocolonialism and the Custom House* (Durham, NC: Duke University Press), 10.

45. Hofmeyr, *Dockside Reading*, 2.

46. Leah Price, "Reading: The State of the Discipline," *Book History* 7 (2004): 303–4.

47. Lisa Gitelman, *Paper Knowledge: Towards a Media History of Documents* (Durham, NC: Duke University Press, 2014), 1, 30. See also Peter Stallybrass, "'Little Jobs': Broadsides and the Printing Revolution," in *Agent of Change: Print Culture Studies after Elizabeth L. Eisenstein*, eds. Sabrina A Baron et al. (Amherst: University of Massachusetts Press, 2007), 340.

48. Gitelman, *Paper Knowledge*, 31. Another example: the editors of the special issue, "Learning by the Book: Manuals and Handbooks in the History of Science," rightly place reception at the forefront of their inquiry, but self-correct to replace "reader" with "user." See Angela N. H. Creager, Mathias Grote, and Elaine Leong, "Introduction: Learning by the Book: Manuals and Handbooks in the History of Science," *BJHS Themes* 5 (2020): 5.

49. See, for example, Abigail Williams, *The Social Life of Books: Reading Together in the Eighteenth-Century Home* (New Haven, CT: Yale University Press, 2017); Kathryne Bevilacqua, "'What a Farmer Reads Shows in His Farm': Performing Literacy with Adult Reading Primers," *PMLA* 133, no. 5 (2018): 118–34.

50. Richard Altick, *The English Common Reader: A Social History of the Mass Reading Republic* (1957; reissue, Columbus: Ohio State University Press, 1998), 149.

51. Daniel Henkin, *City Reading: Written Words and Publics Space in Antebellum New York* (New York: Columbia University Press, 1998), 6. See also Esbester, "Nineteenth-Century," 156–57.

52. Peter Stallybrass, "Books and Scrolls: Navigating the Bible," in *Books and Readers in Early Modern England: Material Studies*, eds. Jennifer Andersen and Elizabeth Sauer (Philadelphia: University of Pennsylvania Press, 2002), 47.

53. Stallybrass, "Books and Scrolls," 42.

54. Victor Nell, *Lost in a Book: The Psychology of Reading for Pleasure* (New Haven, CT: Yale University Press, 1988).

55. Nell, *Lost in a Book*, 1–4.

56. Deidre Lynch and Eve Ender, "Introduction: Time for Reading," *PMLA* 133, no. 5 (2018): 1074.

57. Georges Poulet, "The Phenomenology of Reading," *New Literary History* 1, no. 1 (1969): 57.

58. On reading and identification, see Lisa Zunshine, *Why We Read Fiction: Theory of Mind and Novel* (Columbus: Ohio State University Press, 2006); Blakey Vermeule, *Why Do We Care About Literary Characters?* (Baltimore, MD: Johns Hopkins University Press, 2010); Gitelman, *Paper Knowledge*, 31.

59. For a similar critique, see Matthew P. Brown, "Blanks: Data, Method, and the British American Print Shop," *American Literary History* 29, no. 2 (2017): 228–47.

60. Ben Kafka, "Paperwork: The State of the Discipline," *Book History* 12 (2009): 341. Emphasis in original. Kafka's work on the history of paperwork against the backdrop of the French Revolution forms links with work on the anthropology of bureaucracy, which reminds us that everything, even the most mundane of texts, can have social lives. See Ben Kafka, *The Demon of Writing: Powers and Failures of Paperwork* (New York: Zone Books, 2012).

61. Jon Agar writes, "Nearly every historian forgets about the form of the file and reads the content." See Jon Agar, *The Government Machine: A Revolutionary History of the Computer* (Cambridge, MA: MIT Press, 2003), 1.

62. For representative works on this trend in South Asian studies, see Akhil Gupta, *Red Tape: Bureaucracy, Structural Violence, and Poverty in India* (Durham, NC: Duke University Press, 2012); Matthew S. Hull, *Government of Paper: The Materiality of Bureaucracy in Urban Pakistan* (Berkeley: University of California Press, 2012); Raman, *Document Raj*.

63. Ann Laura Stoler, *Along the Archival Grain: Epistemic Anxieties and Colonial Common Sense* (Princeton, NJ: Princeton University Press, 2009), 1.

64. This reading is inspired by Natalie Zemon Davis, *Fiction in the Archives: Pardon Tales and their Tellers in Sixteenth-Century France* (Palo Alto, CA: Stanford University Press, 1987).

65. On the horizontal relationship between literary and nonliterary texts, see Catherine Gallagher and Stephen Greenblatt, *Practicing New Historicism* (Chicago: University of Chicago Press, 2000). Recent work, propelled in response to Lisa Gitelman's *Paper Knowledge*, has staked a literary function for the "blank." For two examples, see Brown, "Data, Method, and the British American Print Shop"; Barbara Hochman, "Filling in Blanks: Nella Larsen's Application to Library School," *PMLA* 133, no. 5 (2018): 1172–90.

66. For studies of reading and print in South Asia that have a regional focus, see Swapan Chakravorty and Abhijit Gupta, eds., *Founts of Knowledge* (Delhi: Orient Blackswan, 2015); *Moveable Type: Book History in India* (Delhi: Orient Blackswan, 2008); *Print Areas: Book History in India* (Ranikhet, India: Permanent Black, 2004); Rimi B. Chatterjee, *Empires of the Mind: A History of Oxford University Press in India under the Raj* (Delhi: Oxford University Press, 2006); Francesca Orsini, *The Hindi Public Sphere 1920–1940: Language and Literature in the Age of Nationalism* (Delhi: Oxford University Press, 2002); A. K. Venkatachalapathy, *The Province of the Book: Scholars, Scribes, and Scribblers in Colonial Tamilnadu* (Ranikhet, India: Permanent Black, 2012); Rochelle Pinto, *Between Empires: Print and Politics in Goa* (Oxford: Oxford University Press, 2007).

Chapter 1: Reading for Survival

1. For a sense of the media controversy the leaked slide created, see Elisabeth Bumiller, "We Have Met the Enemy and He is PowerPoint," *New York Times*, April 26, 2010, https://www.nytimes.com/2010/04/27/world/27powerpoint.html?hp; Noah Schachtman, "Pentagon's Craziest PowerPoint Slide Revealed," *Wired*, September 13, 2010, https://www.wired.com/2010/09revealed-pentagons-craziest-powerpoint-slide-ever/; Simon Rogers, "The McChrystal Afghanistan PowerPoint Slide: Can You Do Any Better?" *The Guardian*, April 29, 2010, https://www.theguardian.com/news/datablog/2010/apr/29/mcchrystal-afghanistan-powerpoint-slide.

The slide was part of a larger presentation of twenty-nine slides depicting similar strategy diagrams.

2. *Counterinsurgency*. Field Manual 3-24/MCWP 3-33.5 (Washington, D.C.: Marine Corps, 2006), n.p.

3. *Counterinsurgency*, 27. The page number refers to Section 1 of the manual.

4. *Counterinsurgency*, 155–56. See also Paul Dixon, "'Heart and Minds'? British Counter-Insurgency from Malaya to Iraq," *Journal of Strategic Studies* 32, no. 3 (2009): 353–81.

5. Martin J. Bayly, *Taming the Imperial Imagination: Colonial Knowledge, International Relations, and the Anglo-Afghan Encounter, 1808–1878* (Cambridge: Cambridge University Press, 2016), ix.

6. Bayly, *Taming the Imperial Imagination*. See also James Hevia, *The Imperial Security State: British Colonial Knowledge and Empire-Building in Asia* (Cambridge: Cambridge University Press, 2012).

The British fought three major wars in Afghanistan: The First Anglo-Afghan War (1839–42), the Second Anglo-Afghan War (1878–80), and the Third Anglo-Afghan War (1919), in addition to other battles and conflicts.

7. Bumiller, "We Have Met the Enemy."

8. Bumiller, "We Have Met the Enemy."

9. Josh Marshall, "Feel Better Now?" *Talking Points Memo*, December 9, 2009, https://talkingpointsmemo.com/edblog/feel-better-now.

10. Amy Davidson Sorkin, "Close Look: Mapping the War," *The New Yorker*, December 10, 2009, https://www.newyorker.com/news/amy-davidson/close-look-mapping-the-war.

11. David Michod, *War Machine* (United States: Netflix, 2017).

12. Garnet J. Wolseley, *The Soldier's Pocket-book for Field Service* (London: Macmillan, 1869), vi. All references to the *Pocket-book* are to this edition, unless stated otherwise. Spellings of the title vary even within a single edition of the text (*The Soldiers' Pocket Book for Field Service* is another version used). For the sake of consistency, I use *The Soldier's Pocket-book for Field Service*.

13. For Wolseley's life, see Halik Kochanski, *Sir Garnet Wolseley: Victorian Hero* (London and Rio Grande, OH: Hambledon Press, 1999); Joseph H. Lehmann, *All Sir Garnet: A Life of Field-Marshal Lord Wolseley, 1833–1913* (London: Jonathan Cape, 1964).

Wolseley was the face of Sofiano and Foscolo cigarette makers and tobacco importers, an organization that operated in Turkey, Berlin, and London. He was also on the cover of the 1883 almanac of the Chinese Tea Company, among others. See Scrapbook 1, 1874–85, Wolseley Special Collections, Brighton and Hove Libraries, Brighton.

14. Wolseley, *The Soldier's Pocket-book*, vi.

15. Wolseley, *The Soldier's Pocket-book for Field Service* [1869] (London: Macmillan, 1871). For the recipe for beef and mutton pudding, turn to p. 169; for breadmaking advice, turn to p. 38; for mules and how much weight they can carry, turn to p. 36.

16. See Bayly, *Taming the Imperial Imagination*; C. A. Bayly, *Empire and Information: Intelligence Gathering and Social Communication in India, 1780–1879* (Cambridge: Cambridge University Press, 1996); Thomas Richards, *The Imperial Archive: Knowledge and the Fantasy of Empire* (London: Verso, 1993).

17. Wolseley, *The Soldier's Pocket-book*, v. Wolseley was also to write another handbook in later years, *Field Pocket-book for the Auxiliary Forces* (1873), which borrowed from the content of the *Pocket-book* but was aimed, as its title suggests, at the less-trained sections of the army. See Garnet J. Wolseley, *Field Pocket-book for the Auxiliary Forces* (London: Macmillan, 1873).

18. Wolseley, *The Soldier's Pocket-book* (1871), iii.

19. In a letter to Macmillan, Wolseley wrote: "I am sure you will be glad to hear that many of the changes which I laid down in the 'Pocket Book' [sic] . . . have been agreed to, amongst others the small kit for officers." See Garnet Wolseley to Macmillan, April 6, 1871, vol. CDLXVII, Add MS 55252: 1869–1940, Macmillan Archive, British Library, London. See also Wolseley, *The Soldier's Pocket-book* (1871), 9.

20. Garnet Wolseley to Craik, August 18, 1874, vol. CDLXVII, Add MS 55252: 1869–1940, Macmillan Archive, British Library.

21. Leah Price, *How to Do Things with Books in Victorian Britain* (Princeton, NJ: Princeton University Press, 2012), 7.

22. Natasha Glaisyer and Sara Pennell note: "It is indeed an irony of book history that the volumes of didactic material that survive today were those that were often little used or carefully preserved in libraries or closets." Quoted in Francis Dolan, *True Relations: Reading, Literature, and Evidence in Seventeenth-Century England* (Philadelphia: University of Pennsylvania Press, 2013), 158–59.

23. This anecdote is recounted in "New Books: The Soldiers' Pocket Book [sic] for Field Service (Fifth Edition)," *The State*, April 2, 1886, 122. The article is preserved in Scrapbook 3, 1873–95, Wolseley Special Collections, Brighton and Hove Libraries. It appears repeatedly across a range of other articles about the *Pocket-book*, too. See, for example, *Western Daily Press*, June 25, 1883.

24. After its first edition in 1869, the *Pocket-book* went through four more, published in 1871, 1874, 1882, and 1886.

25. An advertisement for the *Pocket-book* touted it as a volume "replete with interest even to those who are not directly connected to the military profession." See "Macmillan and Co.'s List," *St. James's Gazette*, September 30, 1882, 2.

The *Pall Mall Gazette*, too, described it as "pleasant and interesting reading to the public at large." See these comments in "Messrs. Macmillan & Co.'s List," *Pall Mall Gazette*, November 18, 1882, 14.

26. *The Star*, May 5, 1874.

27. Wolseley, *The Soldier's Pocket-book*, v.

28. For a similar theoretical argument, see Roger Chartier, "Intellectual History or Sociocultural History? The French Trajectories," in *Modern European Intellectual History: Reappraisals*

and New Perspectives, eds. Dominick LaCapra and Steven L. Kaplan (Ithaca, NY: Cornell University Press 1982), 39–40.

29. J. H. Lefroy, *Report on the Regimental and Garrison Schools of the Army, and on Military Libraries and Reading Rooms* (London: HMSO, 1859), 58. For a detailed discussion of this report, see Sharon Murphy, *The British Soldier and his Libraries, c. 1822–1901* (Basingstoke, UK: Palgrave, 2016), 109–120.

30. Tabitha Jackson, *The Boer War* (London: Channel 4 Books, 1999), 80–81.

31. Edward Spiers, *The Victorian Soldier in Africa* (Manchester: Manchester University Press, 2004), 2–3.

32. *Report of the Council of Military Education* (London: Eyre and Spottiswoode, 1860), 19–20.

33. W. J. Reader, *Professional Men: The Rise of the Professional Classes in Nineteenth-Century England* (London: Weinfield and Nicolson, 1966), 74.

34. For a comprehensive account of the forms of writing that the British military produced in response to empire, see this excellent study: Hevia, *The Imperial Security State*, especially chapters 4–7.

35. Wolseley, *The Soldier's Pocket-book*, 6.

36. Wolseley, *The Soldier's Pocket-book*, 1.

37. Wolseley, *The Soldier's Pocket-book*, 1.

38. For a discussion of nineteenth- and twentieth-century self-help's evocation of character and self-reliance, see Rebecca Richardson, *Material Ambitions: Self-Help and Victorian Literature* (Baltimore, MD: Johns Hopkins University Press, 2021); Beth Blum, *The Self-Help Compulsion: Searching for Advice in Modern Literature* (New York: Columbia University Press, 2020).

39. Scholarship on soldiers and reading in World War I has been abundant. See, for example, Mary Hammond and Shafquat Towheed, eds., *Publishing in the First World War: Essays in Book History* (Basingstoke, UK: Palgrave, 2007); Edmund King, "E. W. Hornung's Unpublished 'Diary,' the YMCA, and the Reading Soldier in the First World War," *English Literature in Transition, 1880–1920*, 57, no. 3 (2014): 361–87; Amanda Laugesen, "'Boredom Is the Enemy': The Intellectual and Imaginative Lives of Australian Soldiers in the Great War and Beyond* (Farnham, UK: Ashgate, 2012). For the literary lives of Indian soldiers posted in Europe during World War I, see Santanu Das, *India, Empire, and First World War Culture: Writings, Images, and Songs* (Cambridge: Cambridge University of Press, 2018).

For the most part, however, these studies focus on the imaginative potential of fiction reading, rather than technical works such as the *Pocket-book*.

40. Quoted in Sharon Murphy, "Imperial Reading?: The East India Company's Lending Libraries for Soldiers, c. 1819–1834," *Book History*, 12 (2009): 76. See also Murphy, *The British Soldier and his Libraries*, 2–3.

41. *Sixth Report by the Council of Military Education on Army Schools, Libraries, and Recreation Rooms* (London: Eyre and Spottiswode, 1870), 114.

42. For more on the history of the British army in India, see David Omissi, *The Sepoy and the Raj: The Indian Army, 1860–1940* (Basingstoke, UK: Palgrave, 1994); Douglas Peers, *Between Mars and Mammon: Colonial Armies and the Garrison State in India, 1819–1835* (London: Bloomsbury, 1995).

43. Wolseley, *The Soldier's Pocket-book*, 142.

44. Garnet Wolseley, *The Story of a Soldier's Life*, Vol. 1 (New York: Scribner, 1903), 11. Emphasis mine.

45. Wolseley, *The Story of a Soldier's Life*, 29.
46. Wolseley, *The Story of a Soldier's Life*, 7.
47. Lefroy, *Report on the Regimental and Garrison Schools*, 58.
48. Sharon Murphy, "'Quite Incapable of Appreciating Books for Educated Readers': The Mid-Nineteenth-Century British Soldier," in *A Return to the Common Reader: Print Culture and the Novel, 1850–1900*, eds. Adelene Buckland and Beth Palmer (Farnham, UK: Ashgate, 2011), 121.
49. Lefroy, *Report on the Regimental and Garrison Schools*, 57.
50. *Sixth Report by the Council of Military Education*, 107.
51. Garnet Wolseley to Macmillan, August 31, 1871, Vol. CDLXVII, Add MS 55252: 1869–1940, Macmillan Archive, British Library.
52. "Macmillan and Co.'s List," 14.
53. See, for example, Paul R. Rooney, *Railway Reading and Late-Victorian Literary Series* (London: Routledge, 2018).
54. Wolseley, *The Soldier's Pocket-book*, 8. Wolseley notes in a letter to Macmillan that the list was approved by the army. See Garnet Wolseley to Macmillan, April 6, 1871, Vol. CDLXVII, Add MS 55252: 1869–1940, Macmillan Archive, British Library.
55. The *Pocket-book* was a sextodecimo (16°) volume. The weight cited in the chapter is of the first edition of the *Pocket-book* in the British Library's collections. The exact figure is 235.9 grams, though the copy is slightly damaged. Thanks to Nicholas Alen of the British Library for providing me with this information.
56. Garnet Wolseley to Macmillan, September 2, 1871, Vol. CDLXVII, Add MS 55252: 1869–1940, Macmillan Archive, British Library.

In 1878, Wolseley once again wrote to Macmillan, this time suggesting that the edges be blue. No reason was given for this change. See Garnet Wolseley to Macmillan, [month?] 9, 1878, Vol. CDLXVII, Add MS 55252: 1869–1940, Macmillan Archive, British Library.

57. Wolseley, *The Soldier's Pocket-book* (1871), iii.
58. In 1870, Wolseley wrote to Macmillan: "I am very anxious to get through another edition as I wish to add much useful information to it." See Garnet Wolseley to Macmillan, November 4, 1870, Vol. CDLXVII, Add MS 55252: 1869–1940, Macmillan Archive, British Library.

Wolseley followed up the next year to ask for a meeting to discuss the second edition, which would include his experiences of the Red River Expedition in Canada and be a "very great improvement upon the first." See Garnet Wolseley to Macmillan, April 6, 1871, Vol. CDLXVII, Add MS 55252: 1869–1940, Macmillan Archive, British Library.

59. Garnet Wolseley to Macmillan, September 2, 1871, Vol. CDLXVII, Add MS 55252: 1869–1940, Macmillan Archive, British Library.
60. This was not an unusual innovation, and it is possible that the idea for the pencil borrowed from the example of Wilmot-Sitwell's letter packets for soldiers on Foreign Service, an example of which can be found in Wolseley's scrapbook collection. See Scrapbook 19, n.d., Wolseley Special Collections, Brighton and Hove Libraries.
61. In addition to this pencil suggestion, Wolseley wrote to Macmillan to discard the blank pages to compensate for the increased length of the second edition. See Garnet Wolseley to Macmillan, September 2, 1871, Vol. CDLXVII, Add MS 55252: 1869–1940, Macmillan Archive, British Library.

The pencil holder, too, like the blank pages, persists across editions.

62. "War Rumours," *Taunton Courier and Western Advertiser*, November 15, 1876, 5.

63. John J. Wilson, *Construction and Destruction; or The Devilry of War [Being notes on the Third Edition of "THE SOLDIERS' POCKET BOOK FOR FIELD SERVICE," (By Major-General Sir Garnet J. Wolseley)]* (Birmingham, UK: C. Cooper, 1891), 2. The edition Wilson refers to is Garnet Wolseley, *The Soldier's Pocket-book for Field Service* [1869] (London: Macmillan, 1874).

Several editions and versions of the pamphlet exist. The earliest version was published sometime between 1886 and 1887 and references the fifth edition of the *Pocket-book*. See John J. Wilson, *Construction and Destruction; or The Devilry of War: Being Notes on the Fifth Edition of "The Soldier's Pocket Book for Field Service" (By Viscount Wolseley)* (Kendal: n.p., 1886?), 4. Unless stated otherwise, all references in this chapter are to the 1891 version of the pamphlet.

64. Wilson, *Construction and Destruction*, 2.

65. John J. Wilson, *The Devilry of War, or Construction and Destruction: Being Notes on the Fifth Edition of "The Soldier's Pocket book for Field Service," by Viscount Wolseley; "Tactics of Today," by Colonel C .E. Callwell, C.B. (Second Edition, 1909); "Aiming and Firing," by Quarter-Master Sergeant-Instructor J. Bostock, Seventh Edition; "Hints for Soldiers Proceeding to India," (n.d.)* (London: Friends' Peace Committee, 1913).

66. Wilson, *Construction and Destruction*, 5. Emphasis in original.

67. Wilson, *Construction and Destruction*, 3.

68. For an alternative theorization of the Christian soldier, see Trev Broughton, "The Life and Afterlives of Captain Hedley Vicars: Evangelical Biography and the Crimean War," *19: Interdisciplinary Studies in the Long Nineteenth Century*, 20 (2015).

69. Keir Hardie, "Peculiar Animals and How to Train Them," *The Labour Leader*, May 12, 1900, 148.

70. Hardie, "Peculiar Animals," 149.

71. Hardie, "Peculiar Animals,"149.

72. See the *Oxford English Dictionary* entry for "Object Lesson," https://www.oed.com/dictionary/object-lesson_n?tab=meaning_and_use.

73. Wilson, *Construction and Destruction*, 2.

74. These are: an R. G. Chapman followed by an A. G. Chapman, and finally, an H. C. Morland. Wilson, *Construction and Destruction*, 2.

75. Wilson, *Construction and Destruction*, 2–3. I have not found any significant annotations in the copies of the *Pocket-book* I have consulted over the course of my research.

76. Bayard, *How to Talk about Books You Haven't Read*, trans. Jeffrey Melman (New York: Bloomsbury, 2007), 44.

77. Bayard makes a similar comment but to different effect in *How to Talk about Books* on p. 6: "The act of picking up and opening a book masks the countergesture that occurs at the same time: the involuntary act of *not* picking up and *not* opening all the other books in the universe." Emphasis in original.

78. It is only from the third edition that Wolseley listed a chaplain as part of the army. See Wolseley, *The Soldier's Pocket-book* (1874), 119.

79. Wolseley, *The Soldier's Pocket-book* (1874), 91–92.

80. Wolseley, *The Soldier's Pocket-book* (1874), 93.

81. Wilson, *Construction and Destruction*, 6.

82. For other examples from Victorian Britain, see Price, *How to Do Things with Books*.

83. Edmund Calamy, ed., *Cromwell's Soldier's Bible: Being a Reprint, in Facsimile, of "The Souldier's Pocket Bible," compiled by Edmund Calamy, and Issued for the Use of the Commonwealth Army in 1643*; bibliographic introduction and preface by Garnet Wolseley (Boston: Roberts Brothers, 1895).

84. Hardie notes the irony of the binding, too: "In this war of disgusting things, few have been a greater outrage on all good taste and feeling than the issuing of khaki-bound editions of Holy Writ." See Hardie, "Peculiar Animals," 149.

85. Wolseley, "Preface," *Cromwell's Soldier's Bible*, n.p.

86. Hardie, "Peculiar Animals," 149.

87. The volumes form part of the collection of Wolseley's private papers held at the Brighton and Hove Public Libraries. Wolseley Special Collections, Brighton and Hove Libraries.

88. See Scrapbook 18, n.d., Wolseley Special Collections, Brighton and Hove Libraries. It's unclear whether the series contained more than the four sketches preserved in the scrapbook.

For more on soldiers' scrapbooks (albeit in the context of the Crimean War), see Holly Furneaux, *Military Men of Feeling: Emotion, Touch, and Masculinity in the Crimean War* (Oxford: Oxford University Press, 2016), 147–86.

89. This is frequently seen across Wolseley's scrapbooks, especially in the case of newspaper articles, which were often crudely cut and glued on the page in strips.

90. For more on the scrapbook form and its ability to reorder meaning, see Ellen Gruber Garvey, *Writing with Scissors: American Scrapbooks from the Civil War to the Harlem Renaissance* (Oxford: Oxford University Press, 2013), 5.

91. Wolseley, *The Soldier's Pocket-book* (1871), iv.

92. Rudyard Kipling, "The Taking of Lungtungpen" [1887], in *Mulvaney Stories* (Philadelphia, PA: Henry Altemus, 1897), 14–22; "The Courting of Dinah Shadd" [1890], in *Life's Handicap: Being Stories of Mine Own People* [1891] (New York: Doubleday, 1899), 115–43.

93. David Gilmour, *The Long Recessional: The Imperial Life of Rudyard Kipling* (London: John Murray, 2002), 27.

94. Gilmour, *The Long Recessional*, 44.

95. Quoted in David Bradshaw, "Kipling and War," in *The Cambridge Companion to Rudyard Kipling*, ed. Howard Booth (Cambridge: Cambridge University Press, 2011), 81.

96. Gilmour, *The Long Recessional*, 47.

97. Kipling, "The Taking of Lungtungpen," 14.

98. Kipling, "The Taking of Lungtungpen," 15.

99. Kipling, "The Taking of Lungtungpen," 15.

100. Kipling, "The Taking of Lungtungpen," 15.

101. "Silence is Golden," Scrapbook 1, 1874–85, Wolseley Special Collections, Brighton and Hove Libraries. Page numbers and sources have been lost in the scrapbooking process.

102. *Pall Mall Gazette*, May 3, 1886.

103. The five editions of the *Pocket-book* ran to 275 pages (1869), 356 pages (1871), 399 pages (1874), 531 pages (1882), and 551 pages (1886).

104. For example, Gale and Polden, a military textbook series, simultaneously advertised the *Pocket-book* and manuals written by a Mr. Gordon of the 2nd Gordon Highlanders, which they described as "less voluminous." See Henry Doveton, *Military Training in Engl. & Hindustani*, Urdu edition (London: Chatham, 1890), 124.

105. Kipling, "The Courting of Dinah Shadd," 118.

106. Russell appears across Wolseley's correspondence as a much-hated figure. Russell, however, had problems of his own: the failures of the Crimean War had been attributed to him, as his newspaper articles supposedly kept the Russians well-informed of British moves. See Kochanski, *Sir Garnet*, 43.

Wolseley did, however, find other uses for the despised profession of journalists, for example, using them to spread false intelligence and confuse enemy troops. Wolseley, *The Soldier's Pocket-book*, 60.

107. Garnet Wolseley to Louisa Wolseley, January 28, 1874, Wolseley Special Collections, Brighton and Hove Libraries.

108. Wolseley, *The Soldier's Pocket-book*, 60. They were, Wolseley went on to argue in the third edition (1874) on p. 97, "an encumbrance to an army; they eat the rations of fighting men, and do no work at all. Their numbers should be restricted as much as possible."

109. Kipling, "The Courting of Dinah Shadd," 128.

110. "London Club Chat," *Bolton Evening News*, November 16, 1903, 4.

111. Bradshaw, "Kipling and War," 81.

112. "London Club Chat," *Bolton Evening News*, November 16, 1903, 4.

113. Kipling, "The Courting of Dinah Shadd," 128.

114. Kipling, "The Taking of Lungtungpen," 16. The reference here is to the legendary rivalry between Wolseley and Lord Frederick Roberts, and their two army loyalty camps, the Ashanti or Wolseley Ring and the Indians respectively. The groups were divided on questions of military strategy and reform; each accused the other of self-advertisement and unfair play. Wolseley's strong belief in meritocracy made him enemies throughout the army, especially among senior officers who were passed over for promotions. Roberts, by contrast, came across as a much more charming person and so managed to endear himself to the public and the media more successfully than his rival. Kipling's hero worship of him played a considerable role in this. For more on the subject, see Leigh Maxwell, *The Ashanti Ring: Sir Garnet Wolseley's Campaigns, 1870–1882* (London: L. Cooper, 1985). For a discussion of the opposition between Wolseley and Roberts in "The Taking of Lungtungpen" in terms of imperial hybridity and masculinity, see Bradley Deane, *Masculinity and the New Imperialism: Rewriting Manhood in British Popular Literature, 1870–1914* (Cambridge: Cambridge University Press, 2014), 82–84.

115. Kipling, "The Taking of Lungtungpen," 16.

116. Kipling, "The Taking of Lungtungpen," 17.

117. Kipling, "The Taking of Lungtungpen," 21.

118. This is also possibly an authorial jibe at the *Pocket-book*'s silence on the sexual lives of soldiers.

119. Kipling, "The Courting of Dinah Shadd," 127.

120. Kipling, "The Courting of Dinah Shadd," 133.

121. Kipling, "The Courting of Dinah Shadd," 125–26.

122. Andrew Liptak, "The US Army has Released Its First Audiobooks," *The Verge*, July 5, 2019, https://www.theverge.com/2019/7/5/18714713/us-army-first-audiobook-manual-doctrine-operations-training. See also Kyle Rempfer, "Don't Read, Listen! Army Publishes Field Manual Audiobooks," *Army Times*, July 8, 2019, https://www.armytimes.com/news/your-army/2019/07/08/dont-read-listen-army-publishes-field-manual-audiobooks/.

Chapter 2: Reading for the Record

1. Leonard Woolf, *Diaries in Ceylon, 1908–1911: Records of a Colonial Administrator; Being the Official Diaries Maintained by Leonard Woolf while Assistant Government Agent of the Hambantota District, Ceylon during the period August 1908 to May 1911 and Stories from the East: Three Short Stories on Ceylon* [1962] (Dehiwala: Tisara, 2006), 95.

2. "Regulations relating to Rinderpest," *Ceylon Government Gazette*, no. 6317, July 2, 1909, 606–8. The official notices in the *Ceylon Government Gazette* were also translated (and published) in Tamil and Sinhala.

3. "Regulations relating to Rinderpest," 607.

4. Leonard Woolf, *Growing: An Autobiography of the Years 1904 to 1911* (London: Harcourt Brace Jovanovich, 1961), 190–91.

5. Leonard Woolf to Lytton Strachey, January 26, 1905, in *Letters of Leonard Woolf*, ed. Frederic Spotts (London: Weidenfeld and Nicolson, 1989), 75.

6. Leonard Woolf to Lytton Strachey, February 19, 1905, in *Letters of Leonard Woolf*, ed. Frederic Spotts (London: Weidenfeld and Nicolson, 1989), 79. Emphasis in original.

7. Karl Marx, "The Government of India," in *On Colonialism*, eds. Karl Marx and Friedrich Engels (Moscow: Foreign Languages Publishing House, 196-?), 69.

8. For a discussion of this in the context of contemporary India, see Veena Das, "The Signature of the State: The Paradox of Illegibility," in *Anthropology in the Margins of the State*, eds. Veena Das and Deborah Poole (Santa Fe, NM: SAR Press, 2004), 245.

9. Cornelia Vismann, *Files, Law and Media Technology*, trans. Geoffrey Winthrop-Young (Palo Alto, CA: Stanford University Press, 2008), xi.

10. James C. Scott, *Seeing Like a State: How Certain Schemes to Improve the Human Condition Have Failed* [1998] (New Haven, CT: Yale University Press, 2020), 2. The term "legibility effect" was coined by Michel-Rolph Trouillot in response to Scott's work in *Seeing Like a State*. See Trouillot, "The Anthropology of the State in the Age of Globalization: Close Encounters of the Deceptive Kind," *Current Anthropology* 42, no. 1 (February 2001): 132.

11. Max Weber, "Bureaucracy," in *The Anthropology of the State: A Reader*, eds. Aradhana Sharma and Akhil Gupta (Malden, MA: Blackwell, 2006), 49–70.

12. These figures are from the 1911 Census of Ceylon. See E. B. Denham, *At the Census of 1911: Being the Review of the Results of the Census of 1911* (Colombo: H. C. Cottle, 1912), 435.

In 1911, only 31 percent of Hambantota's male population could read and write in any language, whether English, Tamil, or Sinhala. The figure for the female population is substantially lower at 2.2 percent. See Denham, *At the Census of 1911*, 407.

13. Mike Esbester's ongoing project on railway safety explores accidents caused by workers who were illiterate and therefore unable to read railway safety handbooks. See Mike Esbester, "Reading Between the Lines," *Railstaff*, accessed May 15, 2022, https://www.railstaff.co.uk/2019/05/20/reading-between-the-lines.

14. Leonard Woolf to Lytton Strachey, January 8, 1905, in *Letters of Leonard Woolf*, ed. Frederic Spotts (London: Weidenfeld and Nicolson, 1989), 71.

15. Nira Wickramasinghe, *Slave in a Palanquin: Colonial Servitude and Resistance in Sri Lanka* (New York: Columbia University Press, 2020), 70.

16. Ann L. Stoler, *Along the Archival Grain: Epistemic Anxieties and Colonial Common Sense* (Princeton, NJ: Princeton University Press, 2009).

17. My arguments here are inspired by scholarship on the ethnography of paperwork, including: Akhil Gupta, *Red Tape: Bureaucracy, Structural Violence, and Poverty in India* (Durham, NC: Duke University Press, 2012); Richard Harper, *Inside the IMF: An Ethnography of Documents, Technology and Organisational Action* (New York: Academic, 1998); Matthew Hull, *Government of Paper: The Materiality of Bureaucracy in Urban Pakistan* (Berkeley: University of California Press, 2012); Nayanika Mathur, *Paper Tiger: Law, Bureaucracy and the Developmental State in Himalayan India* (Cambridge: Cambridge University Press, 2015).

18. Leonard S. Woolf, *The Village in the Jungle* (London: Edwin Arnold, 1913). All references to the novel in this chapter are to this edition of the text.

19. Woolf arrived in Ceylon in 1904. He worked in various government divisions until receiving the post of Assistant Government Agent of the Hambantota district in 1908, a post he held until his resignation in 1911. For the definitive biographical account of Woolf's life, including his years in Ceylon, see Victoria Glendinning, *Leonard Woolf: A Biography* (New York: Free Press, 2006).

20. Leonard S. Woolf, *The Village in the Jungle* (London: Eland Publishers, 2006).

21. For a similar argument in the context of the Victorian novel, see Sukanya Banerjee, "Writing Bureaucracy, Bureaucratic Writing: Charles Dickens, *Little Dorrit*, and Mid-Victorian Liberalism," *Nineteenth-Century Literature* 25, no. 2 (2020): 134–36.

22. Woolf, *The Village in Jungle*, 31–32.

23. Dinabandhu Mitra, *Nil Darpan, or the Indigo Planting Mirror, a Drama*, trans. from Bengali by a Native (Calcutta: C. H. Manuel, 1861).

24. *Copy of the Report of the Commission Appointed in India to Inquire into the Causes of the Riots Which Took Place in the Year 1875, in the Poona and Ahmednagar Districts of the Bombay Presidency* (London: Eyre and Spottiswoode, 1878), 4.

25. See "Minute," *Ceylon Government Gazette*, no. 6826, September 29, 1916, 771.

Interestingly, the final ordinance, passed in 1918, replaces "intelligible" with "plain words and numerals." See "No. 2 of 1918: An Ordinance Relating to Money Lending," in *A Revised Edition of the Legislative Enactments of Ceylon*, Vol. 3 (1910 to 1923) (Colombo: A. C. Richards, 1923), 585.

26. For double-entry account books and transparency in the context of early modern Europe, see Mary Poovey, *A History of the Modern Fact: Problems of Knowledge in the Sciences of Wealth and Society* (Chicago: University of Chicago Press, 1998), 29–91.

27. *Copy of the Report of the Commission Appointed to Inquire into the Causes of the Riots*, 50. Emphasis mine.

The report goes on to state: "One ryot stated before the Commission that his sowkar had told him he could not spare time to make out an account, and if the ryot insisted he should have to charge him 10 per cent for the trouble." See *Copy of the Report of the Commission Appointed to Inquire into the Causes of the Riots*, 50.

28. Mark Amsler, "Affective Literacy: Gestures of Reading in the Later Middle Ages," *Essays in Medieval Studies* 18, no. 1 (2001): 84.

29. Amsler, "Affective Literacy," 83–84. See also Leah Price, *How to Do Things with Books in Victorian Britain* (Princeton, NJ: Princeton University Press, 2012).

30. Woolf, *The Village in the Jungle*, 121, 122.

31. Woolf, *The Village in the Jungle*, 116.

32. *Copy of the Report of the Commission Appointed to Inquire into the Causes of the Riots*, 52.

33. For a useful parallel to Silindu's difficulties in understanding the differences between documented and oral promises, see D. F. McKenzie, *Bibliography and the Sociology of Texts* (1986; reissue, Cambridge: Cambridge University Press, 1999), 77–128, which contains a detailed study of the Treaty of Waitangi, the document that marked the transfer of Maori lands in New Zealand to the Crown.

34. Woolf, *The Village in the Jungle*, 39, 40.

35. A Ratemahatmaya was an administrative official who would head a revenue district. They were subordinate to the Assistant Government Agent. The title derives from an official position in the Kingdom of Kandy, absorbed into British-held territories of Ceylon in 1815.

36. Woolf, *The Village in the Jungle*, 238.

37. For details of how to obtain a gun license in Ceylon circa 1908, see "Ordinance 31 of 1908: An Ordinance to Amend the Law Relating to Firearms," in *A Revised Edition of the Legislative Enactments of Ceylon*, Vol. 3 (1900 to 1913) (Colombo: H. C. Cottle, 1913), 472–81.

38. See "Ordinance 31 of 1908," 474.

39. Woolf, *The Village in the Jungle*, 15.

40. Veena Das and Deborah Poole, "State and Its Margins: Comparative Ethnographies," in *Anthropology in the Margins*, eds. Veena Das and Deborah Poole (Santa Fe, NM: SAR Press, 2004), 14.

41. For a discussion of the figures of the intermediary and the power broker, see Das and Poole, "State and Its Margins," 14–15.

42. Woolf, *The Village in the Jungle*, 32.

43. Woolf, *The Village in the Jungle*, 38.

44. Woolf, *The Village in the Jungle*, 38.

45. "Missing Stamps on Gun Licenses issued by AGA on Circuit," Lot 27/751 G 261, 1913–15, Records of the Hambantota Kachcheri, Sri Lanka National Archives, Colombo.

46. "Letter," March 19, 1913, "Missing Stamps on Gun Licenses issued by AGA on Circuit," Lot 27/751 G 261, 1913–15, Records of the Hambantota Kachcheri, Sri Lanka National Archives.

47. "Letter," May 8, 1914, "Missing Stamps on Gun Licenses issued by AGA on Circuit," Lot 27/751 G 261, 1913–15, Records of the Hambantota Kachcheri, Sri Lanka National Archives.

48. "Letter," March 29, 1915, "Missing Stamps on Gun Licenses issued by AGA on Circuit," Lot 27/751 G 261, 1913–15, Records of the Hambantota Kachcheri, Sri Lanka National Archives.

49. "Letter from G. F. Roberts," July 5, 1915, "Missing Stamps on Gun Licenses issued by AGA on Circuit," Lot 27/751 G 261, 1913–15, Records of the Hambantota Kachcheri, Sri Lanka National Archives.

50. Das, "The Signature of the State," 227; Gupta, *Red Tape*, 227–31.

51. Woolf, *Diaries in Ceylon*, 42–43. The passage is taken from Woolf's diary entry for January 18, 1909.

While, of course, Woolf's frustrated comment highlights the fractures in the native colonial hierarchy, this should not obscure the fact that a well-established system of checks and balances, whatever its effectiveness, did exist to keep government-employed officials in place. This was in the form of conduct registers—large, unwieldy volumes maintained by the offices of the Assistant Government Agents of each province. There was a register for each district, and several pages for each official employed, noting all the "rewards" and "punishments" they received for their actions over the course of their tenure. These ranged from giving false evidence in court to sending requested information and reports late. Meticulous detail characterized the maintenance of these registers, with the dates, circumstances, and details of actions and their consequences noted. We also see that officials are dismissed for every single one of Babehami's connivances. See, for example, a conduct register that tracks the misdemeanors of headmen working as part of the West Giruwa Pattu police force: Headman Conduct Register from West Giruwa Pattu, 1898–1923, Lot 27/529, Records of the Hambantota Kachcheri, Sri Lanka National Archives.

52. Woolf, *The Village in the Jungle*, 182.

53. Quoted in David Zaret, *Origins of Democratic Culture: Printing, Petitions, and the Public Sphere in Early-Modern England* (Princeton, NJ: Princeton University Press, 2000), 86. For an account of how petitioning was mobilized in early-nineteenth-century Ceylon, see Wickramasinghe, *Slave in a Palanquin*, 82–184.

54. Woolf describes an encounter with a group of petitioners who complained about the appearance of a comet and the bad luck it brought with it, which ranged from a rise in taxes to restrictions on chena cultivation. See Woolf, *Diaries in Ceylon*, 151–52. The story is mentioned in Woolf's diary entry for January 29, 1910.

55. Majid Siddiqui, *The British Historical Context and Petitioning in Colonial India* (Delhi: Aakar, 2005); "Petitioning and Politic Cultures in South Asia," eds. Rohit De and Robert Travers, *Modern Asian Studies* 53, no. 1 (2019).

56. Wickramasinghe, *Slave in a Palanquin*, 183.

57. Ranajit Guha, *The Small Voice of History: Collected Essays* (Delhi: Orient Blackswan, 2010).

58. Akhil Gupta makes a distinction between a complaint, "a demand to redress wrongs committed by a person in power," and a petition, "written by supplicants who desire to obtain something as a favor." See Gupta, *Red Tape*, 167. Gupta's observations are about contemporary India, and such distinctions are less obvious in the historical archive of South Asia. For more on the different kinds of texts that circulated alongside petitions in ways that weren't always distinguishable, see Rohit De and Robert Travers, "Petitioning and Political Cultures in South Asia: Introduction," *Modern Asian Studies* 53, no. 1 (2019): 5–6.

59. Wickramasinghe, *Slave in a Palanquin*, 182.

60. A. Wright, *Baboo English as 'Tis Writ: Being Curiosities of Indian Journalism* (London: T. Fisher Unwin, 1891), 79–80.

61. C. A. Bayly, *Empire and Information: Intelligence Gathering and Social Communication in India, 1780–1879* (Cambridge: Cambridge University Press, 1996), 13. For more scholarship on the history of scribes in South Asia, see among others: Bhavani Raman, *Document Raj: Writing and Scribes in Early Colonial South India* (Chicago: Chicago University Press, 2012), especially 23–52; Hayden J. Bellenoit, *The Formation of the Colonial State in India: Scribes, Paper and Taxes, 1760–1860* (Abingdon, UK: Routledge, 2017).

62. Woolf, *Diaries in Ceylon*, 99. This quotation is from Woolf's diary entry for September 6, 1909.

63. Akhil Gupta notes that assets or the lack thereof play a much more significant role in the perpetuation of structural violence. See Gupta, *Red Tape*, 208.

64. "Letter no. 159," September 21, 1886, Lot 27/147, Records of the Hambantota Kachcheri, Sri Lanka National Archives. All the items in this file pertain to grain commutation taxes.

65. "Petition 841," July 6, 1906, "Petitions to AGA reg[arding]: Buffaloes seized by the Headmen and Corr[espondence] between AGA. Hamb[antota]: and Mudaliyar EGP [East Giruwa Pattu] reg[arding]: the Recovery of Irregular Fees," Lot 27 / 745 G 32, Records of the Hambantota Kachcheri, Sri Lanka National Archives.

66. "Report," July 9, 1906, "Petitions to AGA reg[arding]: Buffaloes seized by the Headmen and Corr[espondence] between AGA. Hamb[antota]: and Mudaliyar EGP [East Giruwa Pattu] reg[arding]: the Recovery of Irregular Fees," Lot 27/745 G 32, Records of the Hambantota Kachcheri, Sri Lanka National Archives.

67. Arjun Appadurai, "Topographies of the Self: Praise and Emotion in Hindu India," in *Language and the Politics of Emotion*, eds. Catherine Lutz and Lila Abu-Lughod (Cambridge: Cambridge University Press, 1990), 92–112.

68. "Petition 706," June 9, 1911, "Petitions Addressed to the AGA Hamb[antota] (reports annexed, nos. 600–797)," Lot 27/399, Records of the Hambantota Kachcheri, Sri Lanka National Archives.

69. Natalie Zemon Davis, *Fiction in the Archives: Pardon Tales and their Tellers in Sixteenth-Century France* (Palo Alto, CA: Stanford University Press, 1987).

70. Julia Stephens, "A Bureaucracy of Rejection: Petitioning and the Impoverished Paternalism of the British-Indian Raj," *Modern Asian Studies* 53, no.1 (2019): 177–202.

71. Leonard Woolf to John Maynard Keynes, November 17, 1905, in *Letters of Leonard Woolf*, ed. Frederic Spotts (London: Weidenfeld and Nicolson, 1989), 107.

72. This was true in Britain, too. For an account of unread bureaucratic reports in Victorian Britain, see Oz Frankel, "Blue Books and the Victorian Reader," *Victorian Studies* 46, no. 2 (2004): 308–18.

73. "Letter," September 8, 1906, "Petitions to AGA reg[arding]: Buffaloes seized by the Headmen and Corr[espondence] between AGA. Hamb[antota]: and Mudaliyar EGP [East Giruwa Pattu] reg[arding]: the Recovery of Irregular Fees," Lot 27/745 G 32, Records of the Hambantota Kachcheri, Sri Lanka National Archives.

74. "Letter," April 26, 1911, "Petitions addressed to the AGA Hamb[antota] (reports annexed, nos. 600–797)," Lot 27/399, Records of the Hambantota Kachcheri, Sri Lanka National Archives.

75. The story leads into a comment on the differential treatment of Indian and European officials: "Of course, this [insisting on legible handwriting] is all right. But there is no knowing in what matters poor Natives might be censured. Even some Europeans write in such a way that it is difficult to make out their writing." See *Report on Native Papers Published in the Bombay Presidency for the Week Ending 16 July 1892* (Bombay: n.p., 1892), 11.

76. *Report of Native Papers Published in the Bengal Presidency for the Week Ending 16 February 1889* (Calcutta: Bengali Secretariat Press, 1889), 155.

77. *Selections from the Vernacular Newspapers Received up to 15 May 1888* (Allahabad: N.W.P and Oudh Government Press, 1888), 313–14.

78. H. E. Beal, *Indian Ink: A Novel* (London: Harrap, 1954).

79. Arnold, *Everyday Technology: Machines and the Making of India's Modernity* (Chicago: University of Chicago Press, 2013), 86. Nira Wickramasinghe, *Metallic Modern: Everyday Machines*

in Colonial Sri Lanka (New York: Berghahn Books, 2014) is an equivalent study for Sri Lanka, thought it doesn't discuss typewriters.

80. Beal, *Indian Ink*, 117.

81. Arnold, *Everyday Technology*, 153.

82. Woolf, *The Village in the Jungle*, 261.

83. Woolf, *The Village in the Jungle*, 261–62.

84. For more on Victorian notions of reading, imagination, and affect, see Rachel Ablow, "Introduction: The Feeling of Reading," in *The Feeling of Reading: Affective Experience and Victorian Literature*, ed. Rachel Ablow (Ann Arbor: University of Michigan Press, 2010), 1–10.

85. Woolf, *The Village in the Jungle*, 1–2. Emphasis mine.

86. Das and Poole, "State and Its Margins," 7.

87. For more on "archive stories" and the value of personal narratives about research, see Antoinette Burton, "Introduction," in *Archive Stories: Facts, Fictions, and the Writing of History*, ed. Antoinette Burton (Durham, NC: Duke University Press, 2005), 1–24.

88. For more on migrated archives, especially in the context of the decolonization of Kenya, see Caroline Elkins, "Looking Beyond Mau Mau: Archiving Violence in the Era of Decolonization," *American Historical Review* 120, no. 3 (2015): 852–68.

89. Maya Jasanoff, "Misremembering the British Empire," *The New Yorker*, November 2, 2020, https://www.newyorker.com/magazine/2020/11/02misremembering-the-british-empire.

90. Sarath Sisira Kumara Wickramanayaka, "The Management of Official Records in Public Institutions in Sri Lanka 1802–1990," (Unpublished PhD dissertation, University College London, 1992), 18.

91. Wickramanayaka, "The Management of Official Records," 58–59.

92. For more on the havoc insects wreaked in colonial offices, see Rohan Deb Roy, "White Ants, Empire and Entomo-politics in South Asia," *The Historical Journal* 63, no. 2 (2020): 411–36.

Chapter 3: Reading for Time

1. All translations in this chapter, unless otherwise stated, are mine.

See https://www.guptapresspanjika.com, accessed July 14, 2014. The website has since been deleted, with the press managing its advertising and publicity via social media outlets.

2. Most of the panjikas in the National Library, Kolkata, were part of the Ashutosh Mukherjee Collection, comprising over eighty thousand books from the personal library of the Bengali educationalist, Ashutosh Mukherjee (1864–1924). A few of these panjikas contain annotations.

3. The first day of the Bengali calendar is April 14 or 15 of the Gregorian calendar.

4. Battala, an area in North Calcutta with the highest density of printing presses in this period, was known for its prolific production of cheap pamphlets and lowbrow literary works, all of which were inexpensive to the point of being disposable. There has been a great deal of work on these publications in Bengal, significantly: Tapti Roy, "Disciplining the Printed Text: Colonial and Nationalist Surveillance of Bengali Literature," in *Texts of Power: Emerging Disciplines in Colonial Bengal*, ed. Partha Chatterjee (Minneapolis: Minnesota University Press, 1995), 30–62; Sumanta Banerjee, *The Parlour and the Streets: Elite and Popular Culture in Nineteenth-Century Calcutta*

(Calcutta: Seagull Books, 1998); Anindita Ghosh, *Power in Print: Popular Publishing and the Politics of Language and Culture in a Colonial Society, 1778–1905* (Delhi: Oxford University Press, 2006).

5. An 1818 almanac was produced by a Durgaprasad of Jorasankho, who hoped that the exercise would bring him "wealth." See Gautam Bhadra, "Pictures in Celestial and Worldly Time: Illustrations in Nineteenth-Century Bengali Almanacs," in *New Cultural Histories of India: Materiality and Practices*, eds. Partha Chatterjee, Tapati Guha-Thakurta, and Bodhisattva Kar (Delhi: Oxford University Press, 2014), 277.

6. The inclusion of such secular information was the reason why, as the present director of the Gupta Press, Arijit Roy Chowdhury, informed me, panjikas may have come to gain a non-Hindu readership as well. Further, as flipping through any volume will demonstrate, the texts also contained some information about key dates of other religions, and woodcuts depicting their festivals.

7. Jason Scott-Warren, "Reading Graffiti in the Early Modern Book," *Huntington Library Quarterly* 73, no. 3 (September 2010): 363–81; Adam Smyth, "Almanacs, Annotators, and Life-Writing in Early Modern England," *English Literary Renaissance* 38, no. 2 (2008): 200–44; William Sherman, *Used Books: Marking Readers in Renaissance England* (Philadelphia: University of Pennsylvania Press, 2008).

8. Projit Mukharji, *Nationalizing the Body: The Medical Market, Print and Daktari Medicine* (London: Anthem Books, 2009).

9. Debjani Bhattacharyya, *Empire and Ecology in the Bengal Delta* (Cambridge: Cambridge University Press, 2018), 18.

10. Bhadra, "Pictures in Celestial and Worldly Time," 275–316. See also Gautam Bhadra, *Nyada Battala Jay Kaybar? [How Many Times Will Baldy go to Battala?]* (Kolkata: Chhatim Books, 2011). See also Parna Sengupta, "Astral Time: Almanacs and Colonial Modernity in Bengal," in *Knowing India: Colonial and Modern Constructions of the Past: Essays in Honor of Thomas R. Trautmann*, ed. Cynthia Talbot (Delhi: Yoda Press, 2011), 213–33.

11. For more on Long's incredible life, see Geoffrey Oddie, *Missionaries, Rebellion and Protonationalism: James Long of Bengal 1814–87* (London: Routledge, 1999); Trpti Chaudhury, "The Reverend James Long and Mass Education in Bengal, 1855–1872," *Proceedings of the Indian History Congress* 40 (1979): 779–88.

The first catalogue, *Granthavali: An Alphabetical List of Works Published in Bengali*, was published in Calcutta in 1852 and was an informal exercise. The next two catalogues were sponsored by the British government in South Asia: James Long, *A Descriptive Catalogue of Bengali Works, Containing a Classified List of Fourteen Hundred Bengali Books and Pamphlets, Which Have Issued from the Press, during the Last Sixty Years, with Occasional Notices of the Subjects, the Price, and Where Printed* (Calcutta: Sanders, Cones, and Co., 1855); James Long, *Returns Relating to Publications in the Bengali Language, in 1857, to Which Is Added, a List of the Native Presses, with the Books Printed at Each, Their Price and Character, with a Notice of the Past Condition and Future Prospects of the Vernacular Press of Bengal and the Statistics of the Bombay and Madras Vernacular Presses* (Calcutta: John Gray, 1859). For a comparative study of all three catalogues, alongside other contemporary efforts at enumerative bibliography, see Roy, "Disciplining the Printed Text," 32–47. Robert Darnton also discusses Long's 1859 catalogue. See Darnton, "Book Production in British India, 1850–1900," *Book History* 5 (2002): 240–45.

12. Long, *Returns Relating to Publications in the Bengali Language*, 8, 20.

13. Long, *Returns Relating to Publications in the Bengali Language*, 20–21.

14. Long, *Returns Relating to Publications in the Bengali Language*, 21.

15. *Act XXV of 1867* (Calcutta: Superintendent of Government Printing, 1890).

16. Similar catalogues were produced for the other presidencies of India.

17. The earliest record in Bengal Library catalogues for a Gupta Press panjika is 1910. Gaps in the quarterly reports have been noted by several scholars. See Abhijit Gupta, *The Spread of Print in Colonial India: Into the Hinterland* (Cambridge: Cambridge University, 2021), 8; Samarpita Mitra, *Periodicals, Readers and the Making of a Modern Literary Culture: Bengal at the Turn of the Twentieth Century* (Leiden, Amsterdam: Brill, 2020), 31–32. The shortfall was due to the uneven nature of book registration. Books were only listed in government records if their printers registered them with the relevant local office: many refused to do so, in fear of censorship or being made to pay extra taxes. Then there were also the absurdities of classification leading to what A.R. Venkatachalapathy calls "instances of bureaucratic stupidity." See Venkatachalapathy, *The Province of the Book: Scholars, Scribes, and Scribblers in Colonial Tamilnadu* (Ranikhet, India: Permanent Black, 2012), 175.

18. Amit Bhattacharya, *Business Politics and Technology: Select Themes in the Economic History of Modern India* (Kolkata: Readers Service, 2005), 71–75.

19. *Bengal Library Catalogue of Books for the Third Quarter Ending 30 September 1899*, in appendix to *The Calcutta Gazette* (Calcutta: n.p., 1900), 26–27.

20. From 1864 to 1884, *The Indian Directory* was published as *The Bengal Directory*.

21. *Bengal Library Catalogue of Books Registered in the Presidency of Bengal during the Quarter Ending 31 March 1920*, in appendix to *The Calcutta Gazette* (Calcutta: n.p., 1920), 122; *Bengal Library Catalogue of Books Registered in the Presidency of Bengal during the Quarter Ending 30 June 1920*, in appendix to *The Calcutta Gazette* (Calcutta: n.p., 1920), 76.

22. Nile Green, "The Uses of Books in a Late Mughal Takiyya: Persianate Knowledge Between Person and Paper," *Modern Asian Studies* 44, no. 2 (2010): 243, 254.

23. Green, "The Uses of Books," 243.

24. Lal Behari Day, *Bengal Peasant Life* [1878] (London: Macmillan, 1926), vii. The novel was first published as *Govinda Samanta, or The History of a Bengal Raiyat* (1874).

25. Day, *Bengal Peasant Life*, 48–54. Day converted from Hinduism to Christianity in 1843, working as a missionary and then an English professor. His religious affiliations perhaps explain some of the animosity his novel levels at astrologers.

26. Parna Sengupta, "Market Predictions: Astrology in Modern India," in *Intersections of Religion and Astronomy*, eds. Aaron Ricket, Christopher J. Corbally, and Darry Dinnell (London: Routledge, 2020), 134.

27. Long, *Returns Relating to Publications in the Bengali Language*, 21.

28. See Ghosh, *Power in Print*, 84.

29. Prathama Banerjee, *Politics of Time: "Primitives" and History-Writing in a Colonial Society* (Delhi: Oxford University Press, 2006), 40.

30. Banerjee, *Politics of Time*, 41.

31. The astrological calculations on which panjikas depended used these "acts of the body" as an index of temporal measurement. Banerjee, *Politics of Time*, 63.

32. See Thomas Trautmann, *The Clash of Chronologies: Ancient India in the Modern World* (Delhi: Yoda Press, 2009), xix, 31; Dipesh Chakrabarty, *Provincializing Europe: Postcolonial*

Thought and Historical Difference (Princeton, NJ: Princeton University Press, 2000); Romila Thapar, *Time as a Metaphor of History: Early India* (Delhi: Oxford University Press, 1996).

33. The colonialist belief that native populations had "no history" is one that is replicated across a range of historical and geographical contexts. It is often evoked, for example, as a way of explaining the violent relationship between white colonizers and indigenous populations in the United States.

34. Chakrabarty, *Provincializing Europe*, 8. See also Johannes Fabian's "denial of coevalness": the relegation of the anthropologist subject to a "time other than the present of the producer of anthropological discourse." Johannes Fabian, *Time and the Other: How Anthropology Makes Its Object* (1983; reissue, New York: Columbia University Press, 2002), 31.

35. Ritika Prasad, "'Time-Sense': Railways and Temporality in Colonial India," *Modern Asian Studies* 47, no. 4 (2013): 1257. For a detailed description of the transition between different kinds of time in colonial South Asia, against a global frame, see Vanessa Ogle, "Whose Time Is It? The Pluralization of Time and the Global Condition, 1870s–1940s," *American Historical Review* 118, no. 5 (December 2013): 1376–402. For examples beyond South Asia, see David S. Landes, *Revolution in Time: Clocks and the Making of the Modern World* (Cambridge, MA: Harvard University Press, 1983), 94; Wolfgang Schivelbusch, *The Railway Journey: The Industrialization of Time and Space in the 19th Century* (1977; reissue, Berkeley: University of California Press, 1986), 43–44.

36. Quoted in Ogle, "Whose Time Is It?" 1389.

37. Bernard Capp, *Astrology and the Popular Press: English Almanacs 1500–1800* (London: Faber, 1979), 15.

38. *Lord Ripon's Panjika for 1884–1885*, compiled by Benimadhab Dey (Chitpore: n.p., 1884); *Notun Victoria Panjika Ebong Brihot Dairektari, 1880–1881* [New Victoria Panjika and Large Directory], compiled by B. M. Bhattacharjee (Kolkata: n.p., 1880).

39. Banerjee, *Politics of Time*, 63–64. The Gregorian calendar was adopted across the British empire in 1752 for official purposes, but Bengali Hindus continued to use their own calendar for religious and practical purposes.

40. Benedict Anderson, *Imagined Communities: Reflections on the Origin and Spread of Nationalism* (1983; reissue, London: Verso, 1991), 35.

41. Sumit Sarkar notes that clocks and watches came to colonial South Asia relatively late, only making an appearance at the turn of the nineteenth century. Sumit Sarkar, *Beyond Nationalist Frames: Postmodernism, Hindu Fundamentalism, History* (Bloomington: Indiana University Press, 2002), 10.

42. Sarkar, *Beyond Nationalist Frames*, 25.

43. For an example of this advertisement, see *Panjika, 1902–1903* (Calcutta: Gupta Press, 1902).

44. Sumit Sarkar, "'Kaliyuga,' 'Chakri' and 'Bhakti': Ramakrishna and His Times," *Economic and Political Weekly* 27, no. 29 (July 1992): 1549. See also E. P. Thompson, "Time, Work-discipline, and Industrial Capitalism," *Past and Present: A Journal of Historical Studies* 38 (1967): 56–97.

45. Sarkar, "'Kaliyuga,'" 1549.

46. *Panjika, 1914–1915* (Calcutta: Gupta Press, 1914), n.p.

47. Stephen Kern, *The Culture of Time and Space: 1880–1918* (Cambridge, MA: Harvard University Press, 1983), 20.

48. Advertisement for West Watch Co., in *Panjika, 1914–15* (Calcutta: Gupta Press, 1914), n.p.

49. *Nutan Panjika* [New Almanac], *1862–63* (Calcutta: Cones and Co., 1862).

50. Sarkar, "'Kaliyuga,'" 1549.

51. The speed of printing could also contribute to the creation of print countercultures. In the case of Victorian Britain, "slow printing," as Elizabeth Miller calls it, was associated with niche, radical periodical presses that sought to position their publications against mass-consumerist ones. Elizabeth C. Miller, *Slow Print: Literary Radicalism and Late Victorian Print Culture* (Stanford, CA: Stanford University Press, 2013).

52. Isabel Hofmeyr, *Gandhi's Printing Press: Experiments in Slow Reading* (Cambridge, MA: Harvard University Press, 2013), 4.

53. Quoted in Bhadra, "Pictures in Celestial and Worldly Time," 278. Emphasis mine.

54. Quoted in Bhadra, "Pictures in Celestial and Worldly Time," 282. Emphasis mine.

55. "Bhumika" [Introduction], in *Bishudda Siddhanta Panjika*, compiled by Srimadhab Chandra Chattopadhyay (Calcutta, n.p., 1890), n.p. Emphasis mine.

56. Saswati Sengupta, *The Song Seekers* (Delhi: Zubaan Books, 2011).

57. Sengupta, *The Song Seekers*, 113.

58. Aparajita Mukhopadhyay, *Imperial Technology and "Native" Agency: A Social History of the Railways in Colonial India, 1850–1920* (London: Routledge, 2018), 30.

59. For more about late trains and unpunctual travelers, see Mukhopadhyay, *Imperial Technology,* 30–34.

60. Mukhopadhyay, *Imperial Technology*, 37.

61. Ritika Prasad discusses the public demand for railway timetables in Urdu and Hindi in the 1870s. The Railway Act of 1879 made the display of timetables in vernacular languages mandatory. See Prasad, "'Time-Sense,'" 1274.

62. Esbester, "Nineteenth-Century Timetables and the History of Reading," *Book History* 12 (2009): 163.

63. www.guptapresspanjika.com, accessed July 14, 2014.

64. Projit Mukharji points out that early advertisements often ran into several pages and had their own self-contained page numbers in many almanacs. See Mukharji, *Nationalizing the Body*, 101.

65. Pages 413–16 are missing. See *Gupta Press Panjika*, 1888–89 (Calcutta: Gupta Press, 1888).

66. Thomas Macaulay, "Minute on Indian Education," in *Archives of Empire: From the East India Company to the Suez Canal*, Vol. 1, eds. Barbara Harlow and Mia Carter (Durham, NC: Duke University Press, 2003), 237.

67. William Sherman, for example, reminds us that early modern English almanacs often contain scribbles that had little or no connection with their content, including and not restricted to shopping lists, drafts of letters and arithmetical calculations. See Sherman, *Used Books*, 15.

68. Smyth, "Almanacs," 218.

69. *Panjika*, 1902–3 (Calcutta: Gupta Press, 1902).

70. See, for example, Sherman, *Used Books*, 23; Juliet Fleming, *Graffiti and the Writing Arts of Early Modern England* (London: Reaktion Books, 2001).

71. Thanks to Abhijit Gupta for pointing this out to me at an early stage of my research.

72. Bhadra, "Pictures in Celestial and Worldly Time," 282.

73. See, for example, Chandrima Pal, "A Bengal Almanac That's Survived 150 Years of History Is Now Counting Its Last Days," *Scroll.in*, April 11, 2017, https://scroll.in/magazine/832408/a-bengali-almanac-thats-survived-150-years-of-history-is-now-slowly-counting-its-last-days;

Barnini Maitra Chakraborty, "Gupta Press Panjika: The Story of an Almanac," *The Telegraph*, April 15, 2022, https://www.telegraphindia.com/my-kolkata/lifestyle/gupta-press-panjika-the-story-of-a-bangali-almanac-essential-for-poila-baisakh-the-bengali-new-year/cid/1860756.

74. Pal, "A Bengali Almanac."

75. *Panjika*, 1943–44 (Calcutta: P. M. Bagchi, 1943), n.p.

Chapter 4: Reading for Company

1. *Saguna* was first serialized in *The Madras Christian College Magazine* between 1887 and 1888. It was first published in book form in 1892. All references in this chapter are to the following edition: Krupabai Satthianadhan, *Saguna: A Story of Native Christian Life* [1892] (Madras: Srinivasa Varadachari & Co., 1895).

2. Satthianadhan, *Saguna*, 127.

3. Satthianadhan, *Saguna*, 127. Emphasis in original.

4. Satthianadhan, *Saguna*, 165.

5. Priya Joshi, *In Another Country: Colonialism, Culture, and the English Novel in India* (New York: Columbia University Press, 2002), 180.

6. "Mofussil," in *Hobson-Jobson: Being a Glossary of Anglo-Indian Colloquial Words and Phrases and of Kindred Terms; Etymological, Historical, Geographical, and Discursive*, by Henry Yule and Arthur C. Burnell (London: John Murray, 1886), 435. The dictionary also notes that the word can be used as both as noun and an adjective.

7. Josephine McDonagh, "Rethinking Provincialism in Mid-Nineteeth-Century Fiction: *Our Village* to *Villette*," *Victorian Studies* 55, no. 3 (Spring 2013): 403.

8. Sumana Roy, "The Provincial Reader," *Los Angeles Review of Books*, April 19, 2020, https://lareviewofbooks.org/article/the-provincial-reader/.

9. This review, reprinted as part of the 1895 edition of the novel, appeared in *The Malabar and Travancore Spectator*. See Satthianadhan, *Saguna*, iii.

10. Kamala Satthianadhan, "Introduction," *The Indian Ladies' Magazine* 1, no. 1 (July 1901): 1.

11. Charles Wood, *The Despatch of 1854 on "General Education in India,"* (reprinted, London: General Council on Education in India, n.d.), 35.

12. For work that explores the history of women's education in South Asia, see, among others: Geraldine Forbes, *Women in Modern India* (Cambridge: Cambridge University Press, 1996), esp. 32–63; Sanjay Seth, *Subject Lessons: The Western Education of Colonial India* (Durham, NC: Duke University Press, 2007), 129–58; Shefali Chandra, *The Sexual Life of English: Languages of Caste and Desire in Colonial India* (Durham, NC: Duke University Press, 2012).

13. Gauri Viswanathan, *Masks of Conquest: Literary and British Rule in India* (1989; reissue, New York: Columbia University Press, 2015), 3.

14. Sanjay Seth, *Subject Lessons: The Western Education of Colonial India* (Durham, NC: Duke University Press, 2007), 129–30.

15. Seth, *Subject Lessons*, 129.

16. An Indian Educationist, "The Present Condition of Female Education in India," *The Indian Ladies' Magazine* 1, no. 1 (July 1901): 5.

17. W. Francis, *Census of India 1901: Madras* (Vol. 15, Part 1) (Report) (Madras: Government Press, 1902), 74.

18. Francis, *Census of India 1901*, 79.

19. Forbes, *Women in Modern India*, 33.

20. As Geraldine Forbes notes: "If learning to read would lead to a husband's death, then pursuing knowledge was tantamount to suicide." See Forbes, *Women in Modern India*, 33.

21. Seth, *Subject Lessons*, 38.

22. See, for example, Antoinette Burton, *Burdens of History: British Feminists, Indian Women, and Imperial Culture, 1865–1915* (Chapel Hill: University of North Carolina Press, 1994).

23. For example, see Forbes, *Women in Modern India*, 43, 44, 51, 67, 286.

24. For example, see Elizabeth C. Miller, *Extraction Ecologies and the Literature of the Long Exhaustion* (Princeton, NJ: Princeton University Press, 2021), 159–69; Barnita Bagchi, "'Because Novels Are True, and Histories Are False': Indian Women Writing Fiction in English, 1860–1918" in *The History of the Indian Novel in English*, ed. Ulka Anjaria (Cambridge: Cambridge University Press, 2015), 59–72.

25. There are a few welcome exceptions. Deborah Logan's *The Indian Ladies' Magazine, 1901–1938: From Raj to Swaraj* (Bethlehem, PA: Lehigh University Press, 2017), which provides a survey of the major thematic threads with which the magazine engages. Tara Puri provides a history of *The Indian Ladies' Magazine* that centers the contributors of Kamala Satthianadhan and her investment in transnational print networks. See Tara Puri, "Kamala Satthianadhan and *The Indian Ladies' Magazine*: Women's Editorship and Transnational Print Networks in Late Colonial India," *Victorian Periodicals Review* 55, no. 3 and 4 (Fall/Winter 2022): 340–72.

26. James Long, *Returns Relating to Publications in the Bengali Language, in 1857, to Which Is Added, a List of the Native Presses, with the Books Printed at Each, Their Price and Character, with a Notice of the Past Condition and Future Prospects of the Vernacular Press of Bengal and the Statistics of the Bombay and Madras Vernacular Presses* (Calcutta: John Gray, 1859), 15.

Swati Moitra's discussion of "communitarian reading" among nineteenth-century Bengali women attends to practices of reading aloud, as well as the spaces of the home where women read. See Moitra, "Reading Together: 'Communitarian Reading' and Women Readers in Colonial Bengal," *Hypatia* 32, no. 3 (2017): 627–43.

27. Shahinda, "Correspondence Column: I," *The Indian Ladies' Magazine* 8, no. 9 (May 1909): 352. Emphasis in original.

28. Padmini Sengupta, *The Portrait of an Indian Woman* (Calcutta: YMCA, 1956), 1. Barnita Bagchi identifies the town as being in the native state of Pithapuram in the Madras Presidency. Today, it is part of the state of Andhra Pradesh. See Barnita Bagchi, "Tracing Two Generations in Twentieth Century Indian Women's Education through Analysis of Literary Sources: Selected Writing by Padmini Sengupta," *Women's History Review* 29, no. 3 (2020): 461.

29. Kamala Satthianadhan was born Hannah Ratnam Krishnamma, but she took the name Kamala after her marriage to Samuel.

30. For more on Kamala Satthianadhan's life, see Eunice D'Souza, ed., *The Satthiandhan Family Album* (Delhi: Sahitya Akademi, 2005). The biography by her daughter, Padmini Sengupta, also provides a useful overview. See Sengupta, *The Portrait of an Indian Woman*.

31. Sengupta, *The Portrait of an Indian Woman*, 8.

32. Sengupta, *The Portrait of an Indian Woman*, 8.

33. Sengupta, *The Portrait of an Indian Woman*, 191.

34. *A Catalogue of Books Printed in the Madras Presidency*, in *Fort St. George Gazette* Supplement (First quarter ending March 31, 1902) (Madras: Government Press, 1902), 32–33. The quarterly reports have no record of *The Indian Ladies' Magazine* for 1901.

35. These statistics are compiled from *A Catalogue of Books Printed in the Madras Presidency*, in *Fort St. George Gazette* Supplement (First quarter ending March 31, 1902) ((Madras: Government Press, 1902).

36. Meredith Borthwick, *The Changing Role of Women in Bengal, 1849–1905* (Princeton, NJ: Princeton University Press, 1984); Gail Minault, "Women's Magazines in Urdu as Sources for Muslim Social History," *Indian Journal of Gender Studies* 5, no. 2 (1998): 201–14.

37. Francesca Orsini, *The Hindi Public Sphere 1920–1940: Language and Literature in the Age of Nationalism* (Delhi: Oxford University Press, 2002), 273; Francesca Orsini, "Domesticity and Beyond: Hindi Women's Journals in the Early Twentieth Century, *South Asia Research* 19, no. 2 (1999): 38.

That said, male involvement was not entirely preempted. See Mytheli Sreenivas, "Emotion, Identity, and the Female Subject: Tamil Women's Magazines in Colonial India, 1890–1940," *Journal of Women's History* 14, no. 4 (Winter 2003): 61. Shobhna Nijhawan also notes that the inclusion of male contributors in the twentieth century was a deliberate move to gain a larger audience and enhance political impact. See Nijhawan, *Women and Girls in the Hindi Public Sphere: Periodical Literature in Colonial North India* (Delhi: Oxford University Press, 2012), 4.

38. For an account of how the practice of selling bound volumes of Victorian periodicals makes us rethink the periodical's status as ephemera, see Laurel Brake, "The Longevity of 'Ephemera': Library Editions of Nineteenth-Century Periodicals and Newspapers," *Media History* 18, no. 1 (2012): 7–20.

39. "Terms of Subscription," *The Indian Ladies' Magazine* 1, no. 1 (July 1901): n.p.

40. Satthianadhan, "Introduction," 2.

41. Satthianadhan, "Introduction," 2.

42. Satthianadhan, "Introduction," 2.

43. Satthianadhan, "Introduction," 2.

44. This piece of information is announced at the start of Isabel Brander, "Food and Its Relations to Health," *The Indian Ladies' Magazine* 2, no. 9 (March 1903): 278.

45. Edwin Arnold, "Indian Ladies," *The Indian Ladies' Magazine* 2, no. 4 (October 1902): 127–28. The article was republished from the *Daily Telegraph*, London.

46. Arnold, "Indian Ladies," 127.

47. Arnold, "Indian Ladies," 127–28.

48. "Opinions of the Press," *The Indian Ladies' Magazine* 1, no. 2 (August 1901): n.p.

49. For example, Besley's April 1903 article, "Social Intercourse between English and Indian Women," the third of three articles with this title, was republished in *Womanhood* in July 1903. See Catherine Besley, "Social Intercourse between English and Indian Women," *The Indian Ladies' Magazine* 2, no. 10 (April 1903): 302–4; Catherine Besley, "Social Intercourse between English and Indian Women," *Womanhood* 10, no. 56 (July 1903): 116–18. It's worth noting that while Besley wrote for both magazines, none of Satthianadhan's own articles appeared in *Womanhood*: she exists in that publication only through citation and reference.

50. J. L. Whiting, "Women in China," *The Indian Ladies' Magazine* 2, no. 1 (July 1902): 27–29.

51. Note that the "News and Notes"-style column was a staple of many Victorian-era magazines, where news from across the world would be recorded in a "Foreign Notes and News" section. These columns—indeed, in both mainstream and radical periodicals as a whole—contained references to and articles about South Asian women. See, for example, Julie F. Codell, ed., *Imperial Co-histories: National Identities and the British and Colonial Press* (Madison, NJ: Fairleigh Dickinson University Press, 2003).

52. "News and Notes," *The Indian Ladies' Magazine* 4, no. 3 (September 1904): 94. The magazine accidently calls her "Marion."

53. "News and Notes," *The Indian Ladies' Magazine* 4, no. 3 (September 1904): 94.

54. "News and Notes," *The Indian Ladies' Magazine* 6, no. 10 (April 1907): 387–88.

55. Antoinette Burton and Isabel Hofmeyr, "Introduction: The Spine of Empire? Books and the Making of an Imperial Commons," in *Ten Books That Shaped the British Empire: Creating an Imperial Commons*, eds. Antoinette M. Burton and Isabel Hofmeyr (Durham, NC: Duke University Press, 2014), 3–5. For an argument about how reprinting shapes literary reception in the context of the United States, see Meredith McGill, *American Literature and the Culture of Reprinting, 1834–1853* (Philadelphia: University of Pennsylvania Press, 2003).

56. For more on the history of the Exchange, see Ellen Gruber Garvey, *Writing with Scissors: American Scrapbooks from the Civil War to the Harlem Renaissance* (Oxford: Oxford University Press, 2013); Ross Harvey, "Bringing the News to New Zealand: The Supply and Control of Overseas News in the Nineteenth Century," *Media History* 8, no. 1 (2002): 21–34; Anke te Heesen, *The Newspaper Clipping: A Modern Paper Object*, trans. Lori Lantz (Manchester: Manchester University Press, 2014).

57. For scholarship on this subject, see Isabel Hofmeyr, *Gandhi's Printing Press: Experiments in Slow Reading* (Cambridge, MA: Harvard University Press, 2013), 13; Priti Joshi, *Empire News: The Anglo-Indian Press Writes India* (Buffalo, NY: SUNY Press, 2021), 49–58; Priti Joshi, "Scissors-and-Paste: Ephemerality and Memorialization in the Archive of Indian Newspapers," *Amodern* 7 (2017), https://amodern.net/article/scissors-and-paste/.

58. Kwame Antony Appiah, "Cosmopolitan Reading," in *Cosmopolitan Geographies: New Locations in Literature and Culture*, ed. Vinay Dharwadker (New York: Routledge, 2001), 224–25.

59. Appiah, "Cosmopolitan Reading," 203.

60. An Englishwoman in India, "Suggestions for English Reading: John Ruskin's 'Sesame and Lilies,'" *The Indian Ladies' Magazine* 2, no. 9 (March 1903): 284. The column was spurred on by a suggestion from a contributor.

61. A. Zechariah, "Books and Reading," *The Indian Ladies' Magazine* 8, no. 6 (December 1908), 193.

62. S. K., "English Novels for Indian Girls," *The Indian Ladies' Magazine* 4, no. 9 (March 1905): 272.

63. Joshi, *In Another Country*, 129.

64. Zechariah, "Books and Reading," 194.

65. S. K. "English Novels," 273.

66. An Englishwoman in India, "Suggestions for English Reading: Sir Edwin Arnold's 'The Light of Asia,'" *The Indian Ladies' Magazine* 3, no. 7 (January 1904): 213.

67. Alfred Nundy, "The Higher Education of Women," *The Indian Ladies' Magazine* 1, no. 8 (February 1902): 229.

68. An Englishwoman in India, "Suggestions for English Reading: Mark Twain's 'The Prince and the Pauper,'" *The Indian Ladies' Magazine* 3, no. 3 (September 1903): 86.

69. This mode of reading English literature for its moral lessons was replicated elsewhere in the colonial world. For an example from twentieth-century Ghana, see Stephanie Newell, *Literary Culture in Colonial Ghana: "How to Play the Game of Life"* (Manchester: Manchester University Press, 2002), 83–97.

70. An Englishwoman in India, "Sesame and Lilies," 285.

71. An Englishwoman in India, "Suggestions for English Reading: Coventry Patmore's 'The Angel in the House,'" *The Indian Ladies' Magazine* 2, no. 11 (May 1903): 353–54.

72. An Englishwoman in India, "Angel in the House," 353.

73. An Englishwoman in India, "Angel in the House," 353.

74. An Englishwoman in India, "Angel in the House," 353.

75. Scholarship on missionary education in colonial South Asia is extensive. For one example, see Hayden Bellenoit, *Missionary Education and Empire in Late Colonial India, 1860–1920* (London: Routledge, 2007).

76. An Englishwoman in India, "Angel in the House," 353.

77. Bankim Chandra Chattopadhyay, "Sakuntala, Miranda and Desdemona," trans. Subha Chakraborty Dasgupta, in *Critical Discourse in Bangla*, eds. Subha Chakraborty Dasgupta and Subrata Singh (Delhi: Routledge, 2021), 84–91.

78. Bankim, "Sakuntala, Miranda and Desdemona," 87.

79. Bankim, "Sakuntala, Miranda and Desdemona," 87.

80. For scholarship on the South Asian reception of Shakespeare, see, among others: Jyotsna Singh, "Different Shakespeares: The Bard in Colonial/Postcolonial India," *Theatre Journal* 41, no. 4 (December 1989): 445–58; Poonam Trivedi and Dennis Bartholomew, *India's Shakespeare: Translation, Interpretation, and Performance* (Newark: University of Delaware Press, 2005); Sharmila Mukherjee, *Shakespeare and the Colonial Encounter in India in the Eighteenth and Nineteenth Centuries* (Unpublished PhD diss., University of Washington, Seattle, 2016).

81. Poetry was a major part of English literature syllabi in South Asian schools. See Joshi, *In Another Country*, 17. Historians of reading in the colonial world have long pointed out the popularity of sentimental novels. For an example from India, see Joshi, *In Another Country*, 83–97; for Ghana, see Newell, *Literary Culture in Colonial Ghana*, 98–119.

82. "A Puzzle Competition: The Shakespeare-Names Competition," *The Indian Ladies' Magazine* 7, no. 10 (April 1908): 333.

83. "New Puzzle Competition: The 'Correct-Passages' Quotations," *The Indian Ladies' Magazine* 7, no. 11 (May 1908): 363.

84. "New Puzzle Competition: Puzzle Verses," *The Indian Ladies' Magazine* 8, no. 1 (July 1908): 21.

85. "Our Prize Competitions," *The Indian Ladies' Magazine* 8, no. 1 (July 1908): 21.

86. Alison Herman, "Previously On: How Recaps Changed the Way We Watch Television," *The Ringer*, July 31, 2018.

87. Herman, "Previously On."

88. Zechariah, "Books and Reading," 195.

89. Zechariah, "Books and Reading," 195.

90. Michael Warner, "Publics and Counterpublics," *Public Culture* 14, no. 1 (2002): 49–90.

91. Patricia Spacks, *On Rereading* (Cambridge, MA: Harvard University Press, 2011), 243.

92. Gillian Silverman, *Bodies and Books: Reading and the Fantasy of Communion in Nineteenth-century America* (Philadelphia: University of Pennsylvania Press, 2012), 6. Emphasis in original.

93. Stephen Balm, "My Impressions of 'East Lynn,'" *The Indian Ladies' Magazine* 1, no. 5 (November 1901): 136–39. The novel's title is misspelt throughout the article.

94. Balm, "My Impressions of 'East Lynn,'" 136.

95. Charles Wood, *Memorials of Mrs. Henry Wood* (London: Richard Bentley, 1894), 296.

96. Wood, *Memorials of Mrs. Henry Wood*, 296.

97. Balm, "My Impressions of 'East Lynn,'" 137.

98. Balm, "My Impressions of 'East Lynn,'" 137.

99. Balm, "My Impressions of 'East Lynn,'" 137.

100. Balm, "My Impressions of 'East Lynn,'" 137.

101. Balm, "My Impressions of 'East Lynn,'" 137.

102. P. R. Krishnaswami, "The Merchant of Venice," *The Indian Ladies' Magazine* 10, no. 11 (May 1911): 319–20.

103. Krishnaswami, "The Merchant of Venice," 319.

104. Kamala Satthianadhan, "The Women of Shakespeare: II. Portia, the Wife of Brutus," *The Indian Ladies' Magazine* 1, no. 9 (March 1902): 256.

105. An Indian Lady, "An Estimate of Shakespeare's Desdemona," *The Indian Ladies' Magazine* 6, no. 6 (December 1906): 187. For an argument about how books are cast as friends in eighteenth-century Britain, see Deidre Lynch, *Loving Literature: A Cultural History* (Chicago: Chicago University Press, 2015).

106. I have consulted the original Bengali version of the novel (1901) and an English translation (1971). See Rabindranath Tagore, *Nashtanirh* [1901], in *Deepika* (Calcutta: Viswabharati, 1963), 142–194; Rabindranath Tagore, *The Broken Nest*, trans. Supriya Bari and Mary Lago (Columbia, MO: University of Missouri Press, 1971). Translations are from the latter.

107. *Charulata* (The Lonely Wife), directed by Satyajit Ray (Calcutta: R. D. Bansal, 1964).

108. Tagore, *The Broken Nest*, 33.

109. Tagore, *The Broken Nest*, 33–34.

110. Tagore, *The Broken Nest*, 49.

111. Tagore, *The Broken Nest*, 22.

112. Tagore, *The Broken Nest*, 21.

113. Tagore, *The Broken Nest*, 90.

114. Tagore, *The Broken Nest*, 28.

Epilogue

1. "Artist Intervention: *File Room*," *Future Anterior: Journal of Historic Preservation, History, Theory, and Criticism* 11, no. 1 (2014): x.

2. "Artist Intervention," x.

3. "Artist Intervention," x.

SELECTED BIBLIOGRAPHY

Almanacs

Offices of the Gupta Press, Kolkata
National Library of India, Kolkata
    Ashutosh Mukherjee Collection
Offices of P. M. Bagchi, Kolkata
Bodleian Library, Oxford
British Library, London

Manuscript Sources and Archives

Brighton and Hove Libraries, Brighton
    Wolseley Special Collections
British Library, London
    Macmillan Archive
Sri Lanka National Archives, Colombo
    Lot 27: The Records of the Hambantota Kachcheri, 1867–1966

Archived Newspapers, Magazines, and Serials

The Bolton Evening News
Ceylon Government Gazette
The Labour Leader
The Pall Mall Gazette
The Star
St. James Gazette
Taunton Courier and Western Advertiser
The Indian Ladies' Magazine
Western Daily Press

Manuals and Handbooks

C., Major. *Indian Horse Notes: An Epitome on Useful Information, Arranged for Ready Reference on Emergencies Specially Adapted for Officers and Country Residents.* Calcutta: Thacker, Spink, and Co., 1885.

Counterinsurgency. Field Manual 3-24. Washington, D.C.: Marine Corps, 2006.
Doveton, Henry. *Military Training in Engl. & Hindustani.* Urdu edition. London: Chatham, 1890.
Hardless, Charles. *The Clerk's Manual: A Complete Guide to General Office Routine.* Calcutta: Thacker, Spink, and Co., 1903.
Wolseley, Garnet. *The Field Pocket-book for the Auxiliary Forces.* London: Macmillan, 1873.
———. *The Soldier's Pocket-book for Field Service.* London: Macmillan, 1869.
———. *The Soldier's Pocket-book for Field Service.* London: Macmillan, 1871.
———. *The Soldier's Pocket-book for Field Service.* London: Macmillan, 1874.
———. *The Soldier's Pocket-book for Field Service.* London: Macmillan, 1881.
———. *The Soldier's Pocket-book for Field Service.* London: Macmillan, 1886.

Government and Bureaucratic Publications

Act XXV of 1867. Calcutta: Superintendent of Government Printing, 1890.
A Catalogue of Books Printed in the Madras Presidency (various quarters). *Fort St. George Gazette Supplement.* Madras: n.p., 1901–6.
Bengal Library Catalogue of Books (various quarters). Appendix to *The Calcutta Gazette.* Calcutta: n.p., 1867–1920.
Denham, E. B. *At the Census of 1911, Being the Review of the Results of the Census of 1911.* Colombo: H. C. Cottle, 1912.
Francis, W. *Census of India 1901, Madras.* Vol. 15. Part 1: Report. Madras: Government Press, 1902.
Lefroy, J. H. *Report on the Regimental and Garrison Schools of the Army, and on Military Libraries and Reading Rooms.* London: HMSO, 1859.
Long, James. *A Descriptive Catalogue of Bengali Works, Containing a Classified List of Fourteen Hundred Bengali Books and Pamphlets, Which Have Issued from the Press, during the Last Sixty Years, with Occasional Notices of the Subjects, the Price, and Where Printed.* Calcutta: Sanders, Cones, and Co., 1855.
———. *Returns Relating to Publications in the Bengali Language, in 1857, to Which Is Added, a List of the Native Presses, with the Books Printed at Each, Their Price and Character, with a Notice of the Past Condition and Future Prospects of the Vernacular Press of Bengal and the Statistics of the Bombay and Madras Vernacular Presses.* Calcutta: John Gray, 1859.
Report on Native Papers Published in the Bombay Presidency for the Week Ending 16 July 1892. Bombay: n.p., 1892.
Report of Native Papers Published in the Bengal Presidency the for the Week Ending 16 February 1889. Calcutta: Bengali Secretariat Press, 1889.
A Revised Edition of the Legislative Enactments of Ceylon. Vol. 3 (1910 to 1923). Colombo: A. C. Richards, 1923.
A Revised Edition of The Legislative Enactments of Ceylon. Vol. 3 (1900 to 1913). Colombo: H. C. Cottle, 1913.
Selections from the Vernacular Newspapers Received up to 15 May 1888. Allahabad: N-WP and Oudh Government Press, 1888.
Report of the Commission Appointed in India to Inquire into the Causes of the Riots Which Took Place in the Year 1875, in the Poona and Ahmednagar Districts of the Bombay Presidency. London: Eyre and Spottiswoode, 1878.

Report of the Council of Military Education. London: Eyre and Spottiswoode, 1860.
Sixth Report by the Council of Military Education on Army Schools, Libraries, and Recreation Rooms. London: Eyre and Spottiswode, 1861.
Tennent, James Emerson. *Ceylon: An Account of the Island, Physical, Historical, and Topographical with Notices of Its Natural History, Antiquities and Productions*. Vol. 2. London: Longman, 1859.

Pamphlets

Wilson, John J. *Construction and Destruction; or The Devilry of War: Being notes on the Fifth edition of "The Soldier's Pocket book for Field Service" by Viscount Wolseley, C. E. Callwell's Tactics of Today (2nd edition 1909), J. Bostock's Aiming and Firing (7th edition) and W. F. Raper's Hints for Soldiers Proceeding to India (n.d.)*]. London: Society of Friends, 1913.

———. *Construction and Destruction; or The Devilry of War:[Being notes on the third edition of* "THE SOLDIERS' POCKET BOOK FOR FIELD SERVICE," [sic] *(By Major-General Sir Garnet J. Wolseley)*]. Birmingham, UK: C. Cooper, 1891.

———. *Construction and Destruction; or The Devilry of War: Being Notes on the Fifth Edition of "The Soldier's Pocket Book for Field Service" (By Viscount Wolseley)*. Kendal: n.p., 1886?.

Film

Michod, David. *War Machine*. United States: Netflix, 2017.
Ray, Satyajit. *Charulata* (The Lonely Wife). Kolkata: R. D. Bansal, 1964.

Primary Sources

Beal, H. E. *Indian Ink: A Novel*. London: Harrap, 1954.
Burnell, Arthur C., and Henry Yule. *Hobson-Jobson: Being a Glossary of Anglo-Indian Colloquial Words and Phrases and of Kindred Terms; Etymological, Historical, Geographical, and Discursive*. London: John Murray, 1886.
Calamy, Edmund, ed. *Cromwell's Soldier's Bible: Being a Reprint, in Facsimile, of "The Souldier's Pocket Bible," compiled by Edmund Calamy, and Issued for the Use of the Commonwealth Army in 1643*. Bibliographic introduction and preface by Garnet Wolseley. Boston: Roberts Brothers, 1895.
Day, Lal Behari. *Bengal Peasant Life* [1878]. London: Macmillan, 1926.
Grierson, George Abraham, ed. *Linguistic Survey of India*. 11 vols. Calcutta: Office of the Superintendent of Government Printing, 1903–28.
Hunter, William Wilson. *The Imperial Gazetteer of India*. 9 vols. London: Trubner, 1881.
Kipling, Rudyard. "The Courting of Dinah Shadd" [1890]. In *Life's Handicap: Being Stories of Mine Own People* [1891]. New York: Doubleday, 1899, 115–43.
———. *Departmental Ditties and Other Verses*. Lahore: Civil and Military Gazette Press, 1886.
———. "My First Book." In *The Idler Magazine: An Illustrated Monthly* 2 (August 1892 to January 1893). London: Chatto and Windus, 1893, 477–82.
———. "The Taking of Lungtungpen" [1887]. In *Mulvaney Stories*. Philadelphia, PA: Henry Altemus, 1897, 14–22.

Macaulay, Thomas. "Minute on Indian Education" [1835]. In *Archives of Empire: From the East India Company to the Suez Canal*, Vol. 1, edited by Barbara Harlow and Mia Carter, 227–38. Durham, NC: Duke University Press, 2003.

Marx, Karl. "The Government of India." In *On Colonialism*, edited by Marx and Friedrich Engels, 62–71. Moscow: Foreign Languages Publishing House, 196-?.

Mitra, Dinabandhu. *Nil Darpan, or the Indigo Planting Mirror, a drama*. Translated from Bengali by a Native. Calcutta: C. H. Manuel, 1861.

Satthianadhan, Krupabai, *Saguna: A Story of Native Christian Life* [1892]. Madras: Srinivasa Varadachari & Co., 1895.

Sengupta, Padmini. *The Portrait of an Indian Woman*. Calcutta: YMCA, 1956.

Sengupta, Saswati. *The Song Seeker*. Delhi: Zubaan Books, 2011.

Tagore, Rabindranath. *Nashtanirh* [1901]. In *Deepika*, 142–194. Calcutta: Viswabharati, 1963.

———. *The Broken Nest*. Translated by Supriya Bari and Mary Lago. Columbia, MO: University of Missouri Press, 1971.

Wood, Charles. *Memorials of Mrs Henry Wood*. London: Richard Bentley, 1894.

Woolf, Leonard. *Diaries in Ceylon, 1908–1911: Records of a Colonial Administrator; Being the Official Diaries Maintained by Leonard Woolf while Assistant Government Agent of the Hambantota District, Ceylon and Stories from the East: Three Short Stories on Ceylon* [1962]. Dehiwala: Tisara, 2006.

———. *Growing: An Autobiography of the Years 1904 to 1911*. London: Harcourt Brace Jovanovich, 1961.

———. *Letters of Leonard Woolf*, edited by Frederic Spotts. London: Weidenfeld and Nicolson, 1989.

———. *The Village in the Jungle*. London: Edwin Arnold, 1913.

———. *The Village in the Jungle*. London: Eland Publishers, 2006.

Wright, A. *Baboo English as 'Tis Writ: Being Curiosities of Indian Journalism*. London: T. Fisher Unwin, 1891.

INDEX

Page numbers in *italics* indicate illustrations.

account books: characteristics of, 64; circulation of, 65; and Deccan Riots of 1875, 16, 64, 65–66; destruction of, 64; and illiterate readers, 64–66; and intelligibility, 65; portability of, 64; in *Village in the Jungle*, 63–67
advertisements: for H. Dey's Wonderful Gonorrhoea Mixture, 120–21; in panjikas, 94, 96, 105, *106*, 194n64; for *Upakhyan Manjari*, 122, *123*; for watches and clocks, 105, *106*; and women readers, 120–21
affective literacy, 16, 65–66. *See also* Amsler, Mark
Afghanistan: M. Bayly on, 26; counterinsurgency in, 26, 27
"Afghanistan Stability/COIN Dynamics" PowerPoint slide, 26, 27, 28–29
African Americans, 15, 176n40
alienation, 146–47
almanacs: collecting of, 12, 91–92; as disposable genre, 12, 95–97; marginalia in, Smyth on, 121–22. *See also* panjikas and dairektari panjikas
Along the Archival Grain (Stoler), 19, 62
Amsler, Mark, 16, 65–66
Angel in the House, The (Patmore), 134, 149–50
Anglo-Indian gentlemen's clubs, 7
annotations. *See* marginalia
anthropocentric, defined, 101
anthropology, 8; of bureaucracies, 177n60; of paperwork, 186n17

Appadurai, Arjun, 79
Appiah, Kwame Antony, 145
Appu, Palawinnege Babun (petitioner), 76–79
archives: destruction and disintegration of, 87, 88–89; digitization of, 12; ephemerality of, 11–12; and *File Room*, 168, 170; and illiterate readers, 61–62; insects in, 11, 89; missing files in, 88; Wickramasinghe on, 61–62; and Woolf, 69
Army Doctrine Publication (ADP) 7-0: Training, 55
Arnold, Edwin, 141, 147
Ashutosh Mukherjee Collection, 190n2
Assistant Government Agent, 57–58, 69, 70, 71, 73, 74, 75, 76, 77, 81–82, 187n35; Woolf as, 56
astrology and astrologers: characteristics of, 101–3; Long on, 102; in panjikas and dairektari panjikas, 90, 93, 94–95, 103, *123*, *124*
audiobooks, 55

Babehami, Manage (petitioner), 76–79
Bankim (author). *See* Chattopadhyay, Bankim Chandra
"bard of empire." *See* Kipling, Rudyard
Battala books, 14, 93, 190n4
Bayard, Pierre, 43, 182n77
Bayly, C. A., 75
Bayly, Martin, 26
Beal, H. E., 83. See also *Indian Ink*

205

Bengal Library Catalogues, 98, 99, 101, 192n17
Bengal Peasant Life (Day), 102, 192n25
Besley, Mrs. C., 142. See also *Womanhood*
Bhadra, Gautam, 96
bhadralok, defined, 14
Bhattacharyya, Debjani, 96
Bible, 43–45, 123, 183n84
blank pages: *Nashtanirh*, 166–167; in panjikas, 94, 123; in *Soldier's Pocket-book for Field Service*, 39–40
Bombay, use of name, xi
book-as-object, and book-as-text, 3, 15–16
Book of Household Management (Beeton), 35
"Books and Reading" (Zechariah), 146, 147, 156–157
Brake, Laurel, 12
Brander, Isabel, 141
British army: and Bible, 44; and commissions, 34, 35; Edgeworth on, 35–36; educational requirements of, 33; as employer, 36; Grove on, 38; Kipling on, 48–49; Lefroy on, 33, 37; libraries for, 35, 36, 37–38; meritocracy and reform in, 34; and middle classes, 35; professionalization of, 34; reading by, 35–38; training of, 45–48. See also Cardwell Reforms
British empire: and literary texts, 13–14, 131; and paperwork and writing, 4, 6–8, 59, 170, 171, 179n11; scale of, 6–8
British Labour Party, 41
British soldiers. See British army
Broken Nest, The (Tagore). See *Nashtanirh* (Tagore)
bureaucracies: affect of, 58–59, 61, 80; anthropology of, 177n60; and conduct registers, 187n51; and delays, 73–74; and *File Room*, 168; and functional archive, 24; genres of, 59; and headmen, 70; and networks, 64, 73–75; and panjikas and dairektari panjikas, 94; universalism of, 6–7
Burton, Antoinette, 144, 190n87

Calcutta: Battala publishing in, 14, 93, 190n4; panjika and dairektari panjika publishers in, *100*; time in, 104; use of name, xi
calendars, 98, 105, 107, 193n39
Cardwell Reforms, 33–34
cattle plague, 56. See also rinderpest
causal loop diagram, 27, 28
Ceylon: bureaucratic offices in, 59, 73–74, 75; illiterate readers in, 75; scribes in, 75; use of name, xi. See also Sri Lanka
Ceylon Government Gazette, 9–10, 56
Chakrabarty, Dipesh, 103
chakri, defined, 105
characters as friends, 162
Charulata (film), 163
Chattopadhyay, Bankim Chandra, 151
chenas, defined, 63
Chennai, use of name, xi. See also Madras
Chowdhury, Arijit Roy, 91–92, 191n6
Civil and Military Gazette, The (newspaper), 1, 2, 49
clerical jobs, and time, 105–7
clocks. See watches and clocks
close attention and reading, 20, 172
coded messages, 44
codex format, 18
coercive subordination, 79, 80, 81
Cohn, Bernard, 8
COIN, 26, 27. See also counterinsurgency
comets, 188n54
commissions, purchasing of, 34, 35. See also British army; Cardwell Reforms
communitarian reading, 196n26. See also reading together
complaints, vs. petitions, 188n58
conduct registers, 187n51
Cones and Company, 92, 102, 111, *108*, *112*
Construction and Destruction; or The Devilry of War (Wilson), 40–41, 42–44
contact zones, defined, 173n7
continuous reading, 18
control, and surveillance state, 8
Corelli, Marie, 13

corrective reading: characteristics of, 95; defined, 117; of panjikas and dairektari panjikas, 95–96, *116*, 117, *118, 119*; and selective reading, 95
Council on Military Education, 34
counterinsurgency: in Afghanistan, 26, 27; in Malaya, 26
courtesan watches, *106*, 107. *See also* watches and clocks
"Courting of Dinah Shadd, The" (Kipling): journalists in, 51; Mulvaney in, 51, 52, 53, 54; plot of, 51–52; resourcefulness in, 54; *Soldier's Pocket-book for Field Service* in, 49, 51, 52, 54; war and sex in, 54; Wolseley in, 51; women in, 54
Crawford, Marion, 13
Cromwell's Soldier's Bible, 44
Culture and Imperialism (Said), 13

Dabdaba-i-Qasari (newspaper), 83
dacoits, defined, 53
Daily Telegraph, The (newspaper), 51, 142
dairektari panjikas. *See* panjikas and dairektari panjikas
Das, Santanu, 15
Das, Veena, 72
Day, Law, and Company, 92, 123, *124*
Deccan Riots of 1875, commission of, 16, 64, 65, 66
delays, and bureaucracies, 73–74
denial of coevalness, defined, 193n34
Departmental Ditties and Other Verses (Kipling): as bureaucratic collection, 3; contents of, 1, 21; dedication of, 2; design of, 2, 3–4, 20; as material poetics of empire, 3; popularity of, 1; as prank, 4; publication of, 2; publication date of, 2–3; purposes of, 1; sale of, 1
despatch diaries, defined, 11
dhruva, defined, 105
Diaries in Ceylon, 1908–11 (Woolf), 56, 72–73, 188n54
discontinuous reading, 18, 109
dispersion, of functional archive, 11

disposable genres, almanacs as, 12, 95–97
Dockside Reading (Hofmeyr), 16
Douglass, Anna Murray, 15

East Baltimore Mental Improvement Society, 15
East India Company, 6, 7, 35, 174n11
East Lynne (Wood), 158–60
Edgeworth, Maria, 35–36
education, 130–131, 148. *See also* British Army; women readers; Woolf, Leonard
egalitarianism, of reading together, 157–58
elite readers: characteristics of, 172; and *Indian Ladies' Magazine*, 138, 141, 152; and literate and illiterate readers, 24, 172; and Shakespeare, 151; women readers as, 132. *See also* nonelite readers
empire and empire building, 26, 28
English Common Reader, The (Altick), 18
English language, in marginalia, 122–125
English literacy: in Bengal, 121; in Ceylon, 60; in Madras, 131
English literature: and anxiety, 128, 129; as character building, 131, 149; and empire building, 13; functional archive of, 25; and inadequacy, 25, 129; in *Indian Ladies' Magazine*, 132, 146–47, 151–52, 154–56; moral lessons in, 149, 199n69; reading together of, 25, 132–33; and self-improvement, 149; and women readers, 128, 148–49
English teachers, in South Asia, 150–51
enumerative bibliographies, 96–97
Esbester, Mike, 185n13
essays: "Estimate of Shakespeare's Desdemona, An" (essay), 162; in *Indian Ladies' Magazine*, 154, 156, 158–62; as literary recaps, 157, 158

fairness, and petitions, 79
Fiction in the Archives (Davis), 79
Field Exercise Book, The, 30
Field Manual (FM) 3-0: Operations, 55
Field Manual (FM) 3-24: Counterinsurgency, 26

File Room (Singh), 25, 168–70
files, in archives, 88
films. *See specific films*
foresight, and panjikas and dairektari panjikas, 104
forgeries, 72
Forster's Education Act of 1870, 33
Frankel, Oz, 174n19
functional archive: aesthetic tropes and effects of, 6, 20–21; and bureaucracies, 24; characteristics of, 9–12; as constellations, 11; contents of, 5, 21, 171, 172; defined, 4–5, 9, 170; destruction of, 11–12; dispersion of, 11; duress created by, 5; ephemerality of, 11–12; fragmentation of, 11; gaps in, 171; generative nature of, 10; as historical formation, 20, 21, 171; and illiterate readers, 15, 16; and literature, 6, 21, 63, 172; location of, 11; materiality of, 20; as network, 9–10, 11, 22, 25; as nonliterary, 21; panjikas and dairektari panjikas as, 94; and power, 10; and readers and reading, 19–20, 171; as required reading, 5; scale of, 12; storage of, 12; as textual construct, 11, 20–21; as transaction, 10; of US military apparatus, 26

Gandhi, Mohandas, 109
Garland of Stories, advertisement for, 123
gender reform: and *Indian Ladies' Magazine*, 136, 148, 163; in South Asia, 131, 149, 150
gentlemen's clubs, Anglo-Indian, 7
Gilmour, David, 49
Gitelman, Lisa, 17
Glaisyer, Natasha, 179n22
Golden Age of Television, 156
graffiti, in panjikas and dairektari panjikas, 122
Gregorian calendar, 105, 107, 193n39
Grove, H. L., 38
Growing (Woolf), 58
Guha, Ranajit, 7, 74
Gun License Ordinance of 1908, 9–10

gun licenses: characteristics of, 67–68; flexibility of, 70; functions of, 68–69; and headmen, 69, 71, 72; and illiterate readers, 68, 69; and legibility, 72; necessity of, 67; and networks, 68–69; renewal of, 79; Roberts on, 71; validity of, 71–72; verification of, 71; and Woolf, 68, 69
Gupta, Akhil, 72, 188nn58 and 63
Gupta, Durga Charan, 98
Gupta Press: collections of, 24; and Gupta, 98; history of, 90, 98; location of, 100; and panjikas and dairektari panjikas, 90, 92, 98, 100–101, 125, 126, 192n17; print runs of, 101; storage shelf in, 92

Hambantota: literacy in, 60, 185n12; and Woolf, 56, 186n19
Hardie, Keir, 41, 42, 43, 44, 45
H. Dey's Wonderful Gonorrhoea Mixture, advertisement for, 120–21
headmen: and bureaucracy, 70; corruption of, 71, 72–73, 77; and gun licenses, 69–70, 72; and "Missing Stamps on Gun Licenses Issued by AGA on Circuit," 71; Woolf on, 72–73
Henkin, Daniel, 18
highbrow reading, and lowbrow reading, 13–14
"Higher Education of Women, The" (Nundy), 148
Hindu: festivals, 107–8; notions of time, 103
history of the book, 16, 19–20; in South Asia, 177n68
history of reading, 14–15, 16, 32, 134, 172; and the novel, 17–19; in South Asia, 13–14
Hobson-Jobson glossary, 129
Hofmeyr, Isabel, 16, 109, 144
Hossain, Rokeya Sakhawat, 132
How to Do Things with Books in Victorian Britain (Price), 16, 17
How to Talk about Books You Haven't Read (Bayard), 182n77

illegibility: and authenticity, 82; of books, 86; characteristics of, 60; *Dabdaba-i-Qasari* on, 83; defined, 87; in *Indian Ink*, 83; and jungles, 86; *Kalapataru* on, 82–83; and literacy, 60–61; of newspapers, 85; of petitions, 82–84; *Sanjivani* on, 83; as strategy and opportunity, 83–84; and typewriters, 84. *See also* legibility

illiterate readers: and account books, 64–65; in archives, 61–62; in Ceylon, 75; defined, 17; of Douglass, 15; and functional archive, 15, 16; and gun licenses, 68; and illegibility, 61; and interpretation, 66; vs. literate readers, 61; and materiality, 16, 64; and paperwork, 61; peasants as, 86; and petitions, 75–76, 77; punishment of, 61; and reading, 61; and reading aloud, 15, 133, 150; women readers as, 131, 132; and Woolf, 61; and writing, 76

Illustrated Directory of India, The, 99

imperial commons, defined, 144

imperial conquest, 36. *See also* British empire

Imperial Gazetteer of India, The (Hunter), 8

In Another Country (Joshi), 13

indexes, to panjikas and dairektari panjikas, 115, 116

Indian Directory, 99–100

Indian Ink (Beal), 24, 83–84

Indian Ladies' Magazine, The (Satthianadhan): Arnold on, 141; and Besley, 142; characteristics of, 138; circulation of, 141; contents of, 130, 132, 134, 144, 163, 196n25; cost of, 141; cover of, *137*; and education, 131, 148; and elite readers, 138, 141, 152; English literature in, 25, 130, 132, 146–47, 151–52, 154–56; essays in, 154–56, 158–62; and the Exchange, 144; and friendship, 133, 162; and gender reform, 136, 163; impact of, 142; imperial commons and, 144; as instruction manual, 150; lectures in, 157; literary recaps in, 156, 157, 158–61; literature in, 136; and loneliness, 133; as luxury object, 138; and men readers, *140*, 141; *Merchant of Venice* in, 161–62; and *Nashtanirh*, 134, 164, 165, 166; and networks, 142, 144–45, 152; "News and Notes" in, 144, 145; nonephemerality of, 138; page of, *143*; politics in, 130; print runs of, 133–34; and provinciality, 134, 142, 145; publication of, 130, 135; purposes of, 25, 130, 141, 165; puzzles in, 152–54, 155; readership of, 130–31; and reading together, 132–33, 138, 142, 144, 145, 147, 150, 160, 161–62, 164, 165; reception history of, 163–64; reprints in, 142–44; as required reading, 138, 158; rereading public of, 152; as scaffolding, 132; as scrapbook, 145; and selection bias, 163–64; Sengupta on, 135; Shakespeare in, 151–52; as source for cultural and literary history, 132; Stopes in, 144; subscriber list of, *140*, 160; table of contents of, 136, *137*, 138; and television show recaps, 156; terms of subscription of, 138, *139*; translations of, 141; Troy in, 144, 145; utopianism of, 141; and *Womanhood*, 142; "Women in China," in, 144; and women readers, 131, 133–34, 136, 138–41, 148, 149; women's achievements in, 144, 145–46; and women writers, 134; Zechariah in, 147, 156–57

Indian Opinion (newspaper), 109

instruction manuals, 48, 150; as unread, 31. *See also Indian Ladies' Magazine, The* (Satthianadhan); *Soldier's Pocket-book for Field Service* (Wolseley); panjikas and dairektari panjikas

intelligibility, and account books, 63, 64–66

interpretation, and illiterate readers, 66

jantri. *See* panjikas and dairektari panjikas

Jasanoff, Maya, 88

Joshi, Priya, 13, 129, 146–47

journalists, 51

jungles, 56, 67, 86

kachcheri offices, 59, 61, 71

Kafka, Ben, 19, 177n60

kaghazi raj, defined, 170

Kalapataru (newspaper), 82–83
Kipling, Rudyard: on barracks life, 48; biography of, 2, 173n2; on British soldiers, 52; Gilmour on, 49; on hierarchies, 49; influence of, 52; and MacNamara, 49; on *Soldier's Pocket-book for Field Service*, 31, 49–54; on "Tommy Atkins," 49; on Wolseley, 50
Kolkata: location of panjika publishers in, 100; use of name, xi
kurakkan, defined, 63

Labour Leader (newspaper), 41–42
learning traditions, as anthropocentric, 101–2
lectures, 157. *See also Indian Ladies' Magazine, The* (Satthianadhan)
Lefroy, J. H., 33, 37
legibility: of account books, 66; characteristics of, 59–60; defined, 59–60; and gun licenses, 72; and imperial management, 60; and nonelite readers, 60. *See also* illegibility
Leonard, Steve, 55
libraries: for British soldiers, 35, 36; Grove on, 38; Murphy on, 35; panjikas and dairektari panjikas in, 24–25
licenses. *See* gun licenses
Light of Asia, The (Arnold), 141, 147
Linguistic Survey of India (Grierson), 8
literacy: awareness of, 75; refusal to exercise, 16; rising levels of, 35; and understanding, 16
literary effects, of reading, 19
literary history, of reading, 19
literary recaps: characteristics of, 159–60; of *East Lynne*, 159; essays as, 157, 158; in *Indian Ladies' Magazine*, 156, 157, 158–61; and memory, 156–57; of *Merchant of Venice*, 161, 162; "My Impressions of 'East Lynn'" as, 159; plot summaries in, 159; purposes of, 160, 162; and reading community, 160, 161; and reading together, 157, 160, 161; and rereading public, 157, 158; structure of, 159; as textual infrastructures, 158; Zechariah on, 157
literary scholars, and close reading, 172

Literary Society, 134–35
literate and illiterate readers: and elite readers, 24, 132; and Forster's Education Act of 1870, 33; in Hambantota, 185n12; and nonelite readers, 23–24; and women readers, 132
literature: aesthetic values of, 148; and functional archive, 6, 14, 63, 172; in *Indian Ladies' Magazine*, 136; Zechariah on, 146, 147. *See also* English literature
loneliness: in *Charulata*, 163; and *Indian Ladies' Magazine*, 133; in *Nashtanirh*, 163, 166, 167; and women readers, 133
"Lonely Wife, The" (film), 163. *See also Charulata*
Long, James: on astrology and astrologers, 102; catalogues by, 96–97, 191n11; and panjikas and dairektari panjikas, 97; on reading together, 133; on vernacular press, 96
lowbrow reading, and highbrow reading, 13–14
lower classes, and lowbrow reading, 14

Macaulay, Thomas, 13, 121
Macmillan (publisher), 38–40
MacNamara, Corporal, 49
Madras: literacy in, 131; publishing statistics from, 135–136; use of name, xi
magazines: characteristics of, 14; languages of, 135–36; male contributors to, 197n37; in *Nashtanirh*, 163, 164, 165, 166; print runs of, 135–36; reception history of, 164; in Victorian era, 198n51. *See also Indian Ladies' Magazine, The* (Satthianadhan)
Malaya, 26
Malayan Communist Party, 26
male readers, 140, 141
marginalia: in almanacs, 94, 194n67; as astral vs. imperial, 123–25; defined, 122; in English language, 122; in panjikas and dairektari panjikas, 115, *116*, 117, *118*, *119*, *120*, 121, 122, 123, 124; and reading, 122; in *Soldier's Pocket-book for Field Service*, 39, 42–43; and unreadability, 24

marriage, in Britain vs. South Asia, 149
Marx, Karl, 58–59
Masks of Conquest (Viswanathan), 13
matra, defined, 103
McChrystal, Stanley, 28, 29
McHenry, Elizabeth, 15, 176n40
medicine: Mukharji on, 96; advertisements for, 120–121
memory, 152, 156–57
Merchant of Venice, The (Shakespeare), 134, 161–62
middle classes, 14, 35
Midnight's Children (Rushdie), 14
migrated archives, defined, 87–88
military training camps, 45
Mill, John Stuart, 6–7
Miller, Elizabeth, 194n51
"Minute on Indian Education" (Macaulay), 25
Mirror of the Indigo Revolt (Mitra), 64. See also *Nil Darpan*
"Missing Stamps on Gun Licenses Issued by AGA on Circuit," 70–72
mofussil, 129, 134
Moitra, Swati, 196n26
moneylenders, 63–66; ordinance for, 65, 186n25
motherhood, and education, 148
mudalali, defined, 63
Mukharji, Projit, 96
multitasking, and books, 14–15
Mumbai, use of name, xi
Murphy, Sharon, 35
"My Impressions of 'East Lynn'" (Balm), 158–61. See also *Indian Ladies' Magazine, The* (Satthianadhan)

Naidu, Sarojini, 132
Nashtanirh (Tagore): Amal in, 164–65, 166, 167; Bengali readers' circle in, 165; Bhupati in, 163, 164, 166; Charu in, 163, 164–65, 166–67; and *Indian Ladies' Magazine*, 134, 164, 165, 166; loneliness in, 163, 166, 167; newspapers in, 163, 166; "Notebook" in, 166–67; periodicals in, 25, 163, 164, 165, 166; reading together in, 164–66
"native almanacs." See panjikas and dairektari panjikas
negotiations. See petitions and negotiations
networks: in British empire, 22; and bureaucracies, 73–74; functional archive as, 9–10, 11, 22; and gun licenses, 68–69; and *Indian Ladies' Magazine*, 142, 144–45, 152
Newell, Stephanie, 13
"News and Notes," 144, 145–146; 198n51. See also *Indian Ladies' Magazine, The* (Satthianadhan)
newspapers, 12, 85; in *Nashtanirh*, 163, 166; in *Village in the Jungle*, 85. See also specific newspapers
New Yorker, The (magazine), 28
Nil Darpan (Mitra), 64. See also *The Mirror of the Indigo Revolt*
nimesha, defined, 103
nodes. See networks
nonelite readers, 24, 60. See also elite readers
nonreading, 43, 52, 89
"not at home in empire," 7, 8
novels: and bureaucracy, 62–63; and reading, 17–18. See also sentimental novels

Odriksiddhanta: defined, 100. See also panjikas and dairektari panjikas
offices, holidays for, 107–8
Okehampton, 45
"Okehampton-1897" (sketch), 45–48
Operation Legacy, 87–88
Orsini, Francesca, 14, 136

palimpsests, defined, 84, 124
pan, defined, 97
panchang. See panjikas and dairektari panjikas
Panchangam. See panjikas and dairektari panjikas

panjikas and dairektari panjikas: advertisements in, 105, *106*, 109, 120, *121*, 194n64; in Ashutosh Mukherjee Collection, 190n2; and astrology and astrologers, 90, 93, 94–95, 100, 103, 123, *124*; and Bengali Hindus, 93; Bhadra on, 96; blank pages in, 123; and bureaucracies, 94–95; and calendars, 105; characteristics of, 95, 97–98; and Cones and Company, 92, 102, 111, *108*, *112*; contents of, 90, 94, 109–10, 127; corrective reading of, 95–96, *116*, 117, *118*, *119*; cost of, 97, 102; and Day, Law, and Company, 92, 123, *124*; death of, 125; defined, 24, 90, 94; English language in, 121; ephemerality of, 115; and foresight, 104; format and layout of, 96, *112*, 113–14; as functional archive, 94; and Gupta Press, 90, 100–101, 125, 126, 192n17; history of, 96–103; impatience and frustration with, 117; indexes to, 115, *116*; indispensability of, 97; layout of, 114–15; length of, 114; in libraries, 24–25; and Long, 97; marginalia in, 115, *116*, 117, *118*, *119*, 120, 121, 122, 123, *124*; market for, 97; mass production of, 102, 103, 104; missing pages in, 117, *118*–*19*; and Mukharji, 96; number of, 99; ownership of, 122; page numbering in, 115–17; and P. M. Bagchi and Company, 100–101, 126; popularity of, 97, 98; as portable and affordable, 97; print runs of, 101; production of, 191n5; publication of, 125; and publishers' locations, *100*, *101*; publishing boom of, 90; purposes of, 24, 90, 93, 104–5, 109–10, 125; and railways, 110–11; and reading, 90, 91, 95, 109, 115, 191n6; registration of, 99; and religion, 103; as required reading, 94; responses to, 126; retooling of, 95; and rituals, 115; and Roy Chowdhury, 91–92, 191n6; selective reading of, 95, 109, 110, 111, 113, 114, 115, 117; sizes of, 92; as templates, 94; and time, 93, 94–95, 103, 104–108, 127; timetables in, 94, 110–114; transliterations in, 122–23; ubiquity of, 93; and women readers, 103; as Yellow Pages, 94

paperwork: and British empire, 6–7, 59, 170, 171; and *File Room*, 168–70; and illiterate readers, 61; Kafka on, 19, 177n60; Marx on, 58–59; and novels, 62–63; parsing of, 60; proliferation of, 59; Vismann on, 59; volume of, 60; Woolf on, 58, 87. *See also* kaghazi raj

peasants, as illiterate readers, 86

"Peculiar Animals and How to Train Them" (Hardie), 41–42, 44–45

pencil holder, in *Soldier's Pocket-book for Field Service*, 30, 40, 181n60

Pennell, Sara, 179n22

periodicals. *See* magazines

permits, 5, 67, 72, 77, 79. *See also* petitions and negotiations; gun licenses

petitions and negotiations: of Appu (petitioner), 76–79; and Assistant Government Agents, 75, 76–77, 81–82; of Babehami (petitioner), 76–79; and coercive subordination, 79, 80, 81; vs. complaints, 188n58; conclusions of, 79; contents of, 79; defined, 74; and equality, 81–82; examples of, 76–79; and fairness, 79; growth and multiplication of, 76; history of reading and, 80–81; illegibility of, 82–84; and illiterate readers, 75–76, 77; industry of, 75; irony of, 76; literary elements of, 79; and negotiations, 74; and networks, 74–75; and oral strategies, 79; and permits, 77, 79; phrasing of, 80; purposes of, 74, 76; and ritual, 79; and scribes, 75, 80–81; in Sri Lanka National Archives, 74–75; and trustworthiness, 81; types of, 76; universality of, 74; vocabulary of, 80; weightiness of, 74; Wickramasinghe on, 74; Woolf on, 75

"Phenomenology of Reading" (Poulet), 18–19

plays, 161–62. See also *Merchant of Venice, The* (Shakespeare)

P. M. Bagchi and Company: history of, 99; location of, *100*; and panjikas, 98, 99, 100–101, 126; print runs of, 101
poetry, in schools, 199n81
Portrait of an Indian Woman, A (Sengupta), 135
Poulet, George, 18–19
PowerPoint slide, 27; audience of, 29; failure of, 28; leaking of, 26; reception of, 28, 29. *See also* "Afghanistan Stability/COIN Dynamics" PowerPoint slide
Power in Print (Ghosh), 13–14
"Pow-Wow, The," 46, 47
prana, defined, 103
Pratt, Mary Louise, 173n7
presence and absence, in *File Room*, 168, *169*
Price, Leah, 16, 17, 31
Prince and the Pauper, The (Twain), 148–49
Print and Pleasure (Orsini), 14
print runs: of *Departmental Ditties*, 1; of *Indian Ladies' Magazine*, 133–34; of magazines, 135–36; of panjikas and dairektari panjikas, 99, 101
provinciality: and English literature, 129; and *Indian Ladies' Magazine*, 134, 142, 145; of South Asia, 129; and time, 129–30
publication, of panjikas and dairektari panjikas, 90, 125
pulp genres, 14. *See also* lowbrow reading
purana-itihas, defined, 103
puzzles, 152–55. *See also Indian Ladies' Magazine, The* (Satthianadhan)

Quakers, 41
Queen's Regulations, The, 30

Railway Act of 1879, 194n61
railways: book stalls of, 38; and illiterate readers, 185n13; and panjikas and dairektari panjikas, 110–14; safety of, 185n13; and time, 104, 105; timetables for, 110–14, 194n61
Ratemahatmaya, defined, 187n35
Reader, W. J., 34

readers and reading: alone, 132, 158; aloud, 15, 133; as aspirational, 35, 148; by British soldiers, 35–36; characteristics of, 17, 18–19; defined, 17–18, 171; under duress, 5, 173n8; of *East Lynne*, 158–59; Edgeworth on, 35–36; and functional archive, 17, 19–20, 171; harmfulness of, 36; and interpretative vs. noninterpretative acts, 5–6; Lefroy on, 37; Leonard on, 55; literary effects of, 19; literary history of, 19; moral purpose of, 149; and nonreading and nonreaders, 43, 52, 89; and novels, 17, 18; reluctantly, 38; transformative potentials of, 36, 43–44; and war, 28. *See also* elite readers; history of reading; illiterate readers; nonelite readers; highbrow reading and lowbrow reading; slow reading
reading community. *See* reading together
reading under duress, 5, 173n8
reading together: egalitarianism of, 157–58; of English literature, 25, 131, 132–33; and *Indian Ladies' Magazine*, 132–33, 138, 142, 144, 145, 147, 150, 160, 161–62, 165; and literary recaps, 157, 160, 161; Long on, 133; and *Merchant of Venice*, 161; in *Nashtanirh*, 164–66; and petitions, 75; and rereading public, 162; Silverman on, 157; Spacks on, 157; Warner on, 157
reception history, 159, 163–64
refusal to read, 23, 32
"Regulations Relating to Rinderpest," 56–58, 59, 87
Report on the Progress of Education in India, 131
reprinting, in *Indian Ladies' Magazine*, 142–44
rereading public: defined, 152; of *East Lynne*, 159–60; of *Indian Ladies' Magazine*, 152; and literary recaps, 157, 158; and reading together, 162; and television show recaps, 156
Revolt of 1857, 7
Reynolds, G.W.M., 13
Richards, Thomas, 6–7

rinderpest, 56, 58. *See also* cattle plague
rituals, 79, 115
Roberts, G. F., 71
Roberts, Lord Frederick, 184n114
Roy, Rohan Deb, 89
Roy, Sumana, 129
Russell, W. H., 51, 184n106
ryot, defined, 65

Saguna: A Story of Native Christian Life (Satthianadhan): acclaim for, 130; reading in, 128–29; Saguna in, 128–29, 132; serialization of, 195n1
Sanjivani (newspaper), 83
Sarkar, Sumit, 193n41
Satthianadhan, Kamala, 130, 134–35, 138, 142, 144, 147, 147, 160, 162, 164
Satthianadhan, Krupabai, 130, 134
schools, 131, 199n81
scrapbooks, 12, 145
scribes, 16, 75, 79, 80–81, 87
Seeing Like a State (Scott), 59
selective reading, 95, 109, 110, 111, 113, 114, 115, 117
Self Help (Smiles), 35
self-improvement, and reading, 35, 149
Sengupta, Padmini, 135
sentimental novels, 13–14, 152. *See also* novels
Sesame and Lilies (Ruskin), 149
sexuality, in *Soldier's Pocket-book for Field Service*, 184n118
Shakespeare, William, 151–52, 162
"Shakuntala, Miranda O Desdemona" (Bankim), 151
Silverman, Gillian, 157
slides. *See* PowerPoint slide
slow printing, 194n51. *See also* readers and reading
slow reading, defined, 109. *See also* readers and reading
"small voice of history," 74
Smyth, Adam, 121–22
soldiers. *See* British Army; *Soldier's Pocket-book for Field Service*

Soldier's Pocket Bible, The, 44
Soldier's Pocket-book for Field Service, The (Wolseley): antihierarchy of, 34–35; appearance of, 39; audience of, 38; on battlefield experience, 48; Bible mentioned in, 44; characteristics of, 31, 39–40; Christians on, 32, 41, 45; circulation of, 31–32, 34; contents of, 29–30, 39, 41; cost of, 38; criticism of, 41–42, 43, 45, 54; editions of, 31, 39, 55; first edition of, 30; format and layout of, 181nn55 and 56; Hardie on, 41–42, 44–45; incoherence of, 50–51; as instruction manual, 41, 48; journalists in, 51; Kipling on, 48–49; lampooning of, 31; leisure readers in, 37; marginalia in, 42–43; as object-lesson, 42; pacifists on, 32; and "Peculiar Animals and How to Train Them," 41–42; pencil holder in, 30, 40, 181n60; portability of, 39; praise for, 179n25; publication date of, 36; public outcry about, 31; purposes of, 29, 30, 34, 39, 40, 41; as railway companion, 38–39; readability of, 39; readers of, 31–32, 40; reading vs. experience in, 48, 53; reception history of, 23, 31, 33, 37, 40, 47, 48, 55; and reeducation, 34; and refusal to read, 32–33; and religion, 43–44; reputation of, 33, 55; as required reading, 31; responses to, 32–33; reviews of, 50–51; as self-improvement text, 35; sex, absence of in, 184n118; static nature of, 40; *Taunton Courier and Western Advertiser* on, 40; technical information in, 29–30, 35; terrain discussed in, 30; as textbook, 31; as unread manual, 31, 45, 48, 49, 51, 52, 53; updating of, 39; and writing, 39–40
Song Seekers, The (Sengupta), 110
South Asia and South Asians: English teachers in, 150–51; and functional archive, 9, 171, 174n19; gender reform in, 131, 149, 150; history of reading in, 13, 22, 177n66; provinciality of, 129; schools in, 199n81; and Shakespeare, 151; and time, 103–4,

110–11; writing for and by, 9, 24. *See also* British empire
sowkars, defined, 65
Spacks, Patricia, 157
Sri Lanka, use of name, xi. *See also* Ceylon
Sri Lanka National Archives, 74–75, 87, 89
Stallybrass, Peter, 18
Stanley, Henry Morton, 31
Stark, Ulrike, 11
Stephens, Julia, 80
Stoler, Ann Laura, 19, 62, 173n8
Stopes, Marie, 144, 145
Stories of Indian Christian Life (Satthianadhan), 134
Story of a Soldier's Life, The (Wolseley), 37, 52
Strachey, Lytton, 58, 80
structural violence, 188n63
"Sultana's Dream" (Hossain), 132
surveillance state, 8
Suryasiddhanta, defined, 100. *See also* panjikas and dairektari panjikas

Tagore, Rabindranath, 134, 163–167. *See also* Nashtanirh
"Taking of Lungtungpen, The" (Kipling): Brazenose in, 53, 54; British soldiers in, 53; context for, 50; Mulvaney in, 50, 53, 54; refusal to read in, 54; *Soldier's Pocket-book for Field Service* in, 49, 50, 53
Tales from Shakespeare (Lamb), 151
Taunton Courier and Western Advertiser (newspaper), 40
telegraph networks, 104
Television, Golden Age of, 156
television show recaps, defined, 156
templates, panjikas and dairektari panjikas as, 94
temporality. *See* time
Tennent, J. Emerson, 7
Things Fall Apart (Achebe), 14
time: astral vs. imperial, 94–95, 107, 123–125, 127; and clerical jobs, 105–7; as cyclical, 103; and Hinduism, 103; as matra, 103; as nimesha, 103; and panjikas and dairektari

panjikas, 94–95, 96, 104–5, 107–8, 109, 110, 125, 126; as prana, 103; and provinciality, 129–30; and purana-itihas, 103; and railways, 104, 105; and South Asians, 103–4, 110–11; and telegraph networks, 104; and watches and clocks, 107
timetables, 94, 111–14. *See also* railways
"Tommy Atkins," 49. *See also* British army
transaction, functional archive as, 10
translations, 141
transliterations, 122–23
Travers, Robert, 174n11
Troy, Agatha, 144, 145
Tudor history, 148–49
typewriters, 83, 84

understanding, and literacy, 16
United Kingdom, and Malaya, 26
unreadability, 24, 28, 29, 83–84. *See also* illegibility
US military and functional archive, 26
utopianism, 141

Vernacular Literature Committee, 98
vernacular press, 96
Victorian melodramas, 158
Village in the Jungle, The (Woolf): account books in, 63–65, 66; agricultural seasons in, 63; Babehami in, 65, 67, 69–70, 73, 82, 83, 84; Babun in, 73; banality of empire in, 62; Buddhists in, 84–85; bureaucracy in, 24, 69; circularity in, 64; corruption in, 64; debt in, 63–64; desperation in, 63; Fernando in, 67, 73, 83, 84; gun licenses in, 67; headmen in, 77; Hinnihami in, 66; illiterate readers in, 64–65; jungle in, 85–86; moneylenders in, 63; newspapers in, 85; paperwork in, 62–63; petitions in, 73; plot of, 62; Punchirala in, 66; reading and writing in, 62, 87; ritualistic pledge in, 66; Silindu in, 62, 64–67, 70, 73, 74, 82, 83, 84–85, 86
Vismann, Cornelia, 59

"waiting rooms of history," 103
war, 28, 41, 53–54
War Machine (film), 28–29
Warner, Michael, 157
watches and clocks: advertisements for, *106*; importance of, 105; Sarkar on, 193n41; and time, 107; for women, *106*, 107
weather, and archival degradation, 88
Wickramanayaka, Sarath, 88
Wickramasinghe, Nira, 61–62, 74
Wilson, John J., 41
Wolseley, Frances (daughter), 45
Wolseley, Garnet: as "All Sir Garnet," 29; background of, 178n13; on Bible, 44–45; career of, 29; characteristics of, 50–51; and correspondence with Macmillan, 38–40; and *Cromwell's Soldier's Bible*, 44; and *Daily Telegraph*, 51; and *Field Pocket-book for Auxiliary Forces*, 179n17; and journalists, 51; Kipling on, 50; letters of, 51; and Macmillan, 39; on Okehampton, 45; on reform and meritocracy, 34; and Roberts, 184n114; and Russell, 51, 184n106; as scrapbooker, 12, 45, *46*; self-aggrandizement of, 50; and *Story of a Soldier's Life*, 37, 52. See also *Soldier's Pocket-book for Field Service*
Wolseley, Louisa (wife), 51
Womanhood (Besley), 142
Woman's Journal (magazine), 144

"Women in China" (Whiting), 144
women readers: education of, 131; as elite readers, 132; and English literature, 128, 148–49; as illiterate readers, 131; and *Indian Ladies' Magazine*, 131, 133–34, 136, 138–41; as literate readers, 132; and loneliness, 133; Orsini on, 136; and panjikas and dairektari panjikas, 103; and reading, 148; and reading alone, 132; in *Report on the Progress of Education in India*, 131; in schools, 131; Wood on, 130–31
women writers, 134. See also specific writers
Wood, Charles, 130–31
Woolf, Leonard: and archives, 69; biography of, 186n19; education of, 86; gun license signed by, *68*, 69; and *Growing*, 58; on headmen, 72–73; and illiterate readers, 61; on paperwork, 58, 87; on petitions, 75; and "Regulations Relating to Rinderpest," 56, 58, 87; and Strachey, 58, 80. See also Assistant Government Agent; *Village in the Jungle*; *Diaries in Ceylon, 1908–1911*.
writing: in British empire, 7, 8–9; as "contact zone," 4; and East India Company, 174n11; material life of, 16; Mill on, 6–7; by South Asians, 9; Tennent on, 7

Yeats-Brown, Francis, 7

Zechariah, Mrs. A., 146, 147, 156–57

A NOTE ON THE TYPE

This book has been composed in Arno, an Old-style serif typeface in the classic Venetian tradition, designed by Robert Slimbach at Adobe.

GPSR Authorized Representative: Easy Access System Europe - Mustamäe tee 50, 10621 Tallinn, Estonia, gpsr.requests@easproject.com